THE LEGACY OF R. D. LAING

The name R. D. Laing continues to be widely recognized by those in the psycho-therapy community in the United States and Europe. Laing's books are a testament to his breadth of interests, including the understanding of madness, alternatives to conventional psychiatric treatment, existential philosophy and therapy, family systems, cybernetics, mysticism, and poetry. He is most remembered for his devastating critique of psychiatric practices and his rejection of the concept of "mental illness."

Most of the books that have been published about Laing have been written by people who did not know him personally and were unfamiliar with Laing the man and teacher. *The Legacy of R. D. Laing: An appraisal of his contemporary relevance* is composed by thinkers and practitioners who knew Laing intimately, some of whom worked with Laing. This collection of papers brings a perspective and balance to Laing's controversial ideas, some of which were never addressed in his books. There has never been a collection of papers that addresses so thoroughly the question of who Laing was and why it can be claimed that he became the most famous psychiatrist in the world.

M. Guy Thompson, PhD, is a personal and supervising analyst at the Psychoanalytic Institute of Northern California and an adjunct professor at the California Institute of Integral Studies, San Francisco. Dr. Thompson received his psychoanalytic training from R. D. Laing and associates at the Philadelphia Association and is the author of numerous books and journal articles on psychoanalysis, phenomenology, and schizophrenia. He currently lives in San Rafael, California.

"M. Guy Thompson has impressively compiled the most authoritative, accessible, and personally revealing book on R. D. Laing ever written, and by contributors who knew him best – his students, trainees, colleagues, and friends. No other book exists that covers the broad range of Laing's legacy including his philosophy, unconventional treatment practices, politics, appeal to popular culture, and his provocative behaviour (including intimate details of his life replete with all the juicy gossip) that shines light on his enigmatic personality. A wonderful piece of scholarship!"

– **Jon Mills**, PsyD, PhD, ABPP, philosopher, psychoanalyst, and psychologist; author of *Underworlds: Philosophies of the Unconscious from Psychoanalysis to Metaphysics*

"Since his death in 1989, R. D. Laing's trenchant contributions to the understanding of human distress have, if anything, grown in their relevance and indispensability. Laing didn't simply treat his patients, he *cared* for and with them in ways imbued with deep interpersonal understanding. *The Legacy of R. D. Laing* collects a number of pivotal essays written by authors and practitioners who knew, worked with and were inspired by Laing. For anyone who has ever been bewitched, bothered or bewildered by Laing, or who is curious to discover what all the fuss is about, this is the book to read."

– **Professor Ernesto Spinelli**, ES Associates, London, UK

"This is an important book! The time has come for a re-evaluation of the legacy of Laing, whose work has been largely neglected by contemporary psychoanalysts and even the existential therapists who owe him so much. Edited by Laing's student and close associate M. Guy Thompson, the book is comprised of contributors who knew Laing intimately and who provide a feel for what he was like as a person, as well as a therapist and thinker. Well written and lively, this book is a compelling *tour de force* that demonstrates why Laing is so relevant for the challenges that confront us in the twenty-first century."

– **Betty Cannon**, PhD, author of *Sartre and Psychoanalysis*, president of the Boulder Psychotherapy Institute, and founder of Applied Existential Psychotherapy (AEP)

"*The Legacy of R. D. Laing* makes you yearn for a time when radical ideas about madness were seen as exciting possibilities to be explored. The conference proceedings also provide a foil for assessing the 'brain-disease' constructs of madness that drive modern psychiatry. Today's conceptions seem particularly impoverished and lacking in all poetry."

– **Robert Whitaker**, author of *Anatomy of an Epidemic*

"This wonderful book, bringing together essays written mainly by people who knew Laing and his teachings personally, uniquely illuminates the life and contributions of one of the true giants of our field."

– **George E. Atwood**, PhD

THE LEGACY OF R. D. LAING

An appraisal of his contemporary relevance

Edited by M. Guy Thompson

Routledge
Taylor & Francis Group

LONDON AND NEW YORK

First published 2015
by Routledge
27 Church Road, Hove, East Sussex, BN3 2FA

And by Routledge
711 Third Avenue, New York, NY 10017

Routledge is an imprint of the Taylor & Francis Group, an Informa business

British Library Cataloguing in Publication Data
A catalogue record for this book is available from the British Library

Library of Congress Cataloging-in-Publication Data
The legacy of R. D. Laing : an appraisal of his contemporary relevance /
   edited by M. Guy Thompson.
      pages cm
   1. Laing, R. D. (Ronald David), 1927–1989.   2. Psychiatrists—Great
Britian.   3. Psychology.   I. Thompson, M. Guy, 1947– editor.
   RC339.52.L34L44 2015
   616.890092—dc23
   2014048137

ISBN: 978-1-138-85014-9 (hbk)
ISBN: 978-1-138-85015-6 (pbk)
ISBN: 978-1-315-72494-2 (ebk)

Typeset in Bembo
by Apex CoVantage, LLC

Printed and bound in Great Britain by
TJ International Ltd, Padstow, Cornwall

For
Ronnie Laing
mentor, troublemaker, friend

CONTENTS

CONTRIBUTORS

Fritjof Capra, PhD, is a physicist and systems theorist, a founding director of the Center for Ecoliteracy in Berkeley, California, and on the faculty of the Beahrs Environmental Leadership Program at the University of California, Berkeley. Dr. Capra is the author of several international bestsellers, including *The Tao of Physics* (1975), *The Web of Life* (1996), *The Hidden Connections* (2002), and *The Science of Leonardo* (2007). He is currently working on a multidisciplinary textbook, *The Systems View of Life*, coauthored with Pier Luigi Luisi, to be published by Cambridge University Press. He lives in Berkeley, California.

Steven Gans, PhD, is Associate Professor of Philosophy at the American Public University and is in private psychotherapy practice at the Center for Relational Psychotherapy in Phoenix, Arizona. He worked closely with Laing for many years at the Philadelphia Association and taught in the psychotherapy training program. Dr. Gans is the coauthor, with Leon Redler, of *Just Listening: Ethics and Therapy* (2001). He lives in Scottsdale, Arizona.

John M. Heaton, MA, MB, BChir, DO, received his medical degree at Cambridge University and was an eye surgeon before training as a psychoanalyst with E. Graham Howe at the Open Way. Dr. Heaton founded the Philadelphia Association Training Programme in Phenomenology and Psychoanalysis in 1971 and continues to serve on its faculty. He is the author of numerous books and journal article on the interrelationship between phenomenology, Greek thought, and psychotherapy, with a particular interest in the sceptics.

Theodor Itten is a psychotherapist and clinical psychologist in private practice in Switzerland. He trained at the Philadelphia Association under the tutelage of R. D. Laing and Francis Huxley in the 1970s, before returning to his native Switzerland, where he is a past president of the Swiss Psychotherapeutic Association and currently is the executive editor of the *International Journal of Psychotherapy*. Mr. Itten is the author of *Rage: Managing an Explosive Emotion* (2011) and coeditor, with Courtenay Young, of *R. D. Laing: Fifty Years Since THE DIVIDED SELF* (2012). He lives in St. Gallen, Switzerland.

Douglas Kirsner, PhD, holds a chair in Philosophy and Psychoanalytic Studies at Deakin University, Melbourne, Australia. He is the author of *The Schizoid World of Jean-Paul Sartre and R. D. Laing* (2003) and *Unfree Associations: Inside Psychoanalytic Institutes* (2009). He lived in one of the post–Kingsley Hall, Philadelphia Association households during the 1970s and has retained a special research interest in Laing's work. His 1980 interview with Laing has recently been published in *The Psychoanalytic Review* (April 2013). He lives in Melbourne, Australia.

Peter Mezan, PhD, is a psychoanalyst in private practice in New York City. He was educated at Harvard College, Harvard Medical School, Christ's College, Cambridge, and the City University of New York. In London, where he lived for many years, he became close to Laing and his circle and, as a freelance journalist, introduced Laing to the American public in cover articles in major American magazines as well as contributions to several books. He has given numerous papers at psychoanalytic conferences around the world on the psychoanalysis of couples and is currently collaborating on a book on that subject. He lives in Katonah, New York.

Andrew Pickering, PhD, is an internationally renowned leader in the field of science and technology studies. For many years, he was Professor of Sociology at the University of Illinois at Urbana-Champaign, and is now Professor of Sociology and Philosophy at the University of Exeter in England. He has held fellowships at the Massachusetts Institute of Technology; the Institute for Advanced Study at Princeton, Princeton University; the Guggenheim Foundation; the Center for Advanced Study in the Behavioral Sciences at Stanford; and, most recently, Institutes for Advanced Study at the Universities of Durham and Konstanz. He is the author of numerous books, the most recent which is *The Cybernetic Brain: Sketches of Another Future* (2010), which includes a chapter on Gregory Bateson and R. D. Laing, which reviews the antipsychiatry movement and the 1960s counterculture. He lives in Great Britain.

Kirk J. Schneider, PhD, is a leading spokesperson for contemporary existential-humanistic psychology, and is an adjunct faculty member at Saybrook University, San Francisco, California, and at Teachers College, Columbia University, New York. Dr. Schneider is a founding member of the Existential-Humanistic Institute and is the author and/or editor of numerous books, including *The Paradoxical Self: Toward an Understanding of Our Contradictory Nature* (1999), *Rediscovery of Awe: Splendor, Mystery and the Fluid Center of Life* (2004), and his most recent, *The*

Polarized Mind: Why It's Killing Us and What We Can Do About It (2013). He lives in San Francisco, California.

Martin A. Schulman, PhD, was editor of *The Psychoanalytic Review* for sixteen years. He is coeditor of *Failures in Psychoanalytic Treatment* (2001, with J. Reppen), *Way Beyond Freud: Postmodern Psychoanalysis Observed* (2004, with J. Reppen and J. Tucker), and *Sexual Faces* (2009, with C. Schwartz. Dr. Schulman has had an enduring interest in the work of Laing and wrote his doctoral dissertation on Laing's early work. He lives in Aventura, Florida. Sadly, Dr. Shulman passed away last year, shortly after submitting his paper for this book.

M. Guy Thompson, PhD, received his psychoanalytic training from R. D. Laing, and Hugh Crawford at the Philadelphia Association in London, and served as the organization's administrator from 1973 to 1980. He is currently Personal and Supervising Analyst and Faculty Member, Psychoanalytic Institute of Northern California, San Francisco, and Adjunct Professor at the California School of Professional Psychology and the California Institute of Integral Studies, Dr. Thompson is founder and director of Free Association, Inc., a non profit organization devoted to the dissemination of Laing's ideas in the U.S., and is the author of more than 100 journal articles, book chapters, and reviews, as well as three other books, *The Death of Desire* (1985), *The Truth About Freud's Technique* (1994), and *The Ethic of Honesty* (2004). A completely revised and expanded edition of Dr. Thompson's first book, *The Death of Desire: An Existential Study in Sanity and Madness*, will be published by Routledge soon. He lives in San Rafael, California.

INTRODUCTION

M. Guy Thompson, PhD

R. D. Laing wore many robes in his career, including psychiatrist, psychoanalyst, philosopher, social critic, author, poet, and mystic, and at the peak of his fame and popularity in the 1970s he was the most widely read psychiatrist in the world. Renown of that magnitude is dependent on the happy coincidence of a multitude of factors, including the right message at the most opportune time. This was no doubt true for Laing, when the student unrest of the Vietnam War intersected with his devastating critique of a society, he argued, intent on subverting the minds of its youth for undisclosed purposes. At a time when authority figures of every persuasion were suspect, members of the counterculture embraced this hip, disarming Scotsman to explain how they were being mystified and why. Arguably the most controversial psychoanalyst since Freud, Laing's meteoric rise in the 1960s and 1970s was the result of his rare ability to make complex ideas accessible with such best-selling classics as *The Divided Self* (1960); *Sanity, Madness and Family* (with Aaron Esterson, 1964); *The Politics of Experience* (1967); *Knots* (1970), and many others. Laing's impassioned plea for a more humane treatment of those in society who are most vulnerable catapulted him into the vanguard of intellectual and cultural debate about the nature of sanity and madness, and inspired a generation of psychology students, intellectuals, and artists to turn Laing into a social icon. His impact on the youth of the 1970s was especially pronounced in the United States, where his renown rivaled even that of the Indian sages that were the rage among the college crowd's cognoscenti.

Yet by the time Laing died of a heart attack at the age of 62 his influence had all but vanished in America. In Europe, where his impact never reached the incendiary proportions it enjoyed in the U.S., his ideas continued to be debated and taken seriously. But generally his writings gradually fell out of favor with the times, and on many occasions during the last decade of his life he showed up for public lectures (always well attended) inebriated, arrogant, and rude. What are we to make of a man who had the world in the palm of his hand yet who apparently despised his notoriety and the fans who accounted for it, who both courted fame and rejected it? Although several biographies have attempted to address this question (most of them written by people who never met him), Laing continues to be an enigma shrouded in mystery. Even his closest friends found him a bewildering and oftentimes exasperating contradiction of character traits. Capable of great warmth and sensitivity – the basis of his uncanny clinical acumen, especially with psychotics – Laing could be painfully provocative and delighted in upsetting his followers' most cherished assumptions about themselves, sometimes to shattering effect. Who was Laing, and how should his legacy and contemporary relevance be assessed? How did he become so famous, and why was his influence so pervasive?

Laing's extraordinary reach into the American zeitgeist was based almost entirely on his devastating critique of conventional psychiatric practices, which he believed were often more sinister than the mental illnesses they presumed to treat. The (albeit reluctant) father of anti-psychiatry,[1] Laing developed a daring alternative to conventional psychiatric treatment in 1965 at Kingsley Hall, the therapy center in London where he conceived the notion of a community where therapists and patients alike could live without clearly defined roles.[2] This controversial treatment regimen was so successful that it continues to operate fifty years later and is even funded by the Local Council in London. Kingsley Hall also inspired numerous residential treatment communities in North America that eventually led to a sea change in contemporary attitudes about the involuntary incarceration of the mentally ill.

Of course, it was Laing's books that made him world famous, some of which continue to sell at an impressive rate. *The Divided Self, Sanity, Madness and the Family, The Politics of Experience*, and *Knots* are now considered classics and continue to serve as the foundation of Laing's unique and disconcerting message. They are just as relevant today, and just as radical, as when they were first published in the 1960s. Some of the papers included in this collection address these books and recapitulate their contemporary relevance and why their message continues to shock and disturb.

On a broader, cultural level Laing's ideas spread far beyond issues concerning psychotherapy and the treatment of the mentally ill. Nearly every American college student in the early 1970s read *The Politics of Experience*, a campus best seller that seemed to encapsulate the undercurrent of social malaise so many young people were then feeling. When the pot-smoking, acid-dropping counterculture intersected with the radical anti–Vietnam War protest movement Laing's critique of how people in power were systematically mystifying them transformed him into a social phenomenon and quasi-spiritual leader. So what was his message and why was its impact so palpable?

I first encountered Laing in the fall of 1972, at the very zenith of his fame and notoriety, at the tail end of a national lecture tour in Berkeley, California, that billed him as "The Philosopher of Madness." The poster announcing Laing's lecture featured a photograph of him, bare to the waist, standing upside down in a yoga position. This was hardly typical of what you expected from a world-renowned psychoanalyst! Was Laing going to talk to us or just engage in some kind of far-out, private meditation? It somehow made perfect sense to expect Laing to shock, seduce, and mesmerize us as we waited for him to let us in on just how crazy our parents and political leaders were. As his presentation commenced, there was nothing remotely conventional about Laing or his lecture. Dressed in dark brown velvet slacks and a matching elegant long-sleeve pullover, hair down to his shoulders, Laing looked more like the kind of poet you would encounter in a North Beach bookstore than a world-famous psychiatrist. Laing was also a strikingly beautiful man, with eyes that seemed to glow in the dark, seeing through the falsity the rest of us hardly noticed. He walked out onto the stage, gingerly approaching the microphone, and for what felt like hours proceeded to shuffle his feet, silently gaze at the floor, looking about as uncomfortable as you might imagine yourself in his position, by now leaving all of us wondering, where is this going? He then proceeded to talk, in that distinctive, slow Scottish burr, conversationally and without notes, about what it was like to travel about America, the craziest culture he had ever set foot in. This was not a penetrating lecture about existential philosophy or anything remotely theoretical and incisive as you might have expected or hoped for from, after all, a *philosopher*. Instead, we got a fireside chat, a conversation among friends, as we were enlisted into something special, intimate, conspiratorial. He had us eating out of the palm of his hand less than thirty minutes into his "performance," and we never looked back. It was then and there that I decided to abandon my graduate studies and move to London to work with him.

This kind of power and charisma made Laing the phenomenon he had become. Like Freud, Laing aimed to change the rules of how the game was played, but where Freud succeeded in changing the way we understood the nature of mental illness, while inaugurating a novel treatment method for neurosis, Laing ultimately failed to conceive a method of treating schizophrenia that could be packaged for universal consumption. Laing did not make it easy to work with him and made it even more difficult to learn what he was doing. There was nothing about Kingsley Hall and the subsequent residential therapy centers that followed in its wake that was overtly elucidated to us. We had come from all over the world, but mostly America, to contribute to the groundbreaking work he and his associates were undertaking, only to find him disconcertingly aloof, disinterested, disengaged. Yet, as Peter Mezan's opening paper and Douglas Kirsner's interview with Laing each demonstrate, there was something irresistible about Laing the person that convinced everyone around him that we were making history together while engaging in the most noble work one could envision. We were helping the most psychotic members of our society recover from their madness, not by "treating" them but by just *living* with them and carrying on in our day-to-day affairs, perfectly normally, as though we had being doing this all our lives. We were not being taught "how" to do therapy with them, nor was any conventional treatment on the table, including medication. Like Alice in Wonderland, we had fallen down the rabbit hole, hanging on for dear life, and loving every minute of it.

During the decade that I lived in London, from 1973 to 1980 (four of those years at Portland Road[3]), Laing's notoriety was legendary. Many of the world's most famous thinkers, gurus, philosophers, psychiatrists, and anthropologists regarded Laing's "scene" at the Philadelphia Association a must-see when in London. Although this was the decade when Laing's writing began to abandon him, his fame was such that all of his books continued to sell in vast numbers, so he remained very much at the center of the conversation everyone was having about the ills of society and how to change it. Like Bob Dylan, Laing had initially been embraced by the Left as one of their own, only to subsequently make clear that he was completely disinterested in politics of any kind, except, perhaps, the politics of *experience*! Laing's distaste for political groups and their agendas eventually led to his falling out with David Cooper, who, by the late 1960s, had concluded that psychotherapy of *any* kind was nothing more than a subtle form of brainwashing.

While working with Laing I was also training as a psychoanalyst and supporting myself by serving as the administrator (and only employee) of Laing's organization, the Philadelphia Association. This was the decade when Laing's organization came out of hiding (when I first arrived there in 1973, its phone number was unlisted!) and mounted an ambitious study program as well as a psychoanalytic training regimen that integrated existential philosophy, phenomenology, Buddhism, yoga, and other spiritual practices into their loosely structured curriculum. I found Laing to be a brilliant administrator, with a very clear concept of what he and his colleagues were about, careful to avoid the pitfall of being mistaken for just another therapy training scheme. This was probably the only genuinely *existential* training program ever undertaken, literally dropping you at the deep end of the pool and letting you fend for yourself, allowing you in that offhand British way to sink or swim. Not an insignificant number of students from America, despite their best efforts, sank, never to be heard from again. This was the era when psychedelic drugs were also an unavoidable component of one's learning experience. But by far the most radical experience offered was living in one of the so-called Laingian houses,[4] about which I elaborate in this collection of papers ("Living at Portland Road"). There was really nothing in the world remotely like these "treatment" centers, which continue to flourish today in London, along with the psychoanalytic training program inaugurated by John Heaton in the early 1970s.

This decade of Laing's work was nothing short of thrilling, and my experience there could not have been more illuminating and transformative. It was at the culmination of my training in 1980 that I decided to return to California and continue Laing's work there. By the end of that decade, however, Laing had still failed to write another best-selling book, and this began to take a toll on him. On his many visits to American during this interlude Laing made deep inroads into various aspects of the therapy culture, including the family therapy movement, humanistic psychology, Kingsley Hall–type houses attempted in California (Soteria, Diabasis, Shadows) and New Hampshire (Burch House), and what was left of the counterculture. The 1980s, however, were not kind to Laing or the counterculture. The political tide turned against the rampant era of experimentation that had characterized the 1970s, and now a new cynicism crept in that was diametrically opposed to the use of street drugs, hippie communes, and the kind of educative experimentation that culminated in dispensing with grades at even the most prestigious universities in America. The pendulum has swung radically in the other direction, as it continues unabated to this day.

Laing's marriage, which had always been on life support, exploded at the beginning of this decade and with it any desire to remain in London and work as a clinician. During this period Laing fell out with his colleagues and opted to go his own way.[5] With no more best sellers with which to connect to a new generation of college students, always his most passionate fan base, Laing's fame began to wane. He nevertheless spent the rest of that decade continuing to write, hoping to crank out at least one more best seller while devoting the rest of his time giving lectures the world over for premium fees, his sole means of support. His drinking, always a factor, increased, and it eventually became obvious to those of us who knew Laing personally that he was seriously ill. He was said to be dying of cancer when the heart attack he suffered in 1989 killed him.

So what of Laing's legacy today? Are his ideas still radical and as relevant to our current situation, or have they become outdated, obsolete, and passé? These were the questions that a few of Laing's former colleagues and I decided to address as we approached the twenty-fifth anniversary of his death. In October 2013, I decided to organize a conference to honor Laing on the twenty-fifth anniversary of his death and to commemorate his impact on American culture, while assessing the contemporary relevance of his ideas. I had organized a similar symposium in 1999, in San Francisco, where we celebrated the tenth anniversary of Laing's death with papers also by former colleagues who had worked with Laing in London.[6] What we envisioned for 2013 was something on a far grander scale and over a greater duration. Many of Laing's former students and colleagues from around the world convened in New York to assess his legacy and his impact on current treatment mores of the mentally ill, and the ills of the culture at large. To this end Wagner College on Staten Island hosted a weekend symposium for the purpose of exploring Laing's legacy with many of Laing's still-living colleagues who knew and worked with him intimately. Representatives from family therapy, existential therapy, phenomenology, psychoanalysis, Buddhism, the treatment of schizophrenia and psychotic process, the humanistic-transpersonal and New Age community, and spiritual practitioners met to discuss Laing's impact on these disciplines and his continuing relevance to twenty-first century attitudes about psychological suffering and the nature of madness.

It is impossible for any conference or collection of papers to do justice to the breadth and depth of Laing's unconventional message, but we believed it was worth giving it a try, to at least get the conversation going, and see where it would lead. As the twenty-fifth anniversary of Laing's death approached, I began to realize how many of Laing's former colleagues and friends had died. A considerable amount of Laing's message and style was never broached in his books and has never been written about by any of his former associates. We decided that we should take advantage of those still-surviving friends and colleagues to meet and share what it was like to know Laing and work with him, and to share our nuggets of wisdom with the world while we still could. Our primary focus was on those Americans who, like myself, went to London to work with Laing, as well as Americans who Laing developed relationships with in the U.S. and who were profoundly impacted by him. With that in mind we put a program together and convened at Wagner College on Staten Island, New York, to share what we learned from him and what it was like to have him as a friend, confidante, and collaborator. The book you hold in your hands is the culmination of that endeavor.

Now let me introduce our contributors and something about their relationship with Laing or his ideas (more detailed biographies can be found elsewhere in this volume).

Peter Mezan, a New York psychoanalyst who opens this volume, was an expatriate American living in London in 1970 when he decided to write a magazine article about Laing in order to begin a writing career. Mezan proceeded to meet Laing and over a number of months of conversations fashioned a riveting article that was published in *Esquire* magazine, just in time to introduce Americans to Laing on the eve of his famous 1972 lecture tour of American college campuses. In his essay, "Who Was R. D. Laing," Mezan recounts what that time was like, as well as the exasperating nature of what it was like to know Laing as a friend. This piece is the perfect introduction to Laing for those who have never read him, but especially for those who have.

In the second piece of this volume, "Laing and the Myth of Mental Illness Redux," I explore one of Laing's favorite topics: What is sanity, and what is madness? Like Thomas Szasz, Laing questioned the efficacy of the concept of psychopathology, or mental illness, and tried to take the question of madness outside of mental hospitals and back to where he thought it belonged: our relationships with each other. To this end I turn to Laing's most important and enduring work, *The Divided Self*, to mine the extraordinary insight into the nature of madness that Laing explicated in his very first publication. I also rely on my personal and professional relationship with Laing and the many conversations we shared on this topic over the course of nearly 20 years.

The next essay features Fritjof Capra, the renowned physicist and systems theorist and the author of *The Tao of Physics* (1975), in which he recounts a series of conversations he enjoyed with Laing in the summer of 1981, during their off moments while attending a conference in Zaragoza, Spain. In Capra's essay, "Laing's *The Voice of Experience* and the Emerging Science of Consciousness," he reviews a debate he enjoyed with Laing about the relationship between experience and science and about whether science has access to something as subjectively personal as experience. What is perhaps most remarkable about this exchange is not only the details of the debate itself but also Laing's style and the method he employed while debating Capra, at one moment hostile and abrasive, the next warm and conciliatory. This is an extraordinary example of what Laing could be like as a friend as well as an adversary.

Next is an essay by John Heaton, one of Laing's oldest colleagues at the Philadelphia Association. Heaton first met Laing in 1960, soon after the publication of *The Divided Self*, and invited him to join him at The Open Way, a therapy and spiritual center founded by E. Graham Howe, an early member of the Tavistock Institute. They collaborated for several years before Laing left to found the Philadelphia Association and Kingsley Hall in 1965. Several years later Heaton joined Laing there and, at Laing's invitation, established the Philadelphia Association's psychoanalytic training program. Needless to say, Heaton knew Laing deeply, and in his essay, "On R. D. Laing's Style, Sorcery, Alienation," shares with us original insights into Laing's style and his lifelong meditation on the concept of alienation, much of which Laing only sporadically discussed in his books. The result is both illuminating and mesmerizing.

Andrew Pickering, the renowned British academic and leader in the field of science and technology studies at the University of Exeter, never knew Laing but was deeply taken with his work and his ideas. In his book *The Cybernetic Brain: Sketches of Another Future* (2010), Pickering explores Laing's pivotal relationship with the American anthropologist Gregory Bateson and how it helped inspire Laing's immersion into the anti-psychiatry movement and the 1960s' counterculture. In his essay, "Nonmodern Selves," Pickering makes the remarkable argument that it was not Laing's *ideas* that were so important but the *work* Laing engaged in at Kingsley Hall and the Philadelphia Association, what Pickering depicts as the "performative" aspect of Laing's legacy. This is an original take on Laing's importance to us as we embark on this brave new world of the twenty-first century.

Douglas Kirsner, the Australian philosopher and Sartre scholar, first met Laing soon after the publication of Kirsner's first book, *The Schizoid World of Jean-Paul Sartre and R. D. Laing* (2003), in London. Kirsner went there to interview Laing for an Australian radio program and, after befriending me, decided to move into Hugh Crawford's house on Portland Road to see firsthand what these Laingian houses were like. I believe that Kirsner was the only academic who was brave (or crazy?) enough to dare such an undertaking! This experience provided Kirsner with a unique and penetrating perspective into Laing's views about madness and its treatment, and Kirsner has written numerous superb papers about Laing's contribution to psychiatry as a result. Kirsner's essay, "Laing's *The Divided Self* and *The Politics of Experience*" reviews the enduring importance of Laing's two most important and best-selling works.

Martin A. Schulman, the New York psychoanalyst and former editor of *The Psychoanalytic Review*, never knew Laing personally, but Laing was a pivotal figure in Schulman's early development and decision to become a psychoanalyst. Laing's early book on *Interpersonal Perception* (1966) was the topic of Schulman's doctoral dissertation and profoundly influenced his approach to psychoanalysis. In his essay, "R. D. Laing: Premature Postmodern Psychoanalyst," Schulman argues that Laing's ideas predated the so-called postmodern turn that subsequently had an impact on the relational psychoanalytic movement in America and that many of the ideas and therapeutic techniques adopted by the relational perspective were anticipated by Laing, although he seldom gets credit for it. This is an important contribution to Laing's impact on American psychoanalysis by one of its most prominent practitioners.

In the next essay, "Awakening to Love: R. D. Laing's Phenomenological Therapy," Steven Gans, the American philosopher who also received his psychotherapy training from Laing and his cohorts at the Philadelphia Association, explores the profound role that Laing's lifelong obsession with the nature of love played in both his life and his clinical work. Drawing from his numerous conversations with Laing as well as Laing's private seminars that only his students had access to, Gans also benefits from his access to Laing's last and unpublished manuscript, *The Challenge of Love*, to get to the depths of Laing's meditation on this pivotal aspect of our existence. Gans's personal relationship with Laing, coupled with his own philosophical background, serves him well in this highly informative exploration of Laing's complicated perspective on the nature of love and its heartbreaking absence.

Next, Kirk Schneider, the prominent American existential therapist and former protégé of Rollo May, who was one of Laing's closest friends, examines in his essay "R. D. Laing's Existential-Humanistic Practice: What Was He Actually *Doing?*", Laing's therapeutic technique. Schneider knew Laing personally and had attended a number of workshops that Laing gave on his frequent visits to California, so he had some considerable experience to draw from in his critique of Laing as a therapist. Schneider was particularly struck by the utter lack of any discernable technique in Laing's work but suggests that appearances can be deceiving. Schneider argues that Laing was a master of what psychoanalysts today are only beginning to acknowledge as an essential part of every therapeutic encounter: the use of the analyst's personality, a far more subtle way of connecting with one's patients than the more familiar transference–countertransference dynamic effectively captures.

In close proximity to both Gans's and Schneider's emphasis on the inherently human side of Laing's clinical style, Theodor Itten, the Swiss psychologist who also trained with Laing at the Philadelphia Association addresses the role of compassion in his essay, "Psychotherapeutic Compassion in the Tradition of R. D. Laing." Itten connects the various world religions' emphasis on the Golden Rule – do unto others as you would have them do unto you – with Laing's oft-repeated admonition to apply this standard in one's work with patients, especially those who are the most difficult and demanding to work with, Laing's particular specialty. Itten draws on his close friendship with Laing in showing the more compassionate side of Laing's notoriously difficult personality, to excellent effect.

The last essay from the Laing Symposium is a synthesis of a panel that was composed of eight people who had all lived in one of Laing's therapeutic households and what that experience was like. In this essay, "A Note on Living in One of R. D. Laing's Post-Kingsley Hall Households: Portland Road," I recount a portion of my own experience of living there, featuring a young man who was a roommate of mine for a year and a half, during which time he refused to leave his bed. The difficulty that all of us had with "Jerome's" intransigence – he also refused to speak to us during the entirety of this period – neatly encapsulates how truly unconventional these households were and the enigmatic nature of what was specifically therapeutic about them. I think you will find this story both shocking and moving in its startling and unexpected resolution.

Finally, the last essay in this volume is a bonus that was not a direct outcome of the symposium. This essay, titled "Human, All Too Human: The Life and Work of R. D. Laing Interview," is an extraordinary interview that Douglas Kirsner conducted with Laing in 1980 and includes an incisive introduction in which Kirsner astutely summarizes Laing's importance today, including Kirsner's own assessment of why Laing's all too human personality was both an asset and a curse. This is one of the best interviews ever conducted with Laing, and we are fortunate that Kirsner has given us permission to include it in this collection.

You will undoubtedly note by the time you have finished reading this volume that the contributors have barely skimmed the surface of Laing's enduring legacy. I hope that this is only the first step in bringing Laing's importance back into play as we embark on a new century, the second century of the psychotherapeutic process, initiated by Freud a hundred years ago. As more books appear in the future addressing Laing's impact and relevance, it is important to remember that, by its nature, Laing's contribution is impossible to capture from his writings alone. Not to have known Laing personally presents a serious impediment to appreciating the full range and paradoxical nature of his message. I am especially appreciative of those contributions from his former colleagues who were able, if only in a relative way, to impart what that experience was like. I hope you will derive as much enjoyment from reading their accounts as I have.

Last but not least, I would like to take this opportunity to thank my collaborators, Steven Gans and Miles Groth, who helped organize the Laing Symposium at Wagner College. Without their help, the conference would not have happened and this volume would have been impossible. Steve Gans has been a friend for more than forty years, going back to the time we both lived at Portland Road in London. He has been a stalwart collaborator and was immensely helpful in conceiving the Wagner conference, from which most of these papers were taken. I also want to thank Miles Groth for making Wagner College available for the Laing Symposium and for hosting the conference for us. His help was indispensable, and I could not be more grateful for the help he provided. And last, I wish to thank Wagner College for their generous hospitality and for ensuring a memorable experience for all who attended. And, of course, to all those individuals who participated in and attended the Wagner Symposium, thank you, for without your involvement this book would not exist.

Notes

1 In fact, it was Laing's close associate in the 1960s, David Cooper, who coined the term and made it popular in his 1967 book *Psychiatry and Anti-Psychiatry*. The term was more political than descriptive, which served Cooper's radical motives well but detracted from Laing's concern to focus his efforts on developing a more humane treatment of persons suffering from debilitating mental and emotional distress, especially schizophrenia. Laing

initially went along with the label, but as Cooper became increasingly disenchanted with any form of treatment, humane or otherwise, and more politically active he and Laing parted ways, at which point Laing pointedly rejected the label. Cooper eventually settled in Paris, where he occupied the center of the then-established anti-psychiatry movement that included Felix Gauttari in France, Franco Basaglia in Italy, and others who shared a loathing for bourgeois attitudes about mental illness and a passion for Marxist ideology and the burgeoning protest movement. Despite Laing's efforts to distance himself from this label, he nevertheless remained on good terms with his Continental cohorts, all of whom looked to him as their leader, due to Laing's fame and charisma which served, if ironically, to legitimize their movement. Laing's argument that he was never an anti-psychiatrist has become a moot point because the term has much wider usage than when Laing was still alive. For all intents and purposes, Laing is regarded as the instigator and champion of any effort to question psychiatric orthodoxy and the involuntary incarceration and treatment of the mentally ill, and the term *anti-psychiatry* has come to epitomize this perspective.

2 See the next to last chapter in this collection, "A Note on Living in One of R. D. Laing's Post-Kingsley Hall Households: Portland Road," for a description of what it was like to live in one of Laing's treatment centers.

3 One of the post-Kingsley Hall households set up by Hugh Crawford, one of Laing's closest colleagues, also from Glasgow, which I talk about at length in the Portland Road essay in this collection.

4 The houses that followed in the wake of Kingsley Hall were never thought of as "Laingian" houses. After closing Kingsley Hall in 1970, Laing invited his colleagues (other members of the Philadelphia Association) to open houses of their own. The way this typically worked was that a member of the Philadelphia Association would procure a house and then establish a relationship with it in his own fashion, which usually meant visiting on a regular basis, but not living there. There were no paid staff to work there, and no "patients." Everyone who chose to live in one of these communities did so on an equal basis, some inevitably crazier than others, some saner. Students like myself had no special prerogative for being there. In fact, it could be a disadvantage. Leon Redler opened a number of houses that had been condemned by the London Council for demolition, but all of them operated as one community called Archway (the town in North London in which they were located). Hugh Crawford subsequently opened a house on Portland Road, and then a second. When I arrived in London in 1973 there was a total of three such houses, and at their peak a few years later there were eight, operated by four or five therapists affiliated with the Philadelphia Association, spread all over London. None of them was called "Laingian" communities because each took on the personality and style of the therapist responsible for setting it up. No one answered to Laing as being in any kind of authority, so the houses' affiliation with the Philadelphia Association was loosely defined as merely under its auspices. This epitomized Laing's management style, which also characterized the way the seminars and training programs were also run. (John Heaton took it on himself to start the training program, so he was ostensibly "in charge.") Looking back on this historically, there is some merit in regarding all of the Philadelphia Association's residential houses as Laingian in nature, if not in fact, because of Kingsley Hall serving as their inspiration.

5 Hugh Crawford, Laing's most trusted confidante, had died the previous year, which only contributed to Laing's growing sense of isolation and estrangement.

6 Two essays in this volume, the ones by John Heaton and Steven Gans, are from that 1999 Laing symposium.

1

WHO WAS R. D. LAING?

*Peter Mezan, PhD**

I met R. D. Laing the end of 1970, beginning of 1971. This was around six months after Kingsley Hall shut its doors and shortly before he closed his Wimpole Street psychoanalytic practice, packed up his family, and went off to Ceylon and India to study yoga and meditation. I don't know how many of you remember 1970. How many of you were even born in 1970? That was 43 years ago – 43 years! Wow, it makes me want to keel over right here and now.

By 1971, Laing had become a major culture hero and the most famous living psychiatrist in the world. To explain how that happened, let me give you a brief reminder of what was going on in those days. Revolution was in the air, everywhere you looked. The political culture, the social culture, the artistic culture, the intellectual culture – all of it was in an uproar. In this country, there'd been the unthinkable assassinations, the Vietnam War was raging, there was the civil rights movement, the women's rights movement, protests everywhere you turned.

All this was following an era of social and political conformity, or what I would call the culture of "Because I Say So": because the president said so, because the generals and politicians said so, because the local draft board said so, because the police said so, because the doctors and the psychiatrists said so, because the teachers and professors said so, because everybody's parents said so. The assumption was that power and authority were benign and could be trusted to be more or less looking after your best interests. And suddenly it seemed they weren't.

Nothing seemed to be working the way it was supposed to. Police who were supposed to be protecting you were beating up students who were protesting the war, civil rights marchers were being beaten and killed on the orders of governors and sheriffs, and the soldiers, who were no more than kids themselves, were either being slaughtered in Vietnam or shooting and killing college students at Kent State, right here at home. And everyone was watching in horror and confusion as all of this played out right in front of them every night on their TVs. It was not very hard to feel as though either the world had gone crazy or you had.

Enter R. D. Laing.

I was living in London at the time. I was an editor of *Nature*, the British science journal, and commuting to Cambridge where I was teaching literature. Somehow I got it into my head that I wanted to try writing for a living and thought I'd start by doing some freelance journalism for American magazines. I had no idea how to go about this, so in a burst of preposterous optimism and naiveté I wrote a letter to Tom Wolfe, one of my literary heroes ever since I'd read *The Electric Kool-Aid Acid Test*, and asked him what I should do. Amazingly, he wrote back. He said all you have to do is get something published in one of the following five magazines, and you'll have a career: *The New Yorker, Esquire, The Atlantic, Harper's* or *Playboy*. No problem.

So I wrote to the editors of all five magazines, told them a little about myself, said I'd be in New York in a couple weeks and had some ideas about articles that I was sure would be perfect for them. All five said great and gave me appointments to meet when I was in the city. I made up a list of subjects I wanted to write about – one of them was to do a profile of R. D. Laing.

Here's one reason I was interested in R. D. Laing. When I was a Harvard medical student, a professor from the psychiatry department took a bunch of us on a tour of the Metropolitan State Hospital in Belmont, Massachusetts. It was reputed to be one of the worst state mental hospitals in the country. I think it was ranked 43rd or 44th. After we spent a couple hours roaming in and out of the wards filled with chronic schizophrenics, some of whom had been there for years, I remember there was a long hallway down in the basement, and three lines of patients quietly waiting. One line was waiting for electroconvulsive therapy, one for insulin coma therapy, and one for a prefrontal leucotomy. As medical students, we were invited to observe each of these treatments in action. By the time I watched some poor woman strapped down and being put into an insulin coma, I was close to throwing up. That was 1966.

Then it was 1968, and I had moved to England, and I came across *The Divided Self*. Me and everybody else. Out of nowhere, as it seemed to me, everybody was talking about R. D. Laing. Radicals were honoring him as a philosopher of revolution. Intellectuals were coming close to blows about him, unsure whether he was a demagogue or a thinker to be reckoned with. Psychiatrists were going berserk with indignation, feeling as though he was not only attacking what they did but also undermining their authority about mental illness of any kind. And then there were the masses of people who felt he was talking directly to them – that he was expressing something they had been feeling but had never articulated to themselves. People from all over the world were actually picking up and moving their whole families to London to be near him and be part of things.

And, of course, there were all the rumors and opinions about him, that couldn't help but make me curious. People who had never met him had it on good authority that he was an illuminated saint, a charlatan, a bourgeois revisionist, a dangerous paranoid-schizophrenic who'd had multiple hospitalizations, that he gave all his patients LSD, that he was in the habit of punching some of his patients in the nose (I kid you not), that his once wonderful mind had been ruined by alcohol or mushrooms or what have you and on and on.

Oh, and one other reason I wanted to write about him. I had actually met him once in a shoe store on the King's Road in Chelsea, and the encounter had stuck in my mind. I recognized him from the spooky cover photograph of *The Self and Others* – deep-set, shadowy, X-ray eyes beneath a high-angled brow. I was returning a pair of fine Italian footwear that had fallen apart in a week, and R. D. Laing was being extremely patient with a longhaired salesman who kept bringing him the wrong sandals. When the salesman went back to the storeroom for the third time, Laing smiled, hunched his shoulders and walked over to me: "I hope you don't mind my asking like this, but I was wondering where you got that bush jacket you're wearing. It's just the sort of thing I could use – lots of pockets." I stifled an impulse to just give it to him right off my back, then and there, and explained it came from Africa. He nodded amiably and went back to dealing with the salesman who had reappeared with yet another pair of the wrong sandals. Laing sighed. "I suppose I could go barefoot, but I'm a doctor, you see, and there are some people who might think it a bit odd."

So fast-forward, and I'm in New York, heading to my appointments with the editors. This was not the New York I remembered from 1966: A computer in Grand Central Station cast my horoscope, people in saffron robes were chanting Hare Krishna in front of my bank, some stockbrokers I knew were playing the market by casting the I Ching (and swearing by it, incidentally), Allen Ginsberg was singing "Om Mani Padme Hum" in a Chicago courtroom and some of the most sober and intelligent of my friends were into the Tibetan *Book of the Dead*, the Kabbalah and the Tarot.

All five editors were enthusiastic about one subject or another, but the editor of Esquire, Don Erikson, was especially excited about a profile of Laing, because since the demise of Kingsley Hall, Laing had withdrawn from the public eye and refused to give interviews to anybody.

"I guarantee you I can get to him," I told Erikson.

How hard could it be? I'd already bumped into him in a shoe store, and I'd had no problem getting a quick response from no less a famous writer than Tom Wolfe.

Three months later I was ready to write an article about how I never got to R. D. Laing. For three months I'd written him letters that disappeared without trace – any of you remember how people used to write actual letters? I'd called his Wimpole Street office umpteen times, and either nobody answered, or somebody answered and said they'd give him a message, maybe they did, maybe they didn't, but I never heard back. Then one day a woman answered who said she was a friend of his who just happened to be in his office and told me she thought Laing probably wouldn't give anybody an interview – ever.

By this time, I had talked to more than two dozen of his colleagues, friends, patients and acquaintances, all of whom had been interesting to meet in their own right but who brought me no closer to the man. Not to mention that the pictures they gave me of him were hard to reconcile, to the point that sometimes I wondered if they were talking about the same person. I was sure some of these people had known him pretty well, and yet they disagreed about whether he was serene or cruel or reckless or cold or warm or compassionate or manipulative or arrogant or humble.

Then one of the Philadelphia Association therapists (this was the umbrella organization of asylum communities that began with Kingsley Hall) said to me, "Why don't you go ask some schizophrenics about him." Okay, I'll go ask some schizophrenics. I went to visit one of the communities in a condemned row house in North London. Understand that, up until then, my assumption from having been a medical student was that patients are sick, doctors are not – or at least patients are sicker than their doctors. So on my way there, I kept reminding myself, "No doctors, no patients – just people."

There was no doorbell, so I just walked in. It wasn't the most welcoming scene. There was none of the social niceties I was accustomed to, which I soon discovered was the norm in the Laing world. No hellos, no good to meet yous, no take a seat, no introductions, so I had to pick up on who everybody was by listening. There was somebody tall by the door sucking like crazy on an unlit pipe, and Mike from Phoenix, and Mary Ann from Kentucky, and Tom from Harvard, and Sadie from Los Angeles, and Gregorio from Buenos Aires and David Bell, a charming schizophrenic gentleman who had formerly been a computer engineer who now went by such names as Little Lamb, My Sweet Blue Angel and Oedipus of the Rex family. The conversation was serious and earnest and like no other conversation I'd ever heard, with a lot of mentions of mystifications and invalidations and reifications, like so many pages out of Laing's books. This I found a little disconcerting, so at a moment of calm, when someone got up to make brownies, I made a mild comment that everybody was sounding a bit Laingianized. Some didn't know what I was talking about. Others maybe yes, maybe no. David Bell, who the whole time was quietly muttering to himself about how Oedipus was a man of no social intelligence, suddenly said to me, "Yes, it's an interesting problem." It was the only normal, thoughtful response I got.

Finally one day, in a last gasp of hope, I called up Leon Redler, an American psychiatrist who was one of the original people involved with Laing in Kingsley Hall, and asked him the next time he spoke to Laing to please mention that I was still here, still trying and eager to meet him. As an afterthought, I also said maybe tell him that we'd met once before: "Tell him I was the guy with the bush jacket in the shoe store last spring."

Later the same afternoon a lady called up claiming to be Laing's secretary: "Dr. Laing will see you tomorrow morning at eleven. Oh, and Dr. Redler said to tell you that the bush jacket helped."

Laing was smaller and slighter than I recalled and looking that day, a bit like a leprechaun. Under a brown suede jacket he was wearing a green work shirt buttoned up to the neck, partly hanging out of green velvet trousers. I, of course, was wearing the bush jacket. He nodded at the jacket. "I remember," he said.

We climbed the stairs to his consulting room and sat down and . . . nothing. He said nothing, waiting for me to begin, watching me from a skew angle, and in a way that let me know he'd be quite content to go right on saying nothing for as long as I cared to be watched.

I knew I had a lot of questions, but I couldn't think of them. So I said, "Who are you, Dr. Laing?" He looked bored and answered immediately. "What you're really asking when you ask me who I am, where I'm at, is who are you."

Uh-oh.

I mumbled something to the effect that anything one asks about anything is in some respect a question about oneself. But I was nervous. I began talking faster and faster, saying god knows what. He was beginning to twitch and roll up his eyes, signs I'd been forewarned ether of impatience or of hard concentration. I was pretty sure it wasn't the latter. Just please let me not give him an asthma attack, I thought. I had heard that some people bring on his asthma. But I couldn't think I was up to that yet either.

Finally he made a sweeping motion with his hand. "I've done nothing original, nothing that hasn't been done before, that people don't already know."

I was pretty sure he was overestimating what people know, but I said, "Maybe people don't know they know."

Finally some kind of agreement, and for a second I felt confident enough to ask if I could turn on the tape recorder. "I don't think so. I'd rather you didn't," Laing said. "I can't exactly explain why, but it's just whatever is going to happen between us isn't going to happen there." He began fidgeting with some lint on his trouser leg. I was beginning to understand why some people found him a difficult man.

I took another stab at trying to find out how he came to be whoever he is.

"Look," he said, his eye rolling flipping into a higher gear, "in a sense I am whoever people observe me to be. I talk with a Scots accent, I wear these clothes, I work here" – gesturing at the analytic couch – "I'm a householder in Belsize Park Gardens with my wife and two children. And also there's my presence – whatever I communicate to people physically."

Suddenly I saw an opening and reminded him of what I'd overheard him telling the shoe salesman about the requirements of acting like a doctor – for instance, not going barefoot, and a passage in *The Self and Others* about a little boy pretending that he was an explorer, then a lion, then a sea captain, then simply himself, just a little boy. And some years later, that he is a grown-up, and some years later, that he is an old man, when suddenly he remembers that it had all been a game of pretend from the start. Laing's point was that we take on different roles and are taught to pretend that we are not pretending and then to forget that we are only pretending that we are not pretending. So I suggested to Laing that, in a sense, he too is pretending – to be a doctor, a householder, a Scotsman, the lot. "So who," I ask, holding my breath, "is doing the pretending?"

Laing's eyes stopped rolling, and he flashed me a smile. "Your diagnosis of my metaphysical disease is very astute." He laughed. I exhaled. And he went over to pick up a fat book with a gray cover. "Let me tell you where I am," he said. And for the next hour and a half, he read me passages from the Brahma-Sutra-Bhasya of Sri Sankaracarya, and we talked about such lighthearted subjects as the nature of mind and the phenomenology of experience. Of course, since he hadn't allowed me to turn on my tape recorder, I had to go right out afterward and find a copy of the Brahma-Sutra to find the passages he'd been reading to me.

He seemed tired. I'd heard he was a bit disillusioned and depressed about Kingsley Hall and about all the rumors and distortions and misunderstandings about what he'd written and said and thought, including by his fans. This was partly why he was going to India and Ceylon, to take a break, collect himself, get away from all that.

Before we parted, he asked if he could try on the bush jacket. It was a loose fit.

The *Esquire* article came out in January 1972.

Given the things I'd heard about Laing's capacity to suddenly turn on people, it was a little worrying how he'd react to whatever I wrote about him. But his only objections to the *Esquire* article were that I had gotten certain facts, certain concrete observations, wrong – like the color of the paint on the walls (it was not the shade of green I said it was) and the location of his desk in the room (it was not by the windows facing some backyards).

When he got back from India, he seemed rejuvenated and agreed to do a coast-to-coast tour of America to straighten people out. I was asked to cover the New York leg of the tour. Laing joked that I was becoming his Boswell. He said that in a way Boswell was more famous than Dr. Johnson, cleverly appealing to my vanity.

I asked him what he was going to say in America.

"I really have no idea at all," he said.

I was hoping it would go better than the first time he'd gone to New York, when he flew out again two hours later, having decided that was an environment he was just not at all ready to enter.

The New York tour headquarters was Suite 608 at the Algonquin Hotel. Aside from the big public talks and lectures and the television interviews, this was where all the one-on-one interviews took place, with Laing usually lounging on the sofa, barefoot (I guess doctors didn't need shoes after all). There was a camera crew filming every moment of the tour, publicists, tour promoters, various other members of his entourage and an endless parade of reporters coming to interview him.

The young woman reporter from *Newsweek* started like this: "This is going to be very superficial, Dr. Laing, because I don't know anything about your work. All we'd like, really, is something witty or shocking, so maybe you could just say what you expect to be doing in America."

"I expect to be spending most of my time in this or that hotel room, alone, doing nothing," Laing replied amiably. I'm pretty sure this was not exactly what she was looking for.

A well-known reporter from *Rolling Stone* walked into Suite 608, pale, quaking, hyperventilating and unable to speak, apparently stricken with awe to be in the presence of R. D. Laing. Laing couldn't have been kinder. He smiled at him with enormous warmth, told him just to breathe and said, "We can wait as long as it takes." This was one of Laing's great fortes as a therapist and as a human being. Whether it was a paranoid schizophrenic in one of the communities who went into a violent psychotic panic and was terrifying all the residents or a freaked-out reporter from *Rolling Stone* – Laing had instant sympathy and an uncanny understanding of people in extreme states of mind and an extraordinary knack for calming them down, just by his presence. (Other than me, that is – I apparently wasn't in an extreme enough state).

He was prepared to talk to anybody about anything on the tour. He was not uncordial; he went out of his way to be sociable, but usually he just sat there, impassive, showing neither expectation nor disappointment, with no agenda of his own, nothing urgent he wanted to say – just waiting for them to tell him what was really on their minds. This was more than even experienced reporters had bargained for. They had come to do an interview and instead found themselves in a psychoanalytic session.

Everybody was a little uncertain around Laing – even Norman Mailer. After they appeared on a television talk show together, Mailer said to me, "I tell you I was feeling very equivocal and uncertain about it. I wasn't sure what to say. Usually it's easy – you have one charged mind and one empty one, and it's just a matter of pouring from one into the other. But this was two charged minds, and I had no idea what was going to happen."

It was a different story when Mrs. Elizabeth Fehr turned up, the matriarch of a Manhattan group of about thirty persons, each of whom she had taken through ritual reenactments of their births. She wanted to tell Laing about her work. He was delighted. The tribulations of intrauterine life and the experience of birth were a major preoccupation of his.

Within seconds, Laing was on the floor, lying on his back with his hands and feet in the air, demonstrating how he imagined the experience of labor and birth from the infant's point of view. Suddenly he doubled up in a convulsive jerk, dramatizing the way an infant must feel the moment the umbilical cord is suddenly cut. Then he climbed back up on the sofa and described to Mrs. Fehr his history of respiratory ailments, culminating in asthma, which he demonstrated with bulging eyeballs and much frightening wheezing. He said he'd come to locate its origins in some part of his own birth experience but felt he had all but managed to free himself of it.

Mrs. Fehr, already late for a meeting with some leading astrologers, reluctantly stood to go. "For years I've wanted to meet you," she said. "You think the way I do. You know, some people think I'm crazy."

Laing smiled. "Well a lot of people think I'm crazy too."

Later that week we visited Mrs. Fehr's loft in the village. There was a thirty-foot-long mattress on the floor, and anyone who wanted was invited to go through the birthing process. So we all took turns. Laing did it. I did it. You'd lie down at the top of the mattress, and there would be one person behind your head and one or two people on each side of you. The first step was inducing a state of pure relaxation and awareness of your body, which they did by gently touching your head, your face, your arms, your sides, and so on. And then little by little, they would start pushing and squeezing and pushing and squeezing you down the mattress. The idea was to reexperience the birth process, feeling the uterus beginning to contract around you, pushing you down into the birth canal, with the pushing and squeezing becoming more and more intense. And finally, when they'd pushed and squeezed and pushed and squeezed you all the way down the mattress, you'd come out the end, and you were born. And Mrs. Fehr would be there, giving you a sip of tea and placing a teaspoon of honey on your tongue to welcome you into the world. The reactions on the way down the mattress were amazing. Some people wept or shook or screamed or hallucinated or were flooded by memories of all sorts. It went on most of the night.

Things didn't go so well with Professor Amitai Etzioni, chairman of the Columbia University sociology department. This was a soiree in a handsome Bank Street townhouse. As people began to gather in the living room to hear and talk to Laing, Professor Etzioni, not realizing that he was addressing Laing's wife, Jutta, said, "Let's see what this little Scotsman, this Dr. Charisma, has to say for himself." It only got worse from there.

All the guests arranged themselves in a circle on the living room floor. Laing demonstrated a yoga eye exercise, which everyone tried. No one spoke. Laing sat, adjusting the muscles of his back. Finally he said, "Look, why don't we talk about ourselves."

Professor Etzioni, the only person not sitting on the floor, folded his arms tightly across his chest and glared. "Why don't you?" he said.

So Laing started in about his history of respiratory troubles in relation to his birth and childhood: ". . . sinusitis and rhinitis and tonsillitis and laryngitis and bronchitis, culminating in asthma," climaxing with a demonstration of truly magnificent wheezing. "We owe it to ourselves to learn to breathe," he said, summing up.

Professor Etzioni was fuming. "Who cares! What makes you think anybody here is even slightly interested in your medical history? Why can't you talk about ideas like any civilized man? You're alleged to have a few. Perhaps you don't think they can stand by themselves . . ."

Laing didn't reply, and the rest of the party erupted into bitter quarreling.

"My God!" Laing exclaimed outside, hovering between offense and delight over the incident. "I haven't gotten into that sort of thing for ten years, and I have no patience with it now. These are people who adulate me from a distance, but when they meet me, they can't stand me. I was teaching them about what they can do, with their eyes, their backs, their breathing. If you can produce an asthma attack at will, then that's an end of asthma. People don't realize how important that is. It means you've disassembled the machinery of asthma."

One day, Laing mused, "I haven't been able to figure out what people are getting, what they're needing to get, from thinking I'm crazy."

Of course, there were ways that he sometimes behaved that contributed to them thinking that he was crazy, and not just the many notorious episodes of drunken misbehavior. Laing told Bob Mullen about the time he gave a lecture at the Burgholzli, probably the most famous mental hospital in the world. A biologist on the staff told him that about a third of the audience at his lecture thought that he was either psychotic or on drugs because of the way he behaved when giving his lecture.

"It was mainly your movements," he told Laing. "When you stood at the dais, I don't know if you realized this, you had your notes in front of you, as you started talking, you leaned over the dais and sort of swayed backwards and forwards as you were thinking, as you talked. And at one point when you were making a point you lifted yourself up on the dais and then you moved away. A Swiss lecturer stands there and delivers a talk from a paper and you were animating yourself in a way with your hands and gestures and facial expressions That sort of thing led them to believe that you were in some sort of dyskinesia."

As Laing often cautioned, you really have to be very careful how you behave in our culture.

And, of course, there was the other side of the coin, all the rumors and opinions that he was a saint. One time I went over to Laing's house and found him entertaining a tall, thin Spaniard dressed all in black, complete with cape and a hat that flops over the side, like Zoro wore. He extended an invitation for Laing to visit Madrid. "You'll be given the keys to the city. You'll meet the king. You are as God to us. No one has read your books. But we all want to meet you. We think of you as Jesus Christ, because you attempted the impossible and failed."

In the years after meeting Laing in 1971 we developed a friendship that went on until I left England in late 1979, a few years before his life started falling apart. I'd like to give you some of my impressions about him over those years I got to know him on a more personal level, but here's the problem. I can't say I knew him. I can't say anybody knew him. In a single evening I saw him run the gamut of human emotions, taking on one distinct persona after another, even changing sex, and in each one appearing to be wholly himself. He could be gallant and courteous, he could be savage and cruel, he could be remote, he could be intimate and he could change from one of these to another within seconds. It was very hard to know what to conclude from experiences like these – maybe that he had no self, or that he himself didn't know what it was, or that he juggled and manipulated self after self like a master puppeteer or an actor.

Even physically, he had a face that seemed to decompose and compose into more ages and expressions, all looking to be equally in repose than any face I'd ever seen.

All this could be very anxiety making. I don't know about you, but I expect a certain constancy of the external world. At least I tend to hope that someone I meet one day will resemble himself sufficiently the next, psychologically as well as physically, that I will recognize him and that if you met him too we'd agree we met the same person. In Laing's case it was not always so certain.

An anthropologist I interviewed, who also happened to be the leader of a prominent London coven of witches, described Laing as a shape-shifter. I came to agree. I was prepared to accept that almost anything anybody thought about him might be as true as not true.

The only thing about which everybody seemed to agree was that, however he appeared to them, was at the time utterly convincing, devoid of sham, unquestionably his real self. Of course, a "real self" was not a concept Laing entertained. As he told Norman Mailer during the television interview, "For quite sustained periods of time I've had the experience, which I simply report as another experience, that my experience of myself is an illusion."

"The contract I've made with my mind," Laing explained to me, "is that it is free to do anything it cares to do."

Think about that for a second. "The contract I've made with my mind is that it is free to do anything it cares to do." This meant that his mind was always in motion. When any structure would appear, it would be fleeting. And Laing didn't take kindly to anyone's interfering with that. This was one of the reasons that people who met him sometimes found him so infuriating or frustrating or disappointing. He disappointed people's expectations. He almost made a fetish of it.

Even gifts – he was intensely uncomfortable and could be extremely ungracious if someone gave him a gift. A gift was an imposition because for him it included a demand for reciprocity – an obligation being imposed on him.

So this contract Laing made with his mind did not contribute to sociability. It made it very hard to know where you stood with him from moment to moment. You could sit with him, and there was a way in which you were always off balance and never knew where you stood, which could be very disconcerting. One moment he would be looking at you with the greatest interest and attentiveness, and the next you'd have an uncomfortable feeling that he was looking at you from a great distance, and the next his eyes would flutter up into his head and you didn't know if he was with you at all. He was with his own mind. Some people thought of this as an annoying tic. I didn't think so. I think he was questioning his own state of mind. He was a skeptic in the deepest sense and completely skeptical about himself and his own states of mind as well as yours. He was constantly interrogating his every thought, his every state of mind, his every assertion. So he, too, didn't know where he stood with himself, because where he stood with himself was always in motion.

This contract he made with his mind also made it very difficult to fulfill the contract I had with Pantheon to write a book about him. The more time I spent with him, the less it felt I really knew him and the harder it seemed to write anything "true" about him. I spent a fortune trying to figure this out with my psychoanalyst. Boswell, I'm guessing, did not have these kinds of troubles about Dr. Johnson. (By the way, the book never got written.)

There was one place where I felt I did know where I stood with him and where I got to know Laing best, and that was music. I was brought up to be a cellist, and Laing had been brought up to be a pianist. One day we were reminiscing about our musical childhoods, and I told him the story of the relationship I'd had with my mother, a Julliard-trained professional pianist. Every day, from the time I was four years old, she accompanied me on the piano as I practiced for recitals. I described to Laing how when I didn't like the way I had played some phrase, I would jump back 8, 10, 15 bars, without saying a word, and there she'd be, just like that. Somehow she knew where I was going in the same moment I did.

Laing loved that story, perhaps because he didn't hear too many happy stories about mothers being attuned to their children. Also, this was a capacity he was reputed to have in spades with his patients and one of the things that made some people regard him as a shaman. It was as though he could absorb someone's world, the way they were experiencing things, and at the same time be in complete possession of himself.

He said, "I don't expect I'll be able to live up to your mother, but why don't we give it a try?" And every week for the next six or seven years, we spent many nights, many of them quite drunken, playing the entire cello-piano repertory, from Bach and Vivaldi and Hayden to Brahms and Schubert and Beethoven.

This was how I learned firsthand just how attuned he could be. It's not possible to play music like this without being totally concentrated not only on what one is doing oneself but also on what the other is doing, and making instantaneous adjustments from sensing where the other is going.

The tensions that sometimes belonged to Laing's relationships were gone. There was a third thing to focus on – the music. The relationship was in the service of the music.

Music, I felt, was a completely unconflicted world for Laing, and it was when he seemed to be the happiest and having the most fun. Sometimes it was Bach, sometimes Billy Holliday, sometimes old, scratchy recordings of the early-twentieth-century soprano Rosa Ponselle, as often as he could getting people around the piano to sing Cole Porter and George Gershwin songs – usually very, very badly and painfully off key. But it didn't matter. When it came to music, he was totally forgiving – of himself as well as others.

Some people think Laing could have been a world-class pianist. He knew that wasn't so. When he was a boy he'd broken some bones in his hand playing rugby, and he knew that was the end of any idea of making a career of it. But music was, I think, the one thing that was able to collect him, so that his mind wasn't moving from thing to thing to thing. The bargain he'd made with his mind could be exhausting. And music gave him freedom from that. And also exercised every part of him – intellectual, sensual, emotional, spiritual.

There was a time when he became obsessed with the clavichord and the extraordinarily intricate compositions of Girolamo Frescobaldi, an early-seventeenth-century composer who had a big influence on Bach. Part of what intrigued and moved him was that the clavichord was the quietest, most private instrument in the world. It made the harpsichord sound like a concert grand piano. The clavichord could only be performed in a little room with a small group of people. You had to strain to hear it. There was something about the intimacy required and the complexity of the music that made no attempt to impose itself on anybody. That fascinated and moved Laing.

I want to say a few words about the issue of charisma and Laing's relationship to his fame – since that was supposed to be the topic of this talk. Traditionally the meaning of charisma was a special gift or power given to an individual by the gods. I'm really not sure what to say about that concerning Laing, other than his having a fiercely original mind – and I mean fierce as well as original – and a certain gift for rhythmic, incantatory prose. He was one of the most erudite people I've ever met. The weekly Philadelphia Association seminars I attended, and by seminars I mean a bunch of people sitting in a circle cross-legged on the floor while Laing ruminated on whatever was on his mind, were astonishing. He could rise to incredible rhetorical heights.

But Laing was very divided about being a charismatic leader, which made anything like a Laingian movement or organization impossible. For one thing, he had an allergy to any form of authority, including his own. As much as he sought it in certain ways, being thrust into a position of leadership drove him nuts, and he kept undermining it or fleeing it. When you're a leader, you have to fulfill certain expectations of your followers. People kept wishing he would be a leader, but this habit of mind of his, of wanting perfect freedom, made him an impossible person when it came to leading an organization or a movement. So his followers were in trouble all the time, thrown off balance and sometimes savagely attacked, either for expecting certain things of him or for anything that smelled to him of inauthenticity, about which he could be terribly unforgiving.

The only time I ever heard him speak directly about charisma was that awful evening with Professor Etzioni, who referred to him insultingly as Dr. Charisma.

"Dr. Charisma! If he'd asked me what charisma was I could have told him," Laing exclaimed on the way out the door. "Max Weber said it years ago. It grows out of a group process just like that one, where one member of the group is endowed by the others with this power or aura. I mean, of all the people there, he was the one who was most impressed with my charisma. He was creating it!" That was Laing's view of charisma – at least in that moment.

Fame, however, was a subject we did discuss. A lot of people seem to think that Laing desperately wanted and needed to be famous.

During a break in one of the interviews in Suite 608, a reporter leaned over to me and said, "He really loves being famous, doesn't he?" I said, "Well, he's very interested in it." I could see he thought that because I was smiling I was apparently agreeing with him. But that wasn't it. I was smiling because I smile a lot. What I meant was that Laing was genuinely interested in fame – that he was curious about it, about the phenomenon of fame in general, about the phenomenon of his own fame, and about his own wish for it.

"I was very much motivated by the whole fame complex, especially in my teens," Laing told me. "I used to compare the lives of famous intellectuals or writers to see when they produced their first books. I noted that Havelock Ellis, for instance, decided when he was nineteen that he'd publish his first book by the time he was thirty. I saw to it that I'd finished *The Divided Self* by then.

"There are some rather tawdry claims to fame." Laing grinned. "The kind I wanted was the fame of a wise man. I figured since I wanted to be wise, and I wanted to be famous, I thought I might as well be famous for being wise . . . and wise to see the vanity of all that. And I consciously pursued both," Laing confessed, gasping with laughter, "and in an equally calculated manner. Now I feel I can take it or leave it."

Sometimes he clearly seemed to be in favor of taking it.

On the first day of the American tour I said to Laing, "You know the airport scene in a *Hard Day's Night*, when the fans tear the Beatles' clothes off? Well, that's what people are expecting you may be in for, that sort of thing."

Laing's eyes lit up. "I'm about to become more famous than I've ever been before, and in a completely different way. A poster – that kind of famous. Up to now I suppose I've been famous mostly to people in psychology or psychiatry or people who generally consort with ideas. I mean, no one like me, to my knowledge, has ever been famous that way before. Not in their lifetime anyway." And then, as it often did, his mind took another turn.

"Funny that it should be happening now, when it means the least to me."

He later told me, "I've arrived at a position now where fame, as far as I can see, looking at it as hard as I can, really means nothing to me at all. It's just fantasy, sheer fantasy. What's the point of putting oneself out just for the hell of being known? I've never really seen any point in it. But then I've done quite a number of things in my life that I didn't see any point in. In fact, I've seldom seen the point in doing anything. But that's never stopped me from doing quite a lot."

So did fame really matter to Laing? Was he just pretending that it didn't? Or was he pretending that it did?

Like anything else with him, it was hard to say, and it came in and out of focus from one day to the next, even one moment to the next. You could see him thinking about his fame and becoming incredibly excited about it, and then his excitement would become just another object that he looked at one moment this way, the next moment that way. You could watch his mind moving from one position to another in in a matter of seconds.

People want to simplify things about Laing – and it's certainly an impulse I understand. If you can't say something absolute about him – that he was this or he was that – then you reach for the next best thing, saying that he is both. For instance, he was a saint and a sinner – a saint and bodhisattva who had attained enlightenment and an unregenerate drunk, sinner and bully. (A lot of saints were terrible bullies, by the way. But that's another matter.) The point I'm trying to make is that this habit of mind, based on binary distinctions, was exactly the habit of mind that Laing was all the time trying to undermine.

On the afternoon of August 23, 1989, I was with friends lounging on a beach in East Hampton on a hot, brilliantly sunny day. Suddenly my friend, Rick

Hertzberg, came running down the beach, out of breath, looking stricken. "Peter, I have terrible news. Laing died." I was speechless; I had an immediate experience of tremendous loss, regret that I had put off more opportunities to get together with him; and it was hard to take in that someone who was so alive could be dead. Then, in the distance, the sound of a bagpipe. And a piper all kitted out in sash and kilt came marching along the beach, right at the edge of the surf, playing one of the most famous of the Scottish funeral dirges. Laing was messing with my mind yet again.

Note

* At R. D. Laing in the 21st Century Symposium October 25, 2013.

2

LAING AND THE MYTH OF MENTAL ILLNESS REDUX

M. Guy Thompson, PhD

The theme of this essay concerns R. D. Laing's conception of psychopathology or, as we typically encounter this term in the media, "mental illness." This is not such a simple matter to explore because Laing was undeniably dubious about the concept and avoided employing it altogether. In *The Politics of Experience* Laing even questioned whether schizophrenia, the form of psychopathology he is most identified with, exists. Yet many of the people who Laing saw in therapy suffered miserably and sought his help hoping that he could relieve them of the most unbearable anguish imaginable. So what, exactly, was it that Laing was hoping to relieve them *of*, if not a psychopathological condition? Surely, if there is such a *bona fide* activity as psychotherapy (i.e., the "treatment of the mind"), then there must be some condition or state, however we have come to name it, that the so-called therapeutic process presumes to relieve. What else is the one person, the patient, paying the other person, the therapist, for?

I will never forget when Thomas Szasz, the author of *The Myth of Mental Illness* (1961 [1974]), in the 1970s accused Laing of betraying the cause of anti-psychiatry (although Szasz hated this term) by advocating the treatment of the mentally ill, despite Laing's condemnation of the psychiatric community for the way they conducted this practice. Szasz accused Laing of wanting it both ways: on one hand, to condemn psychiatry for treating a disease whose existence Laing believed was dubious at best while, on the other hand, advocating his own treatment for it at Kingsley Hall. Szasz built his career around the notion that mental illness is a myth, that there is no such thing as an "illness" of the mind, and that psychiatry had orchestrated a hoax by insisting that mental illness does exist and that psychiatrists are treating it with relative success. Szasz argued that Laing was merely advocating a more benign form of treatment than, say, drugs, lobotomy, or electric shock but that he was advocating *treatment* nonetheless and, by it, perpetuating the same hoax as the psychiatrists Laing condemned. The gauntlet that Szasz threw down was nothing if not direct: "Do you believe in psychopathology or not? And if you don't, then what is it exactly you claim to be relieving, if not mental illness?"

Laing, in fact, did not believe in psychopathology or mental illness, but he took a more nuanced and less polemical approach to the problem than did Szasz. Whereas Szasz insisted that the entire structure of psychiatry, including its psychological derivative, psychotherapy, should be abolished, Laing believed that however flawed psychiatry is, we still need it, or something like it, to help those people who need someone to relieve them of their unremitting emotional and mental distress. Laing took issue with the way these people were being helped, not with the fact that they needed help, even if what they needed help with is not a mental illness. Although this distinction is not an easy one to articulate, I hope that the following will help to bring some clarity to the problem.

Let us begin with the term itself. The word *psychopathology* derives from the medical term *pathology*, which in turn derives from the Greek *pathos*, meaning suffering. The term was also employed by the Greeks to connote passions or feelings more generally. The first psychotherapists were physicians, and the term *psychiatry*, which was only coined in the nineteenth century, became the medical specialty of doctors whose mandate was to treat the psyche or the soul, or, as we say today, the mind. Laing's first book, *The Divided Self* (1960 [1969]), was his most concerted effort to show why psychiatrists, and for the most part psychoanalysts, have misunderstood the kind of suffering that people labeled schizophrenic, say, are experiencing, and why psychiatric nomenclature does little to help us understand the phenomena so labeled. If what psychiatrists believe they are treating is, as Laing suggested, not schizophrenia, or *any* form of psychopathology, then what is it they are treating? And why do we, whether psychiatrists, psychologists, psychoanalysts, or lay psychotherapists, still refer to the conversations we conduct with our patients *treatment*, or its derivative, psychotherapy?

In order to ponder these questions I explore some of the arguments Laing put forward in *The Divided Self* and then try to explain why Laing believed what we psychotherapists do, though not a medical activity, is nonetheless a kind of "therapy," so-called. Whereas some of my comments are based on Laing's published writings, for the most part I rely on my personal relationship with Laing, which included being supervised by him while I was training as a psychoanalyst in London, and over the course of numerous informal conversations I enjoyed with him until shortly before his death in 1989.[1]

It is instructive to note that the subtitle Laing assigned to *The Divided Self* was "an existential study in sanity and madness." It was not an existential study in *psychopathology*. Why is this distinction important? Are the two terms, *madness* and *psychopathology*, not the same thing? In order to answer this question, let us first take a look at what Laing set out to accomplish in that study, why he qualifies it as a study that is specifically *existential* in nature, and how this classic work laid the foundation for everything that Laing would write subsequently.

As Laing says in the preface to that work, this book is "a study of schizoid and schizophrenic persons," and its basic goal "is to make madness, and the process of going mad, comprehensible" (1960 [1969], p. 9). At the outset, the diagnostic language Laing employs is readily familiar to every psychiatrist and psychoanalyst who works with this population. Terms such as *psychotic, schizoid, schizophrenic, paranoid* – all standard nosological entities with which therapists the world over are familiar – proliferate throughout this book. He is speaking *their* language, but the meaning he is assigning to these terms is anything but ordinary. Laing explains that he has never been particularly skillful in recognizing the diagnostic categories that are standard in every psychiatric diagnostic manual in the world, including the *Diagnostic and Statistical Manual* (5th ed.; *DSM 5*; American Psychiatric Association, 2013) that is the bible of the mental health community in America. Laing had trouble recognizing the subtle nuances that are supposed to distinguish, for example, the various types of schizophrenia, of which there are many, or even what distinguishes schizophrenia from other forms of psychotic process, including paranoia, bipolar disorder (previously manic-depressive syndrome), or dementia.

None of these terms is written in stone. In fact, they are constantly changing and undergo revision in every new edition of the *DSM*. So what is Laing saying here? Is he suggesting he is too stupid to understand the complexity of these entities? I don't think so. Rather, he is suggesting that because there is no agreement in the psychiatric community as to how to recognize these symptoms and the mental illness they are purported to classify, it is impossible to take them literally, or seriously. No two practitioners agree on how to diagnose a person, and given the never-ending revisions to these categories, practitioners often change their own minds as to how to recognize what it is they are proposing to diagnose and treat. This is hardly the science it is purported to be.

What did Laing conclude from this disarray in categorization? That there is no such thing as mental illness, or psychopathology, so no wonder there is no agreement as to what *it* is. When a doctor sets out to diagnose a typical medical illness, he or she customarily looks for physical symptoms in his or her patient. The color or tone of one's skin, dilation of the pupils, body temperature, and so on may indicate an abnormality. Additional tests may be administered that examine the blood or urine, and if that fails to provide conclusive results, perhaps X-rays, CAT scans, EKG's, heart stress tests, mammograms – all ways of examining the chemistry or interior of the body – may be utilized in order to hone in on what is malfunctioning. For so-called psychiatric symptoms, however, such tests will be useless, because no one has ever been able to locate the symptoms of psychopathology inside or on the surface of the body. Even an examination of the brain, which is now the darling of neuropsychiatry and neuropsychoanalysts, has yet to locate the presence of any form of mental or emotional disturbance that we can label a mental illness. (Organic conditions such as Alzheimer's or drug-induced psychosis are not labeled as "mental illnesses," because they are specifically organic in nature, meaning they can be detected inside the brain or because there is a direct correlation between ingesting a drug and the resulting psychotic symptom.)

When seeking signs of mental illness, what we are able to examine, according to the *DSM 5*, is the *behavior* of the person being diagnosed, whether, for example, that person is suffering from delusions or hallucinations, confusion, disorganization, incoherent speech, withdrawal, flights of fancy or depression, anxiety, dissociation or maladaptation, or perhaps a persistently elevated, expansive, or irritable mood, and so on. This list is hardly inclusive, but what all these symptoms share in common is that they refer to experiences that *everyone* has, at one time or another, some more than others and some less. Even delusions and hallucinations, the gold standard for schizophrenia, are common in dreams, and not that uncommon when we are awake. Yet most people who exhibit or experience these so-called symptoms are never subjected to a formal diagnosis or are not treated for them. So why is it that some people are and some people are not? Why are some people deemed crazy and others sane, when they exhibit the same symptoms?

The principal mode of treating psychotic conditions today is in fact not psychotherapy, but "medication." Medication is typically prescribed for a medical illness or condition, so why is it prescribed for mental illnesses that do not really exist? How is it that drugs are used to treat people who do not suffer from a *bona fide* medical condition? There is nothing about drugs, inherently, that possess medicinal properties, though some do. Drugs were around a long time before they were adopted by medicine, and most of the drugs we use today are not the kind you need a prescription for, and do not claim to "medicate" illnesses. Alcohol, marijuana, opium and its derivatives, coffee, sugar, tea, and tobacco are only some of the traditional mind-altering drugs that nearly all cultures throughout history have employed. For what purpose? For the most part, to reduce anxieties and, perhaps, the tedium of an unsatisfying life or a stressful occurrence. There is nothing wrong with this. Drugs have always been used to enhance our lives, though some in desperation have erred in believing they can be used to obliterate their problems. We call such people "addicts." What distinguishes the drugs they become addicted to from the kind promoted by psychiatry is that street drugs are used episodically, when the need arises, usually prompted by anxiety. Prescription drugs, such as Prozac, Paxil, Zoloft, Wellbutrin, Thorazine, Haldol, Abilify, Lithium, Adderall, or Xanax, are employed variously for depression, psychosis, manic episodes, attention-deficit disorder, or anxiety and are ingested daily in order to remain in the nervous system *continuously*. Whereas street drugs are ingested in *response* to anxiety or boredom, prescribed drugs are ingested to *prevent* such feelings from arising, or to keep them in check. Virtually all drugs, if ingested habitually, are addictive, including those prescribed by a doctor.

What all these drugs share in common, whether prescribed or recreational, is not that they are good for treating a medical condition, but that they are capable of altering our *states of consciousness*, depending on the state of consciousness we wish to alter, and to what degree it is distressing. We like to say that alcoholics are self-medicating their depression or anxiety, but in fact they are not *medicating* anything. They are simply using a drug to mitigate their suffering whenever they feel unable to cope with it. Again, there is nothing wrong with this, nothing immoral or sick about it. We all draw the line somewhere. Some of us are able to handle a lot more anxiety than the next person, and some of us are fairly astute at solving our problems before they get out of control. We don't know why some people manage the stress and strain of everyday life more ably than others, but whatever the root cause or causes might be, we are nonetheless left with a choice when confronted with such feelings: we can either examine why life is making us so anxious and adjust our behavior accordingly, or we can render ourselves senseless with this or that drug. What do we gain by calling these problems incidents of mental illness? I don't think one has to ponder that question for very long in order to arrive at the obvious answer. There is a massive and highly lucrative drug industry that makes enormous amounts of revenue selling so-called remedies to an unwary public who don't know any better. This is nothing new. The desperate have been victimized by unscrupulous vendors throughout history. We have simply become more sly about it, and sophisticated.

These are only some of the questions that Laing alluded to in *The Divided Self*, and even more forcefully in *The Politics of Experience* (1967), but he never arrived at a conclusive solution for them. In matters of the mind, the act of diagnosis can just as often be a political as medical ceremonial. Laing believed that we will never succeed in understanding such phenomena as long as we persist in looking at people from an alienating, and an alienated, point of view. It is the *way* that we look at each other, the way psychiatrists and psychoanalysts typically see a patient when they look at him or her, that Laing believed is the crux of the problem. The reason Laing called *The Divided Self* an existential study instead of, say, a psychiatric, or psychoanalytic, or even psychological study is because the existential lens is a supremely *personal* way of looking at people, a person-to-person manner of regarding others and recognizing them, as Harry Stack Sullivan once said, as more human than otherwise. This is another way of saying that the person, or the patient I am treating, is not a sick person but is a person *like me*. And it is the fact that he is just like me that makes it possible for me to understand and empathize with him in the first place.

Laing began writing *The Divided Self* while still working at a mental hospital in Glasgow, when he was just in his twenties. It doesn't sound like he had an opportunity to do much psychotherapy there, but he did have lots of time to hang out with the patients under his charge, all of them diagnosed as schizophrenic. Instead of looking for symptoms of recognizable forms of psychopathology, Laing sought instead to simply talk to his patients, as he was fond of saying, "Man to man," and to listen to what they had to tell him. What he heard, which he recounts in *The Divided Self*, is nothing short of amazing. They told him stories about their life, their belief systems, and experiences, the things that worried them and the things they thought about, day in and day out. The thing that I remember standing out for me when I first read this book – and I have probably read it a dozen times in the past forty years – was that I felt he was talking to *me*. This, from what I have subsequently gathered from others, is not an unusual experience. It is this reaction that has made this book the classic that it is.

Instead of trying to determine what makes "us," the sane ones, so different from "them," the ones who are crazy, Laing sought to explore what we share in common. Laing used the term *schizoid* – quite common in Britain but only marginally employed in the U.S. – to depict a state of affairs that lies at the heart of every person labeled schizophrenic, as well as many who are not so schizophrenic, in fact all of us to varying degrees. The common thread is this: that the person so labeled, in his or her personal experience, suffers from a peculiar problem in his relationships with others: *He cannot tolerate getting too close to other people but at the same time cannot tolerate being alone.*

This is a terrible dilemma to be faced with. Most of us either hate to be alone and throw ourselves into the social milieu with others (Jung would have called them extroverts) or cannot bear social situations and opt instead to spend most of our time by ourselves. These more introverted, private individuals may be gifted writers or artists or scientists or psychotherapists, well suited to their relative isolation, whereas the extroverts among us make excellent politicians or salespeople or actors or any number of other callings that entail contact with others. We tend to incline in one direction or the other and either may be a perfectly viable way of existing and living a happy, contented life. The person who is schizoid, however, doesn't excel at either. He cannot tolerate isolation, nor can he get genuinely close to others. He is caught in a vise, a kind of hell that is rife with unrelenting anxiety, what Laing calls *ontological insecurity*, because simply existing is a serious and persistent problem for him. Intimacy is such a problem that in his relations with others this person must, in effect, hide himself behind a mask by pretending to be somebody else, a phenomenon Laing termed a "false self," living incognito among others, like a spy. In speaking of a person this way we are not really diagnosing him, we are simply describing what it is like to be him.

Laing makes a careful distinction between the kind of person who struggles with schizoid character traits and the kind of person who is labeled schizophrenic. The so-called schizophrenic is at the extreme end of the pendulum, though it is notoriously difficult to generalize about this for reasons I have already explained. It is often impossible for a person who struggles with schizophrenia to work at a job or enjoy satisfying sexual relationships. The reason is due to the extreme anxiety that close proximity to people, which is a given with jobs or sexual relationships, exacts. We all find the work environment stressful, but the person who struggles with paranoia often finds these stresses and strains intolerable, even with medication. Better to avoid such relationships altogether than to risk being at the mercy of somebody else. There are exceptions to this, usually the consequence of many years of psychotherapy, but even with that caveat intimacy can be an ongoing problem. The schizoid person shares a similar repulsion to intimacy, but is much better at *acting the part* of an employee, a lover, or a spouse, and can often function perfectly well in work situations in which the expectation of intimacy is mitigated. The problem is that there is always a part of him that is held back, the part that struggles with paranoid worries about the power others may have over him. This is the kind of person who, like the neurotic, is much more likely to seek therapy and, in time, even benefit from it. Indeed, Laing wondered if the schizoid condition is the *normal* condition in the present age, due to the extraordinary alienation that has become the norm.

When I first read this I couldn't help but wonder how many of us are really all that comfortable being alone, and how many of us are truly at ease in our relationships with others, which is to say, free from anxiety. Isn't this a problem, for example, that psychotherapists typically share with their patients? Psychotherapy is a fabricated relationship whose purpose is to achieve uncommon intimacy with another person, while placing extraordinary constraints on it, conducted by two people who, to a considerable degree, have problems getting close to others. Isn't this rather like the lame leading the blind? Laing didn't think so, but he was acutely aware of the paradox, of how wounded a person must be to even want to spend all of his or her professional time in the company of people who are so obsessed with their problems.

Laing, however, was not the first to recognize this paradox. Nor was he the first to accuse psychiatrists of employing means of helping others that are for the most part ineffectual. For that Sigmund Freud would have to be credited, arguably the first anti-psychiatrist. Freud was a neurologist, not a psychiatrist, and he was scathing in his commentary about the psychiatrists of his day who, Freud believed, knew nothing about why their patients suffered and how to help them. Freud believed that people develop symptoms of hysteria and neuroses, or worse, because they have been traumatized by unrequited love in their childhoods. He was the first to recognize the powerful effect that our parents, in fact all our social relationships, have on us and how our capacity to love is also the source of our most profound suffering. Freud was also the first to recognize that our demand for love is unremitting and insatiable, no matter how much we get, and that we are most vulnerable when at the mercy of the person we love. Laing loved this about Freud and was writing a book on love when he died. He was also planning to write a book about Freud.

Yet Freud was not interested in the kind of person Laing described in *The Divided Self*, because he did not believe that a person who suffers from psychotic anxiety is capable of attaching him- or herself to the person of the psychotherapist who is treating him. Freud was correct in recognizing how incredibly vulnerable such people are, but mistaken in his prognosis about their treatment. It has been argued that Laing accomplished for the so-called schizophrenic what Freud accomplished for the neurotic: a way of establishing an intimate relationship with them that may, *in itself*, serve as a vehicle for healing. Freud was unhappy with the brutal way that the hysterics of his day, mostly women, were typically treated and even less happy with the prevailing conception of psychopathology. Unlike psychiatrists, Freud did not believe in an us-versus-them mentality. He did not believe, for example, that some people are neurotic and that some people are not. He believed that *everyone* is neurotic and that this is an essential aspect of our human condition. He also believed that neurotics may, on occasion, become psychotic if pushed far enough. So if everyone is neurotic and curing us of neurosis is not feasible, then what is psychotherapy good for?

Freud was never able to definitively answer this question, at least not as definitively as we would like, but he thought it could help.[2] If you read between the
lines, you can't help concluding that Freud viewed anxiety, and the other forms of
alienation that Laing was so good at describing, as an essential aspect of our human
condition. So what we call "ill" versus "healthy," or crazy versus sane is not black
or white, but a matter of degrees. If all of us are neurotic, and on some occasions
even psychotic, some more, some less than others, then all of us are also healthy
and sane, to varying degrees. Although he was reluctant to admit it, Freud rejected
the concept of psychopathology as it is commonly understood, *and replaced it with
an existential perspective that emphasized the management of anxiety as an inescapable
aspect of living.*

Freud's invention of psychoanalysis was a huge step forward in treating people
we think of as nuts or crazy as human beings like ourselves. But once it was
embraced by psychiatrists, psychoanalysis became yet one more weapon – and, in
America, a very popular one – in the war on mental illness. Whereas psychiatrists
had depersonalized the relationship between doctor and patient by pretending
that it wasn't the person, but rather his or her illness, being treated, psychoanalysts
depersonalized the treatment relationship by insisting that it wasn't the person
who was responsible for his or her condition, but his or her *unconscious.* Though
psychoanalysis made extraordinary gains in humanizing the treatment relationship over prevailing psychiatric practices, Laing believed that both disciplines
seem strangely incapable of formulating a genuinely symmetrical therapy relationship between equals. There have been notable exceptions to this, and Laing
himself stood proudly on the shoulders of practitioners such as Sullivan, Fromm-
Reichmann, Winnicott, and other psychiatrists and psychoanalysts who advocated
a more personal way of treating their patients, not treating them for illnesses but
treating them like they would want to be treated themselves were they in a similar
predicament, which, of course, they all had been, at one time or another.

This isn't to say that Laing was advocating simply being nicer, or kinder, to his
patients, as though that alone was sufficient. Instead, his concern was with being
more real, or authentic, with them, in a word, more honest. That is considerably
more difficult than just being nice. This, he believed, could only happen if we
stop objectifying our patients into diagnostic categories that only serve to alienate
them from us. Perhaps the model that best exemplifies what Laing advocated is
not a relationship between therapist and patient, per se, or parent and child, but
one between friends. After all, friends confide in each other, and confiding is an
essential aspect of what therapy entails. In one of his more mischievous moments
Laing suggested that therapists might even call themselves prostitutes, because
what patients are buying is not treatment, *per se,* but a *relationship.* Whether we
think of ourselves as friends or prostitutes to our patients, or neither, Laing didn't
have a problem with calling the people who paid to see him his "patients" any
more than he resisted calling what they were doing "therapy," both undeniably
medical terms. But isn't this inconsistent with what Laing has been saying about
the myth of psychopathology?

Whatever problem Laing had with the institution of psychiatry, he never had a problem with being a *doctor*. He was proud of his medical training, and while such training is not necessary to practice psychotherapy, he thought it was as good a preparation as any to enter the field with. After all, what doctors share in common is that they want to help people. This is also basically what therapists want to do. Laing was fond of pointing out that the word therapy is etymologically cognate with the term *attention* or attendant. In ancient Egypt a religious cult called the Therapeutae were literally attendants to the divine, the first psychotherapists.[3] So the term *therapy* predates the subsequent medical appropriation of it by the Greeks. *If we take the term literally, a therapist is simply a person who is attentive, or pays attention, to the matter at hand, the suffering of his patient.* Similarly, a patient is literally a person who "patiently" bears his suffering without complaint. The term doesn't necessarily refer to someone in *medical* treatment because the kind of suffering is not specific. Laing concluded that if you put these two terms together you get one person, the therapist, who is attentive and attends to the other person's, or patient's, suffering. To what end? Hopefully, such attention, with enough patience, good will, and, most important, time will lead to something, to a point at which the patient no longer requires such attention and can get along perfectly well without it. This is something that Thomas Szasz never understood. He seemed more interested in the legalities of the issue than he was with helping people.

According to Michel Foucault (personal communication, 1980), a close friend of Laing's, it was purely by chance that medical doctors became responsible for treating crazy people in the first place, in eighteen-century Europe. In fact, it is very recent in history that mad people were deemed mentally ill. Historically, people who acted crazy were thought to be possessed, either by evil spirits or by the gods. In the seventeenth century Europeans began to feel unsafe with the crazy people in their midst, who wandered the streets (not unlike the homeless people who wander about our cities) and began to confine them as a means of protection. Not surprisingly, such confinement made them even crazier and their jailors began chaining them to the walls of the lunatic asylums they were in. They soon developed diseases, which only escalated their problems further until the French physician Philippe Pinel was brought in to attend to their specifically *medical* maladies. Pinel couldn't help but observe that the way they were being treated was inhuman. Pinel argued that they should instead be treated more compassionately, as sick people who deserved the kind of attention and consideration that any sick person would expect. It was then, according to Foucault, that mad people were first deemed mentally ill.

This was a remarkable step forward in treating such people as human beings who warranted society's help, but it also initiated the slippery slope that occasioned the birth of psychiatry and, with it, the diagnostic universe we now live in. Laing was proud of being a physician but recognized that we now find ourselves in an historical quandary. Like the Europe that invented the lunatic asylum, our society feels the need to protect itself from crazy people, some of whom are undeniably dangerous and capable of savage violence, even murder, but most of them are perfectly harmless, and even more vulnerable than you or me. When the violence does erupt, if indeed it does, someone needs to make the call: Is the person in question crazy enough to lose, if only temporarily, his or her constitutional rights and be confined to treatment, which is to say, "medication," intended to render him or her senseless or, worse, to have it done against his or her will? Whether we like it or not, that task has been assigned to psychiatrists, and it has given them enormous power over those it deems dangerous, whether to themselves or others. Laing had no ready or easy remedy to this problem but believed that all of us is implicated in it.

Laing never formulated an overarching theory of psychopathology to replace the edifice that psychiatry and psychoanalysis have built. For the most part, his focus was on schizoid phenomena and schizophrenia, not as specific diagnostic categories but, like Freud's conception of neurosis, as a metaphor for varieties of mental anguish that compromise our ability to develop satisfying relationships with others, prompted by unremitting anxiety. As the subtitle of *The Divided Self* suggests, Laing was more comfortable thinking in terms of sanity and madness than of psychopathology. But what does it mean to be crazy? And what does it mean to be sane?

Terms such as *madness* and *crazy* lack precise definition when compared, say, with the plethora of diagnostic categories in the *DSM 5*. Because they are used colloquially, in a manner of speaking, it is up to each of us, individually, to determine how to employ them. Laing thought that the essence of what it means to be crazy, in the way this term is ordinarily used, can be broken down into three components, the combination of which will tell us just how crazy a person is. The first concerns how a given person exercises his or her judgment, the second concerns how agitated that person may be, and the third concerns the lengths a given person will go to mitigate his or her anxiety.

Our use of judgment is probably the most critical of the three, because it determines how we make sense of things, including the situation we are facing at a given moment. The judgment of a person suffering a manic episode, for example, is said to be seriously compromised but so is that of a person who suffers from acute paranoia or hallucinations. Our judgment is where we live, and there's no escaping it, though we can improve it if, and only if, we have the presence of mind to realize that we cannot trust it. Yet, who gets to decide whether a given person's judgment is impaired or sound? If I judge that I need help in improving my judgment and take my plight to a therapist, can I trust the judgment of that therapist over my own? I'm not going to get much out of therapy if I am unable to trust his or her judgment, but who is to say that my therapist's judgment is more sound than mine is? How can I render such a judgment if, say, I don't trust *my own* judgment? This is a problem, and one that Laing thought makes therapy almost, but not quite, impossible.

A person's judgment is for the most part a private affair. The person who is crazed is often in a state of agitation, which others can't help but notice. It is this state than usually makes my judgments public, when, for example, I am about to leap off a tall building or assault someone for no discernable reason. This is the prototypical image we all have of the crazy person, who is acting crazy, and often in a manner that not only gets our attention but also frightens us, because we don't know what he is going to do next. Each of us has been crazed at some time or other, but the moment usually passes before any real harm has been committed. If it persists, that is a different matter, and things can quickly spiral out of our control. This is when I am most likely to be taken to a mental hospital, whether I wish to be taken there or not.

The third way I may feel or appear crazed concerns what psychoanalysts call defenses, the mind games I employ to mitigate my anxiety.[4] This was the issue that Laing was most concerned with in *The Divided Self*, evidenced in the so-called schizoid person. We see the person's defenses in the way he or she engages social space. As we noted earlier, this is a person who cannot tolerate being isolated from or being intimate with others because either position makes him or her intolerably anxious, so the person walks a tightrope in the middle where he or she feels the least amount of anxiety but still too much to navigate his relationships effectively, which is to say satisfactorily, in a way that is pleasing to him- or herself. Much of what we do to cope with our anxieties does not appear crazy to others and does not feel crazy to ourselves, and works for us, more or less. It is the most severe states of anxiety, such as ontological insecurity, that are the most problematic and result in extreme measures to mitigate, such as catatonic withdrawal.

Not all states of craziness, however, occasion distress. Schizophrenia and schizoid states generally occasion various degrees of anxiety and the unpleasant, even haunting, sense of distress that drives us into treatment. We feel distressed when we have reached the end of our tether and can no longer cope. When we arrive at this point we *need help*, and we turn to others to assist us. Manic states are usually contrary to this, because the person experiencing a manic episode does not typically feel *distressed*. Indeed, he or she usually feels the opposite; he feels excited, happy, and alive. The world is a wonderful place, and he is the master of it. This would appear to be the ideal state to be in. After all, don't we all aspire to happiness, even giddiness, as a measure of how happy we are with our lives? Feeling good *is* good, isn't it?

Unfortunately, it isn't as simple as that. We cannot always rely on our feelings to tell us if we are behaving in a sane way or a way that is crazy. It is easy to determine when we feel bad that we are in a bad way. But feeling good does not always indicate that things are well in the world. The manic state depicts a person who *feels* good but who has lost all sense of proportion and self-control. In a word, his judgment has become completely impaired, despite the complication that he feels so good. The reason bipolar disorder was once called manic-depression is because when a person experiences a manic episode, it doesn't last. Before long, it reaches a terminus, and then gives way to profound, sometimes suicidal depression. One way of understanding this phenomenon is to regard the manic "high" as a *defense against depression* and its accompanying anxiety. It is a sort of denial, an escape from an unacceptable or intolerable development in one's life (such as divorce or other catastrophic loss). Manic episodes often occasion intense sexual activity, profligate spending, in short, unreasonable, highly risky, and often self-destructive behavior.

If you happen to know someone who is exhibiting such behavior, you may also note that this person is not being "him- or herself," and you soon realize that something is the matter. But if you do not know this person and meet him or her for the first time when in the throes of this episode, you might even think of him as a perfectly interesting, charismatic, even an exciting person to be with. Given the intensity of this person's libido, you might even fall in love with him. Don't be fooled. This behavior is nothing more than a mask, intended to camouflage the underlying anguish that, for whatever reason, this person cannot, in their current state, handle.

People suffering from manic episodes are not the most promising candidates for psychotherapy. The reason is simple. They do not feel that they need help, so why should they seek it? If a family member tries to persuade them to seek help, they will often resist, because they feel perfectly fine. How do you reach a person who is incapable of self-doubt, who is under the illusion that everything is okay in the world, when you can see that he or she is behaving crazy? Not very easily, if at all. Yet not everyone who suffers a manic episode enjoys the experience. People may feel agitated, anxious, or angry, but the thing they have in common with the person who relishes it is that they, too, are impervious to therapeutic intervention. Just because a person acts crazy doesn't mean that he or she recognizes it and accepts your judgment over his. A person who does not want help and does not seek it cannot, by definition, benefit from psychotherapy. He may, however, and often does, respond to "medication." And how motivated is this person to voluntarily take this medication when he doesn't believe there is anything the matter with him? I think you can guess the answer to that.

Even under the best of circumstances, determining what it means to be crazy, and who can be deemed to be crazy, is not so simple. Sometimes a person who is behaving in a way that you think is crazy happens to feel crazy him- or herself and doesn't like the experience one bit. Sometimes that person, behaving the same way, feels that there is nothing the matter with him. How do you convince a person, who does *not* believe he is crazy, that he is? This dilemma sometimes comes down to just how much craziness a given society is willing to tolerate amongst its citizens, and how much is perfectly acceptable, as long as it isn't harming anyone. Some cultures are more tolerant than others; some, less so. This is where the psychological leaks into the political, the place where we are confronted with how tolerant we are of our fellow human beings, despite their obvious eccentricities.

If these criteria offer a rough and ready means of discerning what it means for me, or you, to be crazy, what does it mean to be sane? It would more or less approximate the exact opposite of feeling crazy. Our judgment would be sound, relatively speaking; our use of defensive maneuvers would be minimal because we would bear our anxieties with relative ease; and we would not find ourselves in a state of panic or agitation but one of serenity and of being at peace with ourselves and with the world. When we weigh the two, there are no crazy people or sane people. Every single one of us goes from one state to the other over the spectrum of our lives and oftentimes in the course of a single day. By this definition, all of us have been crazy, no matter how sane we are most of the time. If this were not so there would be no way for a psychotherapist to connect with or empathize with a person who has been diagnosed, say, schizophrenic. *We can only help people with problems we ourselves can relate to, and have experienced ourselves.* This doesn't mean that one has to be schizophrenic in order to empathize with someone who is, but the underlying experience that all persons diagnosed schizophrenic suffer is something we all share in common, a sense of *alienation.* Not everyone is in touch with his or her alienation, and for the most part we mask it, but every psychotherapist worth his salt is acutely aware of it. This is all it takes to recognize a fellow traveler who, by the grace of God, may, under different circumstances, be me.

What about the genetic theory? It is commonplace to believe that "mental illness" runs in families, so it must be genetically inherited, from one generation to the next, right? There is no denying that many of these diagnostic entities, including schizophrenia, bipolar disorder, and depression do show up with remarkable regularity in family members. So how does that happen? It is quite possible that temperaments, predispositions, and certain character traits are somehow "passed on" from *some* fathers, to *some* sons, but not others, in ways that we simply cannot detect. We have no way of knowing if some of these traits or characteristics are discreetly modeled and adopted by regular contact with a parental figure, in other words, environmentally. Perhaps some of us are born with considerably greater sensitivity to our environment than the next person and this sensitivity, while it may predispose some, under certain environmental triggers, to become artists or thinkers, may predispose others, with different triggers, to become psychotic. But even if some are genetically transmitted, why call them *mental illnesses*? Do we regard political dynasties, which tend to run in families, genetically transmitted? Is the Irish proclivity to drink and literature, which I share, a mental illness? I don't think so.

Laing never developed an etiological theory of what causes us to become neurotic, or psychotic, or just plain crazy, though he clearly favored the environmental thesis over the biological. Neither model, he concluded, is satisfactory and, like the good sceptic he was, Laing believed that our mental states and what accounts for them are for the most part a mystery, and may always be. We may never know why this person is crazier than the next person or why, in fact, all of us are crazy in some contexts and not in others. It seems that some people are capable of driving others crazy, but there are those who appear to be perfectly capable of becoming crazy on their own. Laing thought that common deception is a problem but is difficult to recognize.[5] The bottom line, given the inherent ambiguity of the situation we are in, is to proceed cautiously, with a degree of humility, in how we treat such people when we meet them.

This is because Laing's principal concern, when all is said and done, was not explanatory, but *ethical.* What is the right way to treat people who are the most vulnerable members of our society? Whenever Laing addressed this topic, whether in writing or in public, he often invoked the Golden Rule. How would you, if you lost your wits and fell apart with grief or consternation, want to be treated by those who have you at their mercy? When the shoe is on the other foot, shouldn't you treat them the way you would like to be treated yourself? It is impossible to separate Laing's thinking about psychopathology from the work of psychotherapy. If he met a mad person on the street who was threatening him, Laing would defend himself without hesitation and, if need be, ask the police to confine that person. But if you made an appointment to see him, no matter how crazy you were, and wanted his help, and you were not trying to assault him, that was another matter. And that was the matter that concerned him, for the most part, over the course of his life. How to meet another person in dire straits, whether you are that person's therapist, family, or friend, and how to treat that person in such a way that, in the name of the Hippocratic oath, you do no harm.

And what of today? Twenty-five years after Laing's death, are we more humane and compassionate in our treatment of those at our mercy? It is difficult to say. But one thing we cannot deny, our culture has become even more "medicalized" than at any time in history. The medical metaphor that Laing found more or less acceptable when explaining what he thought therapy is has become effectively literal. In California, we even have medical marijuana. Pot is not just a pleasing way of altering one's consciousness; it has become *medicine*. When you imbibe you are not getting high; you are medicating yourself for whatever ailment you believe you are "treating." You are no longer a recreational pot smoker; you are a "patient." More and more, anything that pains us is treated as a "condition" that can, indeed must, be treated as such. If you are caught having extramarital affairs with a dozen women, you are not necessarily a philanderer. You may simply have a sex addiction, which – you guessed it – is a medical condition for which you can seek treatment, perhaps mandated by the courts. This means you are not responsible for this behavior, because you are suffering from a condition that has "caused" you to behave in this way. This seems to be the one thing our culture, in the era in which we live, is most concerned about: to escape responsibility for who we are and the mischief or confusion we sometimes get up to.

I find this trend in our culture creepy, because it implies that just about anything we do that might get us into trouble or prove embarrassing is nothing more than a condition for which we bear little if any responsibility. Is this a sane way of proceeding? Is this what our capacity for judgment has come to? I think you can guess what Laing would have had to say about that.

Notes

1 For more on my critique of Laing's contemporary relevance, see Thompson (1996, 1997, 1998, 2000, 2006) and Thompson and Heaton (2012).
2 For Freud's most succinct thought about treatment outcome, see Freud (1937 [1964]) and Thompson (1994).
3 For a lucid discussion of these ancient therapists see Meier (1967).

4 For a phenomenological discussion of the true meaning of "defense mechanisms" see Laing (1961 [1969], pp. 17–32).
5 See Laing and Esterson's brilliant *Sanity, Madness and the Family* (1964 [1970]) for a detailed study of deceptive practices in families of schizophrenics. See also Thompson (1996).

References

American Psychiatric Association. (2013) *Diagnostic and Statistical Manual of Mental Disorders* (5th ed.). Washington, DC: Author.

Freud, S. (1937 [1964]) Analysis Terminable and Interminable. *Standard Edition of the Complete Psychological Works of Sigmund Freud* (Ed. & trans., James Strachey) London: Hogarth Press, Vol. 23:209–253, 1964.

Laing, R. D. (1960 [1969]) *The Divided Self.* New York and London: Penguin Books.

Laing, R. D. (1961 [1969]) *Self and Others* (Revised Edition). New York and London: Penguin Books.

Laing, R. D. (1967) *The Politics of Experience.* New York: Ballantine Books.

Laing, R. D. and Esterson, A. (1964 [1970]) *Sanity, Madness and the Family.* New York and London: Penguin Books.

Meier, C. A. (1967) *Ancient Incubation and Modern Psychotherapy* (Trans., Monica Curtis) Evanston, IL: Northwestern University Press.

Szasz, T. (1961 [1974]) *The Myth of Mental Illness* (Revised Edition). New York: Harper and Row.

Thompson, M. G. (1994) *The Truth About Freud's Technique: The Encounter with The Real.* New York and London: New York University Press.

Thompson, M. G. (1996) Deception, Mystification, Trauma: Laing and Freud. *The Psychoanalytic Review,* Vol. 83, No. 6:827–847.

Thompson, M. G. (1997) The Fidelity to Experience in R. D. Laing's Treatment Philosophy. *Contemporary Psychoanalysis,* Vol. 33, No. 4:595–614.

Thompson, M. G. (1998) Existential Psychoanalysis: A Laingian Perspective. From *Psychoanalytic Versions of the Human Condition and Clinical Practice* (Eds., Paul Marcus and Alan Rosenberg). New York: New York University Press, 332–361.

Thompson, M. G. (2000) The Heart of the Matter: R. D. Laing's Enigmatic Relationship with Psychoanalysis. *The Psychoanalytic Review,* Vol. 87, No. 4:483–509.

Thompson, M. G. (2006) A Road Less Traveled: The Hidden Sources of R. D. Laing's Enigmatic Relationship with Authenticity. *Existential Analysis,* Vol. 17, No. 1.

Thompson, M. G., & Heaton, J. M. (2012) R. D. Laing Revisited: A Dialogue on his Contribution to Authenticity and the Skeptic Tradition. In *Existential Psychotherapy: Legacy, Vibrancy, and Dialogue* (Eds., Laura Barnett and Greg Madison). London and New York: Routledge.

3

LAING'S *THE VOICE OF EXPERIENCE* AND THE EMERGING SCIENCE OF CONSCIOUSNESS

Fritjof Capra, PhD

I met R. D. Laing in May 1977, and I last saw him in the summer of 1988, a year before he died. During these eleven years, we met many times, either just the two of us or with our families and friends, and we saw each other at conferences, gave joint seminars, and together participated in panel discussions.

In these reminiscences, I want to concentrate on my longest and most intensive encounter with Laing in September 1980 at a conference on "The Psychotherapy of the Future" in Spain, sponsored by the European Association for Humanistic Psychology.

The central subject of our discussions at that conference was the nature of experience and the challenge of formulating a future science of experience. I want to tell you how I experienced Laing's radical and often dramatic methods of inquiry, which many of you have also experienced, and I also want to share some of his prescient ideas, which began to be realized by cognitive scientists a decade later.

The conference in Spain took place near Saragossa at the Monasterio de Piedra, a beautiful twelfth-century monastery, which had been converted into a hotel. The array of participants was very impressive. In addition to Laing, there was Stanislav Grof, Jean Houston, and Rollo May, and the group would have also included Gregory Bateson had he not died two months earlier.

During that entire week, I experienced a wonderful feeling of community and adventure generated by the extraordinary group of participants and the magnificent setting of the conference. Lectures were held in the old refectory of the monastery, often by candlelight; there were seminars in the cloister and in the garden and informal discussions on a large balcony until late at night.

Laing was the animating spirit of the entire conference. Most of the discussions and happenings revolved around his ideas and the many facets of his personality. He had come to the conference with a large entourage of family, friends, former patients, and disciples, including even a small film crew. He was active day and night and never seemed to tire. He gave lectures and seminars and arranged filmed dialogues with other participants. He spent many evenings in intensive discussions with small groups of people, which usually ended in long monologues when everybody else had become too tired to continue the conversation, and he would often end up at the piano, long after midnight, and reward those who had held out that long with superb renditions of Cole Porter and Gershwin.

During that conference I really got to know Laing. Up to then our relationship had been cordial and our discussions very inspiring for me, but it was not until the Saragossa conference that I really got close to him on a personal level. That's also when I began to call him "Ronnie," following the example of his friends. On the day I arrived at the Monasterio, Laing invited me after dinner to join him and a group of friends for a glass of cognac and discussions. We all sat down on the balcony, surrounded by the balmy breezes of a beautiful Mediterranean summer evening, Laing and I side by side, leaning against the white stucco wall with a fairly large circle of people in front of us.

Laing asked me what I had been up to in the past two years. I told him that I was working on a new book, *The Turning Point*, and that, lately, I had become interested in the nature of mind and consciousness. The next thing I knew Laing was attacking me extremely vigorously. "How dare you, as a scientist, even ask about the nature of consciousness," he said indignantly with a scowl. "You have absolutely no right to ask that question, to even use words like *consciousness* or *mystical experience*. It is preposterous of you to dare mention science and Buddhism in the same breath!" This was not a joking, teasing confrontation. It was the beginning of a serious, vigorous, and sustained attack on my position as a scientist, voiced passionately in an angry and accusing tone.

I was shocked. I was not prepared at all for such an outburst. Laing was supposed to be on my side! Indeed, he had been, and I was especially taken aback by his attacking me like this on the day I had arrived, and in front of a large group. At the same time, I felt his intellectual challenge, and my shock and confusion soon gave way to intense mental activity, as I tried to understand Laing's position, evaluate it, and prepare myself for responding.

In fact, as he continued his passionate diatribe against science, which he saw me as representing, I found myself becoming very excited. I have always enjoyed intellectual challenge, and this was the most dramatic challenge I had ever encountered. Laing had placed our dialogue in a spectacular setting. Not only was I leaning against the wall of the balcony facing Laing's tribe of friends and disciples; I also felt pushed against the wall metaphorically by his relentless attack. But I did not mind. In my state of excitement all traces of embarrassment and discomfort had disappeared.

The main point of Laing's attack was that science had no way of dealing with consciousness or with experience, values, ethics, or anything referring to quality. "This situation derives from something that happened in European consciousness at the time of Galileo and Giordano Bruno," Laing said, beginning his argument. "These two men epitomize two paradigms – Bruno, who was tortured and burned for saying that there were infinite worlds, and Galileo, who said that the scientific method was to study this world as if there were no consciousness and no living creatures in it. Galileo made the statement that only quantifiable phenomena were admitted to the domain of science. Galileo said: 'Whatever cannot be measured and quantified is not scientific,' and in post-Galilean science this came to mean 'What cannot be quantified is not real.'"

"This has been the most profound corruption," Laing continued, "from the Greek view of nature as *physis*, which is alive, always in transformation, and not divorced from us. Galileo's program offers us a dead world: Out go sight, sound, taste, touch, and smell, and along with them have since gone esthetic and ethical sensibility, values, quality, soul, consciousness, spirit. Experience as such is cast out of the realm of scientific discourse. Hardly anything has changed our world more during the past four hundred years than Galileo's audacious program. We had to destroy the world in theory before we could destroy it in practice."

Laing's critique was devastating, but as he paused and reached for his cognac, and before I could say anything in reply, he leaned over to me and whispered under his breath so that nobody else could hear it, "You don't mind me setting you up like that, do you?" With that aside he instantly created a conspiratorial mood and shifted the whole context of his attack. I just had time to whisper back, "Not at all!" and then I had to concentrate fully on my response.

I defended myself as well as I could, being put on the spot with hardly any time for reflection. I said that I agreed with Laing's analysis of Galileo's role in the history of science. I also agreed with him that there was no room for experience, values, and ethics in the science of today. However, I then went on to say that my own endeavor was precisely to help change today's science in such a way that these considerations could be incorporated into the scientific framework of the future.

To do so, I emphasized, the first step had to be the shift from the mechanistic and fragmented approach of classical science to a holistic paradigm, in which the main emphasis was no longer on separate entities but on relationships. This would make it possible to introduce context and meaning. Only when one had that holistic framework, I concluded, could one begin to take further steps in response to Laing's concerns.

Laing was not immediately satisfied with my response. He wanted a more radical approach, going beyond the intellect altogether. "The universe was a vast machine yesterday," he said sarcastically. "It is a hologram today. Who knows what intellectual rattle we'll be shaking tomorrow." And so the argument went back and forth for quite a while, and in the midst of it Laing leaned over to me once more and said softly, in a confidential tone, "You realize the questions I am asking you are all questions I am asking myself. I am not just attacking you, or other scientists out there. I am tarred with the same brush. I could not get so curled up over this if it were not a personal struggle."

The discussion went on until very late that night, and when I finally went to bed I still could not sleep for a long time. Laing had presented me with a tremendous challenge. I spent most of the next day pondering the problem, and in the evening I was ready to see him again. "I have thought a lot about what you said last night, Ronnie," I told him at dinner, "and I would like to respond to your critique in a more complete and systematic way tonight, if you feel like sitting down with me for another glass of cognac." Laing agreed, and so we settled down on the balcony again after dinner in the same setting as the night before.

"I would like to present to you tonight," I said, "as completely and systematically as I can, the view of mind and consciousness that I see emerging from the conceptual framework that I am now developing. This is not a framework in which your critique can be fully satisfied, but I believe, as I said last night, that it is a necessary first step toward that goal. From the vantage point of my new framework, you can actually begin to see how experience, values, and consciousness might be incorporated into science in the future."

Laing simply nodded and kept listening attentively with intense concentration. I then proceeded to give him a concise summary of my ideas. I began with the view of living organisms as self-organizing systems, explained Prigogine's notion of dissipative structures, and emphasized especially the view of biological forms as being shaped by underlying processes. I then wove in Bateson's concept of mind as the dynamics of self-organization. (At that time I was not yet familiar with Maturana's more detailed concept of cognition as the process of life).

I then specified that what I meant by "consciousness" was the property of mind characterized by self-awareness. "Awareness," I argued, "is a property of mind at all levels of complexity. Self-awareness, as far as we know, manifests itself only in higher animals and fully unfolds in the human mind; and it is this property of mind that I mean by consciousness.

"Now, if we look at theories of consciousness," I continued, "we can see that most of them are variations of two seemingly opposite views. One of these views I will call the Western scientific view. It considers matter as primary and consciousness as a property of complex material patterns, which emerges at a certain level of biological evolution. Most neuroscientists today subscribe to this view."

I paused for a moment, and seeing that Laing had no intention of interjecting anything, I proceeded: "The other view of consciousness may be called the mystical view, since it is generally held in mystical traditions. It regards consciousness as the primary reality, as the essence of the universe, the ground of all being, and everything else – all forms of matter and all living beings – as manifestations of that pure consciousness. This mystical view of consciousness is based on the experience of reality in non-ordinary modes of awareness, and such mystical experience, they say, is indescribable. It is . . ."

"Any experience!" Laing shouted, interrupting me forcefully, and when he saw my puzzled look, he repeated, "Any experience! Any experience of reality is indescribable! Just look around you for a moment and see, hear, smell, and feel where you are."

I did as he told me, becoming fully aware of the mild summer night, the white walls of the balcony against the outline of trees in the park, the sound of crickets, the half-moon hanging in the sky, the faint strains of a Spanish guitar in the distance, and the closeness and attention of the crowd surrounding us – experiencing a symphony of shades, sounds, smells, and feelings, while Laing continued: "Your consciousness can partake all that in one single moment, but you will never be able to describe the experience. It's not just mystical experience; it's *any* experience." I knew that Laing was right, and I also knew immediately that his point needed much further thought and discussion, even though it did not directly affect my argument, which I was about to conclude.

"Okay, Ronnie, *any* experience," I agreed. "Now, since the mystical view of consciousness is based on direct experience, we should not expect science, at its present stage, to confirm or contradict it. Nevertheless, I feel that the systems view of mind seems to be perfectly consistent with both views and could therefore provide an ideal framework for unifying the two."

Again I paused briefly to collect my thoughts, and as Laing remained silent I went on to clinch my argument: "The systems view agrees with the conventional scientific view that consciousness is a property of complex material patterns. To be precise, it is a property of living systems of a certain complexity. On the other hand, the biological structures of these systems are manifestations of underlying processes. What processes? Well, the processes of self-organization that we have identified as mental processes. In this sense, biological structures are manifestations of mind. Now, if we extend this way of thinking to the universe as a whole, it is not too far-fetched to assume that *all* its structures – from subatomic particles to galaxies and from bacteria to human beings – are manifestations of the universal dynamics of self-organization; in other words, of the cosmic mind. And this, more or less, is the mystical view.

"I realize," I concluded, "that there are several gaps in this argument. Still, I feel that the systems view of life provides a meaningful framework for unifying the two opposing views of the age-old questions of the nature of life, mind, and consciousness."

Now I fell silent. My long monologue had been a tremendous effort for me. For the first time I had laid out, as clearly and concisely as I could, my entire framework for approaching the questions of life, mind, and consciousness. I had presented it to the most knowledgeable and forceful critic I knew and had been as inspired, spontaneous, and alert as I would ever be. So this was my answer to Laing's challenge of the previous evening, and after a while I asked him, "How does that sound to you, Ronnie? What do you think of it?"

Laing lit a cigarette, took a sip of cognac, and finally made the most encouraging comment I could have hoped for. "I will have to think about it," he said simply. "This is not something I can address myself to right away. You have introduced quite a few new ideas, and I will have to think about them."

With this comment the tension that had persisted for the last hour was broken, and we spent the rest of the evening in a very relaxed and warm conversation in which Ronnie and I were joined by many of our group.

During the next two days, I spent most of my time with Laing and his friends in a relaxed and playful mood without ever mentioning our discussion. After a couple of days of relaxation and some more thinking, I found a way in which quality and experience might possibly be incorporated into a future science, and the next day after lunch I invited Laing to join me for coffee.

"A true science of consciousness," I proposed, "would have to be a new type of science dealing with qualities rather than quantities and being based on shared experience rather than verifiable measurements. The data of such a science would be patterns of experience that cannot be quantified or analyzed. On the other hand, the conceptual models interconnecting the data would have to be logically consistent, like all scientific models, and might even include quantitative elements. Such a new science would quantify its statements whenever this method is appropriate, but would also be able to deal with qualities and values based on human experience."

"I would add to this," Laing replied, "that the new science, the new epistemology, has got to be predicated upon a change of heart, upon a complete turning around; from the intent to dominate and control nature to the idea of, for example, Francis of Assisi, that the whole creation is our companion, if not our mother. That is part of your turning point. Only then can we address ourselves to alternative perceptions that will come into view."

As I reflected on Laing's comment, several of our friends entered the café, and Laing asked me whether I minded if they joined us. Of course, I did not mind, and Ronnie invited them to sit down. "Let me just tell these people what you and I have been talking about," he said. "If you don't mind, let me just reiterate what you have been saying." He then proceeded to give a brilliant summary of what I had said three nights before and during the last hour. He summarized the entire conceptual framework in his own words, in his highly idiosyncratic style, with all the intensity and passion that were characteristic of him. After this brilliant discourse, which amounted to an exhortation, there was no more doubt in my mind that Laing had accepted my ideas.

The question of how experience might be approached within a new scientific framework, which had been the main subject of my discussions with Ronnie Laing in Saragossa, came into full focus in cognitive science a decade later.

During the 1970s and 1980s, the study of consciousness as lived experience was still taboo among most scientists, but during the 1990s, the situation changed dramatically. While cognitive science established itself as a broad interdisciplinary field of study, new noninvasive techniques for analyzing brain functions were developed, which made it possible to observe complex neural processes associated with mental imagery and other human experiences. And suddenly, the scientific study of consciousness became a respectable and lively field of research.

The central challenge of this research was, and still is, to explain the experience associated with cognitive events. Different states of conscious experience are sometimes called *qualia* by cognitive scientists, because each state is characterized by a special "qualitative feel," as Laing emphasized in our discussions. The challenge of explaining these *qualia* is often called "the hard problem of consciousness study," an expression coined by the philosopher David Chalmers.

In the mid-1990s, biologist and neuroscientist Francisco Varela proposed a new approach to this "hard problem" that embraces both brain physiology and the analysis of first-person experience. Varela called this new school of thought "neurophenomenology." Phenomenology, as you know, is an important branch of modern philosophy, founded by Edmund Husserl at the beginning of the twentieth century and developed further by many European philosophers, including Martin Heidegger and Maurice Merleau-Ponty. The central concern of phenomenology is the disciplined examination of experience, and the hope of Husserl and his followers was, and is, that a true science of experience would eventually be established in partnership with the natural sciences.

Neurophenomenology is an approach to the study of consciousness that combines the disciplined examination of conscious experience with the analysis of corresponding neural patterns and processes. With this dual approach, neurophenomenologists explore various domains of experience and try to understand how they emerge from complex neural activities. In doing so, these cognitive scientists are indeed taking the first steps toward formulating a true science of experience.

Prominent neurophenomenologists today include Walter Freeman and Antonio Damasio. I don't know to what extent these scientists were influenced by Laing's views on the centrality of experience in human consciousness, which he published in 1982 in his book *The Voice of Experience*. All I know is that my own attempts over the past thirty years to map out a science of qualities, integrating the biological, cognitive, social, and ecological dimensions of life, were triggered by my dramatic discussions with Ronnie Laing under the starry sky of Saragossa.

4

ON R. D. LAING'S STYLE, SORCERY, ALIENATION

John M. Heaton, MA, MB, BChir, DO

Ronnie (R. D. Laing) meant many things to many people. I elaborate on some aspects of his thought and practice as I knew them.

Style

What struck me on first meeting Ronnie was his style; he stood out from most people because of his unique style or way of being. This was not merely a matter of the way he dressed, the music he liked, his conversation, his looks, and his rather dry and sometimes cruel humor, but his style conveyed something of great importance that can only be conveyed by style. This was crucial in his psychotherapy, and one of the things he can teach us is the vitality of style in the practice of psychotherapy and counseling.

Style conveys something above and beyond what can be explicitly said by means of interpretation and other interventions. For what there is to understand in being human is richer than what it becomes when put into the jargon of therapeutic speech. Intelligibility depends on dialogue, on the way things are said and to whom; there is more to dialogue than what is said.

Style is not just an aesthetic matter. We must distinguish style from stylish; the latter is a matter of aesthetics. A stylish person is consciously concerned about his or her appearance and tends to conform to the latest fashion. Style, on the other hand, is unconscious; we all have a style, a way of being that is visible to others, and this is what Foucault (1988, p. 6) called ethics, or the practice of freedom as opposed to morality. The difference between them is that morality presents us with a set of rules that we can either obey or disobey; a person who is only moral is a "goody," a type that Ronnie particularly disliked. Ethics, on the other hand, is a way of existing, a possibility of life, so what we say or do is assessed in relation to the ways of existing involved. Thus, there are things one can do or say only out of mean-spiritedness, a life based on hatred or bitterness toward life. Sometimes it takes only a gesture or word that can kill. Other styles convey a generosity of spirit. It is our style of life that makes us this or that, what we are capable of seeing or doing and the particular morality and its interpretation that attracts us. Concepts and rules do not act alone; their rhythm and scintillation act on us, and the atmosphere in which they are grasped are vital to their meaning.

Tillich, a theologian who Ronnie knew and admired wrote that love is "the style of life that is willed in and through each of the virtues" (1959, p. 144). Each virtue derives its virtuousness from its participation in love, and each is a particular mode of love. Ethics is the fundamental thinking of authentic love.

Style is a fundamental disposition. It is the way in which each of us holds his or her own prior to positive rules and laws for practical behavior that he or she may follow. Ethics as mere doctrine and exhortation is impotent before style, which is in a fundamental relationship with Being. Style does not result in a relationship to Being; style starts from it.

A fine style comes from precise sensation and full realization in experience. If you sense and experience things precisely you will think precisely and so have a fine style.

Style is unique; one cannot copy it. Some people would try to copy Ronnie's style with disastrous results; he could be withering about people who did this. Style is not just "mental"; it is expressed and so embodied; it transcends the body–mind split; it can never be understood by a psychology that only studies the mind or by a physiology that concentrates on the body. Merely putting a hyphen in *psycho-somatic* is no solution unless we are clear exactly what the hyphen means. Ronnie was very attentive to people's gestures and the extent to which they measured up to their words. I have often sat with him at a lecture when he would point out to me the dissociation between what the lecturer said and his gestures and facial expression – his style.

Style resists any ideal of correctness; it cannot be measured so it is individuating; it sets one apart from the general. It has its own necessity and cannot be adopted at will or on a whim. Style is a movement, a vital substance, not something that you can pick and choose. It is not a property of the individual, or a personal matter; it does not belong to one and so is not egoic. It is useful to recall a term from Duns Scotus – *haecceity*, which translates as "thisness."

Ronnie came across this notion from reading the poet Gerard Manley Hopkins, who was an admirer of Scotus (1265–1308). In *The Self and Others* (1961), he quotes from Hopkins:

> When I consider my self-being, my consciousness and feeling of myself, that taste of myself, of I and me above and in all things, which is more distinctive than the taste of ale or alum, more distinctive than the smell of walnut or camphor, and is incommunicable by any means to another man. . . . Nothing else in nature comes near this unspeakable stress of pitch, distinctiveness, and selving, this selfbeing of my own. Nothing explains it or resembles

it, except so far as this, that other men to themselves have the same feeling. . . . And even those things with which I in some way identify myself, as my country or family, and those things which I own and call mine, as my clothes and so on, all presuppose the strict sense of self and me and mine and are from that derivative.

(p. 18)

Even in 1978 Ronnie was still reading Hopkins, especially his poem "The Windhover: To Christ Our Lord." I quote Adrian, his son: "If Ronnie read this out once he read it a hundred times – sober, drunk, tired, exhilarated" (A. Laing, 1994, p. 198). His own poems show the influence of Hopkins.

Now Scotus's work shows that experience is not something that a person has, or even has happen to one; it is rather what one is made of. So experience is not a property of the individual, it is not personal, it does not belong to me in the sense that my money does; thus, I can lose all my money, but I cannot lose my experience, although I can lose touch with my experience, a disaster Ronnie was particularly interested in. So experience is individuating and is expressed in style.

Style is a force, an anonymous affective force; this is why it is so important in psychotherapy. A vivid style is a power of demystification because it undoes the knots of dead concepts and obsessive verbalizing, that is, concepts and linguistic formulas that one may possess and so possess one. *Haecceity* must be understood in terms of "speed," "feeling" and "intensity," which break up the established affective rhythm and verbalizing within a teaching or learning process. Ronnie had a refined sense of the right timing to break up blocked responses to a patient – a boring case history, thoughtless repetition of psychoanalytic jargon.

A great modern stylists was Nietzsche, greatly admired by Ronnie. To quote Deleuze,

> In relation to Zarathustra, the laugh, the game, and the dance are affirmative powers of transmutation: the dance transmutes the heavy into the light, the laugh transmutes suffering into joy, the game of dice throwing transmutes the low into the high. But in relation to Dionysus, the dance, the laugh, and the game are affirmative powers of reflection and development. Dance affirms the becoming and the being of becoming; laughter affirms the multiple and the 'one' of the multiple; the game affirms chance and the necessity of chance.
>
> *(1983, p. 193)*

Laughter, game and music were all affirmative and transmutive powers used by Ronnie. They could reach the intensity of *haecceity* and so become independent of any affect or sentiment linked to the person, that is, if the person allowed them to reach him or her. These becomings demystify representational thought such as "I am mad" or "I am no good," or "I am giving a correct case history" – beliefs in some totalization of the self or the other. A style, like a *haecceity*, is an *asignifying* sign, that is, a sign that has become a pure event and that no longer signifies anything outside of that which it is. It is not the same as a social interaction which can be represented and conceptualized; rather, it is iconic, so Ronnie at times could talk about nothing yet have a forcible affect. A style and a *haecceity* are focused vibrations, creating a resonance, an invisible force, and so are not discursive; they cannot be put down in propositions, which have a reference and associated states of affairs.

This powerful demystifying force explodes the belief in a totalizing unity, which arises from preconceived representations. It challenges to create new forms of expression and so moves away from self-created knots. More important than what we think is what forces us to think. Style can trigger the metamorphosis from propositions to expressivity, to reach one's own style, to harness one's own forces.

Sometimes Ronnie would forget this as for example when he became fascinated with Bateson's double bind hypothesis as an explanation for some of the manifestations of schizophrenia. This theory assumes the theory of types which depends on a view of language as a purely calculative system, the very opposite of how Ronnie understood language in his better moments. Of course, few are interested now in the theory of types, which has been shown to be fatally flawed, and Ronnie, according to Bob Mullan's interviews, was less enamored of it when he was older.

Sorcery

Haecceity and events are ways of sorcery because they move one through the power of intensity rather than logical argument. Logic treats of propositions, and in its modern form, symbolic logic, the judgment is dissolved into a system of mapping and interconnecting. It becomes the object of a calculus and so of a derivative structure, a concern with entities that conceals the roots of formalized languages in natural language. A calculus is a formal system consisting of a set of specified symbols and a finite set of formation rules that regulate how the symbols are to be connected.

Ronnie was for a time rather enamored with applying symbolic logic to human relationships as is shown in his interest in double-bind theory, dyadic relationships (R. Laing, 1961, 1970). But he had doubts even fairly early on in its value; for example, "*It is doubtful if the Logical Type theory, which arises in the course of the construction of a calculus of propositions, can be applied directly to communication*" (R. Laing, 1961, p. 129). He turned more and more to what was nearer his heart – sorcery:

> Sorcerers have always had an anomalous position, at the edge of the fields or the woods. They haunt the edges. They are at the border of the village, or in between two villages. The important thing is their affinity with the alliance, with the pact, which gives them a status opposite to that of filiation. The relationship with the anomalous is one of alliance. The sorcerer is in a relationship of alliance with the demon as the power of the anomalous.
>
> *(Deleuze, 1988, p. 246)*

Ronnie certainly came to inhabit an anomalous position in relation to his contemporaries. He was a famous psychiatrist and psychoanalyst but at the same time known to be involved with illicit drugs and drunkenness. He was a considered "expert" on the family, on filiation, but at the same time a critic of the family and forming alliances with thinkers such as Sartre and Foucault.

He had a sensitivity to the forces of the "outside" that is critical for the sorcerer; he or she must be able to harness these forces to enable the individual to "deterritorialize" in Deleuze's language. The *haecceity's* combination of speed and feeling, which can, in suitable circumstances, create the power to dismantle the "hang-ups," preventing movement and becoming are easily avoided, however. Psychotherapy now has almost completely succumbed to the "voices of objection." One important means of "objection" to the power of sorcery in our society is to glamorize it, and I think at times Ronnie allowed this to happen. He became enamored of sorcery, a very dangerous position because sobriety is an essential discipline for a sorcerer.

The account of sorcery among one of the tribes of the Jivaro Indians, the Achuar, who are headhunters of the Amazonian forest is enlightening (Descola, 1996). The Achuar were aware that to openly embrace the career of a shaman exposes one to deadly danger. The murder of a sorcerer is considered legitimate by just about everybody – including his closest relatives, who accept that this is more or less the destiny to be expected in this dangerous profession. Sorcerers must live an ascetic existence because it is essential for them to have allies and ritual friends because they are exposed to the threat of summary execution at all times.

Contrast this with the picture of the modern therapist who is cozy and safe, caring, "ethical" and professional. I think that applying any of these words to Ronnie would be problematic.

Alienation

What provokes thought is the holes and gaps in people's lives, and Ronnie had a keen nose for these in his own life and in others. In most lives there are catalepsies or a kind of sleepwalking through a number of years but somewhere there is a hole. Kierkegaard in *The Sickness unto Death* (1989) explored this phenomenon, and Ronnie was greatly influenced by him. He gave the book to Jock Sutherland – a leading psychoanalyst – who looked at it for an hour or so and declared that "it was a very interesting example of 19th century psychopathology." Ronnie was shocked at Sutherland's response, as I remember him telling the story a number of times. It illustrates the huge gap in sensibility between him and most psychoanalysts.

In one of his other books Kierkegaard (1983, pp. 38–41) described the knight of faith. He pointed out that it is his movements that are unique, for they express the sublime in the pedestrian. To look at him one would notice nothing, a bourgeois, nothing but a bourgeois. But actually he is a "becoming"; Kierkegaard shows that the plane of the infinite, which he calls the plane of faith, must become a pure plane of immanence that continually and immediately imparts, reimparts and regathers the finite, a *haecceity*, a style. There is no longer a relation between a subject and an object but, rather, a movement serving as the limit of that relation, in the period associated with the subject and the object.

This is not the place to go into the complexities of *The Sickness unto Death*. It is a phenomenological account of various types of despair-angst based on Hegel's *Phenomenology of Spirit*. For our purposes the most important form of despair is the despair which is ignorant of being despair, or the despairing ignorance of having a self and an eternal self. This applies roughly to the person who considers him- or herself to be successful, who knows what's what, who has most things sussed out, who can put people who obviously are in despair and distress in neat categories that he or she thinks defines them and distances them from their own state of successful mediocrity. It is a state of spiritual mediocrity, a state Ronnie loathed.

But to show how *The Sickness unto Death* had a profound influence on Ronnie's thought and practice I must refer to the master–slave section of *Phenomenology of Spirit* (Hegel, 1977, pp. 111–119). When we started seminars for therapists interested in phenomenology and existentialism the first seminars were given on this section of the *Phenomenology of Spirit* on both Ronnie's and David Cooper's suggestion. Why did they think this so important?

The point is that Hegel undermines the ordinary assumption that the slave is a helpless being, a victim if you like, whereas the master knows all and that the slave depends on the master for his freedom. Hegel shows that, actually, the master is in a blind alley and it is the slave, through his or her suffering, who can go on his or her journey to freedom. Transfer this thought to mental suffering. The patient is a slave to his or her depression, obsessions, phobias, and so on. The psychiatrist or psychotherapist often see themselves as in the position of the master, the one who knows, who is to free the patient from his slavery and, of course, the patient often sees him- or herself as a victim, depending on the psychiatrist to free him or her. The result is the patient becomes a slave to psychiatry or psychoanalysis.

Thinkers on the nature of human freedom from Kant via Hegel and Sartre to Laing have shown that freedom is not merely freedom from but essentially freedom to and that this requires some sort of dialectic or in more modern terms conversation to attain it. In other words neurosis and even schizophrenia, in Ronnie's opinion, depended on some sort of decision, often fairly early in life, not to be free but rather to take up the position of a slave. This decision results in all sorts of confusions and mystifications that the therapist and the patient together have to disentangle to a greater or lesser degree before the patient can realize the untenability of his or her position and can act in a fulfilling way.

Now this way of understanding the nature of being human is completely at odds with conventional thought in psychiatry and psychotherapy. For if freedom is dialogical it is not something that one person possesses and another does not. One cannot make people free, although one can free them from something; for example, if I were tied up by a rope someone might be willing to untie the rope and free me from it. Ronnie's whole practice was deeply influenced by this insight.

If therapy and freedom are necessarily dialogical, then there can be no one technique or group of techniques that is essential to help people on their way. So this distanced him from dogmatic forms of psychoanalysis and nearly all the 400 or so psychotherapies. Let me give an example. Twenty or so years ago I was consulted by the parents of a man who had had a lot of psychiatric treatment and who had been advised to have a leucotomy; they wanted a second opinion. I saw him and couldn't make head or tail of much of what he said except that it was clear he was intelligent, was a devout Muslim and was referring, I thought, to certain Sufi experiences with which I was familiar. I was sure I could not take him on for treatment. I asked Ronnie what I should do. He thought a bit and said he had a friend who knew a lot about Sufi communities. So in the end we arranged for him to go to Egypt to join a suitable Sufi community. Two years or so later I got a letter from the man thanking me and saying that he was now much clearer about his life and had entered training to become a dervish.

Ronnie's skepticism about particular techniques in psychotherapy was many years ahead of his time and, of course, was bitterly attacked. In the last 20 years or so there has been a vast amount of research backing up his position. Briefly what has been found is that it is the credibility (the style?) of the therapist to the patient that is important not the theories and techniques that the therapist believes in (Christensen & Jacobson, 1994). For example, if you match phobic patients, sending one lot to a trained psychoanalyst who sees them 4 times weekly and a matched lot to an intelligent counselor or a cognitive therapist, then there is no difference in the cure rate; the counselor may have no theory whatsoever about phobias but will get just as good results as the psychoanalyst who has highly elaborate theories about phobia. This applies to depression, obsessions and other neuroses.

Worse still for traditional psychoanalytic therapy is that it has been found that supportive therapy produces just as much structural change as non-supportive therapy, so giving the lie to the belief that only psychoanalytic therapy produces real change and other therapies are only suggestive. Furthermore, in psychoanalysis itself it was found that structural change occurred as much with non-interpretive supportive means as with interpretations. For a general review see Erwin (1997).

These observations were done by hard-nosed clinicians and statisticians not by crazy existentialists, but actually confirm what existentialists have been saying for years.

As Freida Fromm-Reichmann (1950), who Ronnie greatly admired, once said, the patient needs an experience, not an explanation. This is conveyed by style and sorcery rather than by treatments that are the application of some theories.

Another aspect of Ronnie's dialogical approach was his way of sharing his cultural sensibilities with his patients. For example, the residents of Philadelphia Association houses would often be interested in phenomenology and existentialism; they would be part of the general enterprise of studying what it is to be human instead of being treated as victims who are having "good" done to them. The central question, "What is good?" would be kept open instead of being decided by a group of self-styled experts and then being applied to people – passive victims of power-hungry knowledge.

Ronnie had a deep understanding that human communication involves not merely the movement of the message from a sender position to a receiver position but that one has already to be in communication with the person to be addressed before one starts speaking. That is why conversational discourse involves paralinguistic elements designed to create interaction and integration.

Transgression

I now want to change the subject and discuss the influence of Nietzsche and Foucault on Ronnie. Nietzsche receives more mention than any other philosopher in *Mad to Be Normal* (Mullan, 1995). I remember him reading extracts from Nietzsche – quite an experience because Nietzsche is very quotable and Ronnie was magnificent at reading aloud. Ronnie was ahead of his time, for in the 1960s, Nietzsche was not much read in England. Now he is one of the most widely read and discussed philosopher. It was Nietzsche's critique of our culture and his style of writing that were important to Ronnie. Nietzsche realized you cannot separate a person's "mind" from his or her culture and so alienation from the culture in which he is alienated. Is it the person or the culture that is alienated?

And, of course, Nietzsche was the most important influence on Foucault, and Ronnie published four of Foucault's books in his World of Man series.

There are many influences running between these three thinkers. I want to discuss their interest in transgression. Foucault's fine essay "A Preface to Transgression" (1977, pp. 29–52) is a good introduction to his thinking on this. Much of Nietzsche's writing shows his interest in transgression. The reason why it is so important to psychiatry is that psychiatrists see people who have transgressed in one way or another and have to take into account its anomalous position. For transgression can be creative or destructive, and the unanswerable question is what makes it sometimes one and sometimes the other; that is a question Nietzsche, Foucault and Laing were interested in.

Take art, for example. Nearly all great art transgresses rules, but not every transgression of rules is great art. If I sent a chamber pot to an exhibition of art I doubt if anyone would be impressed, but when Duchamp did in the 1920s it was highly significant. Great moral thinkers such as Buddha, Jesus Christ and Socrates were thought of by most of their contemporaries as exceptionally wicked transgressors of the law, as was Freud in his time. Socrates was considered a perverter of the young; presumably, nowadays he would be fitted with an electronic device telling the powers that be where he is – such is progress! Lister was thought mad or bad when he suggested that midwives should wash their hands before examining a woman in labor.

Take madness and loss of reason, for example. What is reason? Rarely do psychiatrists or therapists question it; they assume, of course, that they are reasonable and that anyone who deviates much from them is unreasonable or has perhaps "lost" it. But what is "it"?

Ronnie was very surprised at the vehemence of the reaction to his questioning of madness. Many people have questioned the notion, for example, Plato in the *Phaedrus*. That pillar of the establishment Samuel Johnson said of Christopher Smart – the mad poet – "I do not think he ought to be shut up. His infirmities were not noxious to society. He insisted on people praying with him; and I'd as lief pray with Kit Smart as any one else. Another charge was, that he did not love clean linen; and I have no passion for it" (Boswell, 1901, pp. 263–264).

Ronnie refused to be a servant of the state and have to treat people as the state ordered so he left the National Health Service and tried to help people according to their and his best judgment – in a dialogue with them. He knew that a professional person in the old sense of the word could give judgments that were against the majority opinion and the government, as lawyers do to this day. It is ironical that therapists now go cap in hand to the government in order to get recognition as a profession, the direct opposite of how professions were originally formed and of the origins of psychoanalysis. Imagine the response of the British government in the 1920s if Ernest Jones had gone, cap in hand, to ask it to legitimize psychoanalysis! Yet this is what the "profession" is doing now. Questions of sanity and madness and their treatment are subtle and controversial questions, and it is doubtful if a government official is the best person to judge who the best people to deal with it are.

A reading of Nietzsche and Foucault would also show why neither Ronnie nor Foucault were keen on embracing anti-psychiatry. They both knew and argued that things are much more complicated than taking up a pro or an anti position in these matters; Ronnie, like Foucault, was a dialectical thinker. In *Mad to Be Normal* (Mullan, 1995) he talks sympathetically of ECT, saying he could well understand some people wanting it; it is the casual use of it and the forcing of people who do not want to have it that he objected to. He certainly did not think that psychotherapy or psychoanalysis were the sole answer to mental pain and despair.

Ways of being

Nietzsche and Foucault were both very aware of the complexities and subtleties of language and the play of negativity; what can be said and what cannot be said but only shown are crucial. Ronnie, too, was in that tradition; that is why he so liked Dionysius's works, the tradition of negative theology, Zen Buddhism, Beckett and so on. If one had no sense of irony then I think Ronnie would be very difficult to understand – a complaint he made about Americans and humanistic psychologists, perhaps a little unfairly.

In teaching he was fond of Confusius's saying "I show them one corner." I once told him the Zen story of the mayor of a district who visited a Zen master. He went into the room, and the master drew a circle in the air. The mayor said, 'Wait a minute, I haven't even sat down yet." The master shut the door, which meant that he accepted him as a genuine pupil. The ordinary person would have tried to work out what the circle meant and so become endlessly mystified! The mayor, on the other hand, was ontologically secure. Ronnie liked the story.

He was an admirer of Thomas Reid, the great Scottish philosopher of common sense; it was, he thought, "a refined, cultivated common sense; an attempt to steer a way out of solipsism or, on the other hand, crude materialism" (Mullan, 1995, p. 310). Note the profundity of that remark. The field of "mental health" is completely bedeviled by this dichotomy. On one side are most psychoanalysts and therapists who are idealists and solipsistic, although they may not be aware that this is where their theories led. To give one example, Freud (1984, p. 170) assumed that consciousness only makes us aware of our own states of mind, that other people possess a consciousness is an inference only; this assumption leads straight to solipsism or idealism. On the other side are most psychiatrists who think that chemistry eventually will solve human despair.

Ronnie had a great ability to see his way through the maze of nonsense that issues from the mouths of therapists and students. He could be rather savage at times however. He called himself "a provisional sceptic" (Mullan, 1995, p. 310) and was close to the Greek Pyrrhonian sceptics (Heaton 1993). He had no use for any *ism* that closes off into dogmatism and exclusivity. *"The world within us and outside us is beyond us, in both directions"* (Mullan, 1995, p. 313).

I should mention here Ronnie's interest in neuropsychiatry and those great pioneers such as Schilder, Goldstein and Strauss – all German Jews who had read Heidegger – and Freud and, of course, were familiar with neuropsychiatry. They all had to flee Germany when Hitler came to power, so their influence became lost. I was interested in the visual agnosias and to understand them had read Goldstein and Strauss, this common interest was one of my first links with Ronnie. Both of us agreed that one can never understand the 'mind' without taking into account the changes that occur with brain injury; psychoanalytic theories of the mind entirely neglect this. Oliver Sacks, of course, is pursuing this field and refers to the authors I have mentioned. But note the care and modesty of his writing compared with that of most therapists. The basic idea we got from Strauss and others was to walk and talk with these patients and to note how they managed instead of merely submitting them to a battery of psychological tests.

Ronnie was a master of the unspoken. He was attentive to that in language that exceeds the order of signification. For example, in the early sixties LSD was being used in the clinic I was working in. I said to Ronnie that I would like to use it. He said the responsible thing would be for me to take it first and that he would accompany me on the first trip. So on a Saturday afternoon he gave it to me, sitting opposite him. After an hour or so I began to feel depersonalized and began to murmur was I real, was he real, and so on. Ronnie said no words but began to slowly and deliberately light his pipe. I watched fascinated and then suddenly everything somehow clicked into place and the rest of the trip was enjoyable. I talked to him later about it and he said how important Heidegger's point about *zuhandenheit*, handiness, versus *vorhandenheit*, objective presence, was (Heidegger,

1962, pp. 91–107); we are in the world with things ready-to-hand long before any conceptual language develops; it is attention to *zuhandenheit* that is so important in "trips" and with psychotic people. I have found in treating many psychotic people that this is the best advice I have ever received on this topic.

It was not only the use of family therapy but attention to that which exceeds signification that marked our treatment of psychosis from that of Kleinians such as Rosenfeld who were treating psychotic people. To Klein and Rosenfeld everything must be explainable in their theoretical terms. Ronnie, on the other hand, was concerned with how language reveals and conceals. Language comes to the word in *logos* and holds thought in its grip, but it does not speak its essence in that word. Ronnie's love of poetry, and his belief in its importance to psychotherapy was connected with this insight. As he once remarked to me he could not imagine a person with less sense of the poetry of life than Klein.

The vital importance of the poetics of experience, the volatility of our being with, its intangibility, especially evident in the person-to-person encounter, were central to Ronnie's thinking. He realized that the essential meaning of lived experience cannot be captured by assertions and so put into a theory; it is attuned understanding that he sought to develop. This is of course a very Nietzschean theme. I should mention Nietzsche's linking of music and philosophy, and Ronnie would often break up philosophical discussions by playing the piano. He would have agreed with Plato, who wrote that "the supreme music is philosophy."

Conclusion

I think Ronnie was a close student of the poetry of experience and its relevance to psychiatry. He was especially interested in transgression, its nature and its limits; of the relationship between reason and loss of reason, madness and sanity; what is right and what is wrong, what can be said and what cannot be said; of mind and body. He tried to teach that these matters should be of central concern to psychiatry.

References

Boswell, J. (1901) *The Life of Samuel Johnson*. Vol. 1. London: J. M. Dent and Sons.

Christensen, A. & Jacobson, N. (1994) Who (or What) Can Do Psychotherapy: The Status and Challenge of Nonprofessional Therapies. *Psychological Science* 5:8–14.

Deleuze, G. (1983) *Nietzsche & Philosophy*. Trans. H. Tomlinson. London: Athlone Press.

Deleuze, G. (1988) *A Thousand Plateaus*. Trans. B. Massumi. London: Athlone Press.

Descola, P. (1996) *The Spears of Twilight*. Trans. J. Lloyd. London: HarperCollins.

Erwin, E. (1997) *Philosophy and Psychotherapy*. London: Sage.

Foucault, M. (1977) A Preface to Transgression. In *Language, Counter-memory, Practice*. Trans. D. F. Bouchard & S. Simon. Ithaca, NY: Cornell University Press.

Foucault, M. (1988) *The Final Foucault*. Ed. J. Bernauer & D. Rasmussen. Cambridge, MA: MIT Press.

Freud, S. (1984) The Unconscious. In *On Metapsychology*. London: Penguin.

Fromm-Reichmann, F. (1950) *Principles of intensive psychotherapy.* Chicago, IL: Chicago University Press.

Heaton, J. M. (1993) The Sceptical Tradition in Psychotherapy. In *From the Words of My Mouth: Tradition in Psychotherapy.* Ed. L. Spurling. London: Routledge.

Hegel, G. W. F. (1977) *Hegel's Phenomenology of Spirit.* Trans. A. V. Miller. Oxford: Clarendon Press.

Heidegger, M. (1962) *Being and Time.* Trans. J. Macquarrie & E. Robinson. London: SCM Press.

Kierkegaard, S. (1983) *Fear and Trembling.* Trans. H. V. Hong & E. H. Hong. Princeton, NJ: Princeton University Press.

Kierkegaard, S. (1989) *The Sickness unto Death.* Trans. A. Hannay. London: Penguin.

Laing, A. C. (1994) *R. D. Laing.* London: Peter Owen.

Laing, R. D. (1961) *The Self and Others.* London: Tavistock Publications.

Laing, R. D. (1970) *Knots.* London: Tavistock Publications.

Mullan, B. (1995) *Mad to Be Normal.* London: Free Association Books.

Tillich, P. (1959) *Theology of Culture.* Ed. R. C. Kimball. New York: Galaxy Books.

5

LAING BEYOND WORDS

Antipsychiatry as performance

Andrew Pickering, PhD

I am interested here in the work of R.D. Laing and antipsychiatry more generally. My starting point is to distinguish between two Laings – the verbal, textual,
theoretical, cognitive Laing, the man of ideas, and the nonverbal, performative, as
I would say, Laing, the man who did things. I also explain why I am more interested in the performative Laing than his cognitive twin. I should say in advance
that words such as *performance* and *performative* are intended to point to something
very simple and straightforward, namely, action, behavior, and doing things in the
world. My suggestion is that the singularity of antipsychiatry is located precisely
in the centrality of its performative rather than its cognitive/intellectual aspects.[1]

·

I read some of Laing's work in the 1960s, but I first took a scholarly interest in him
in the 2000s. I followed the usual academic route, reading his books and papers
and books and papers about him. When you do that you arrive very quickly at the
cognitive Laing, the man of ideas, and, to tell the truth, I find his ideas interesting but not that interesting. The 1950s and 1960s were a time of great academic
interest in psychiatry and mental hospitals, and the work that Laing draws on by
social scientists such as Erving Goffman and Harold Garfinkel was already well
known. Laing differs from them in taking madness seriously, one could say, as
something important in the world rather than a social construction imposed on
an amorphous substrate. This explains his interest in philosophical approaches
to phenomenology as a way of getting at the inner experience of madness (and
sanity). There is an interesting confluence here of sociology and philosophy, but
nothing earthshaking.

What about the performative Laing? Of course, he did things. He didn't just
write about madness; he interacted with the mad, most famously, and along with
the other members of the Philadelphia Association, at Kingsley Hall in the second

half of the 1960s. And one remarkable fact is that it is hard to find out about Kingsley Hall. As far as I know, Laing himself wrote almost nothing about it.[2] The books that made him rich and famous tell you more than you want to know about phenomenology and social theory – and politics too – but almost nothing about his practice. Academic studies again focus on his ideas as if they developed in some textual outer space. There is a pattern here. Since the Enlightenment, words, ideas, and reason, have been taken in the West as the defining feature of humankind. They are what sets us apart from the beasts and inanimate matter, and it is this sort of human exceptionalism, as I call it (Pickering, 2008), that manifests itself in Laing's own writing and that of his commentators: ideas are what we value in the West, not actions. This is what fascinates me about antipsychiatry – my argument is that it dwelled in this shadowy zone of action.

If we refuse to be dazzled by ideas, however, it turns out that we can find out quite a bit about Laing's practice in roundabout ways. He was, for example, exceptionally good at establishing relations with schizophrenics:

> [In the US] Laing was taken to a psychiatric ward . . . where there was a girl, sitting naked on the floor and rocking. She had not spoken to anyone for months. The staff wanted to see how Laing . . . would handle this case. Laing went into the room, stripped off naked, sat next to the girl and started rocking with her. Within twenty minutes they were chatting.
>
> *(Kotowicz, 1997, 73–74)*[3]

I want to emphasize several points about this story. First, it is purely about performance, doing things – sitting and rocking next to someone else. The talk, the chatting, comes at the end, after the action (or inaction). Second, we should see Laing's performance as situated. The point of the story is not that sitting around naked is a general or universal way to treat schizophrenia; it helped in this instance. And this leads to the third point, which has to do with emergence and unpredictable becoming as integral to performance. We interact performatively with people (and things), and they act back, but we don't know what form that reaction will take until we try it. So performance is relational and experimental, a continual and open-ended process of finding out what the other will do and reacting to that – a process I call a dance of agency (Pickering, 1995). Laing tried it and found out that, in this instance, sitting rocking on the floor was a way of latching onto the other.

I could add two further points. We could note, fourth, a sort of incommensurability and untranslatability between the two Laings. There is nothing in this anecdote that goes over easily into social theory or phenomenology. It is not about meanings or values or social structure or whatever; Laing sat down and something happened in the world, and that was it. And the Enlightenment traditions are not interested in performances like that. Sitting naked on the floor for twenty minutes does not speak to human exceptionalism, to what is special about humanity – cats and rocks do it all the time – it does not fit into hymns of praise to our wonderful cognitive abilities. No wonder Laing the intellectual could not bring himself to write about it. Fifth, I think one can argue that this thread of nonverbal performance was nevertheless the hallmark of Laing's practice and antipsychiatry in general. Now I want to run through some examples to establish this point.

•

Laing's first scholarly publication appeared in 1955 and reported on the so-called rumpus room experiment at Glasgow Royal Mental Hospital (Cameron, Laing, & McGhie, 1955). Laing's idea here was simply to suspend the standard rules and routines of mental care and set in motion an open-ended dance of agency between the patients and the nurses – to see what would happen if they were free to come to terms with one another and establish their own form of life. The point of the paper is simply that they did find a new form of life, with fewer locked doors and less sedation, which, as it happened, proved beneficial for all concerned (though not for the wider institution). David Cooper's (1967) Villa 21 experiment at Shenley Hospital in the early 1960s had just the same character and upshot, an emergent reciprocal adaptation of the practices of inmates and staff. We can understand Laing's use of LSD on himself and his clients likewise, as, in fact, an attempt to stretch the parameters of performance and the dance of agency, taking the performers into new spaces, something we can come back to.

At Kingsley Hall, the story of Mary Barnes and Joe Berke (1971) is again very largely one of open-ended performative interaction. Berke experimented with ways of latching onto Barnes – bathing her when she soiled herself, feeding her with a bottle, being punched and punching her a couple of times, inventing animal games of fighting and biting – and no doubt Barnes was finding ways of latching onto Berke too. As I just said about LSD, we can think here of Berke as expanding the variety of his own performances to find out what would register with Barnes. In David Burns's (2002) very insightful account of life in the Archway communities that followed Kingsley Hall in the 1970s, he talks about the evolution of a strategy he calls twenty-four attention, in which residents would arrange continuous personal nonverbal care for their fellows, either physically preventing them from wandering onto the street and getting into trouble, for example, or to sustain their isolation in "inner voyages." As Burns also notes, the Archway communities were increasingly permeated by wordless bodily practices associated with Eastern spirituality such as dance, meditation, yoga, massage, and a vegetarian diet, thanks largely, as I understand it, to Leon Redler.

Laing's psychiatric practice post-Kingsley Hall is again hard to find out about, but it is clear that in the early 1970s it remained determinedly performative, including an inarticulate "rebirthing" process –a reenactment of emergence from the womb – featuring "all sorts of mini-freakouts and birth-like experiences, yelling, groaning, screaming, writhing, contorting, biting, contending." He also commented, "When I go into one of our households for an evening usually music, drumming, singing, dancing starts up" (quoted in A. Laing 1994, 180). This is the performative, not the cognitive, Laing.[4]

My inclination, therefore, is to see anti-psychiatry as a sort of ground-zero approach to therapy, centered on performance and dances of agency –nonlinguistic, noncognitive, performative actions and interactions – and thus as nonmodern, in the sense of lying outside the space of the Enlightenment West. This is the root of its strangeness and of Laing's inability to speak about his own practice. Of course, one should not exaggerate the wordlessness of it all. No doubt there was plenty of talk at Kingsley Hall, and Laing himself was a great talker. But we should follow Laing's friend, the cybernetician Gregory Bateson, and understand the talk as itself performative – a mode of social action and interaction, rather than the transmission of information (Pickering, 2010, Chap. 5). By all accounts, speech at Kingsley Hall and Archway was often drowned out by inchoate shouting.

•

Why am I so interested in this performative aspect of antipsychiatry? This needs some explanation. My earlier work in the history of science (Pickering, 1995) convinced me that performance and dances of agency are everywhere, all the time – they are the grounds of our being in the world. Everything else, including knowledge, has to be understood in relation to performance. So there is a puzzle here for me: How can I say that the singularity of antipsychiatry resides in its emphasis on performance if performance is everywhere? The answer is that there are different ways of conducting dances of agency, most of which somehow obscure, marginalize, or deny their existence, make them invisible.

Conventional sciences such as physics, for example, depend on finding islands of relative stability in the flux of becoming, and tell us stories not about a world of emergent performance but of regular predictable mechanisms (Pickering, 2011). This is the high status, culturally approved Enlightenment way of going on. I used to think it is how it has to be – I could not imagine any alternative – but then I started to find examples of another way – raw, direct, somehow vaguely embarrassing – in which dances of agency are thematized and traded on and in which performative experimentation is the central methodological principle rather than something to be hidden away in a cupboard. A friend once said I was interested in human beings acting like pigs wallowing in a trough, but I find these other ways politically attractive. I prefer talking pigs to bankers. Our usual modes of being tend to be projects of mastery and domination, command and control, and this contributes a lot, I think, to the increasing grimness and joylessness of the world we live in. I prefer this other way of being that thematizes rather than hides performance and emergence, open-ended exploration of what the world has to offer us. And this, then, is why antipsychiatry interests me so much – as a striking and important example of an approach to psychiatry that makes performance, emergence and the dance of agency its center and its method – that shows us that the trick can be done.

•

Two contrasts might help now. We can think first about psychoanalysis, the talking cure. This is at the opposite, Enlightenment, pole from anti-psychiatry.

Bodies are absent in psychoanalytic therapy; the patient and therapist do nothing, or, better, the only doing in psychoanalysis and the only interaction is at the magical level of talk, words, themselves, processed by the analyst via an elaborate theory of mental structures. So if, as I think, dances of agency are everywhere, it makes a big difference to how we act whether we recognize and foreground them, as in antipsychiatry with performance as method, or we smother them in a detour through words, as in psychoanalysis. These are two visibly very different ways of doing psychiatry. Antipsychiatry was singular, therefore, in just the sense that it foregrounded emergent performances, putting them center stage in therapy rather than detouring away from them into words and thought. And we can just note the obvious: in the Enlightenment tradition Freud is spoken of as a great revolutionary in the lineage of Newton, Darwin, Einstein, and all of our other cultural heroes, while antipsychiatry figures as an embarrassing aberration, to be reviled in retrospect. We could, however, if we liked, look at this differently: Laing as the real revolutionary, upsetting the whole cognitivist Enlightenment paradigm.

Now for a second contrast. Antipsychiatry unfolded against a backcloth of the great and desperate cures of 1940s and 1950s psychiatry: lobotomy, electroshock, and, increasingly, psychoactive drugs (starting with chlorpromazine in the mid-1950s). What can we say about that? First, that, like antipsychiatry, the great and desperate cures also thematized performance. Their history, again, is one of performative experimentation – finding out that suitably adjusted jolts of current through the brain indeed affect people's behavior without killing them. But still, there are illuminating differences here that again illustrate the fact that there are different ways of conducting dances of agency and that these differences matter. I can mention four that are worth thinking about:

1   These cures are enmeshed in scientific talk. Cybernetics, for example, began as a science of psychiatry, offering explanations for the efficacy of lobotomy and electroshock. Nowadays we have neurochemistry, neurobiology, and fMRI images as the discursive penumbra of Prozac. These sciences carry us away from performance and back into the world of words and theory (and, not coincidentally, to big science and big pharma). In contrast, it is hard to imagine what kind of science could take us away from Laing sitting naked next to a noncommunicative schizophrenic, or Joe Berke punching Mary Barnes. It is as if antipsychiatry was rooted at performative ground zero, stuck there, resistant to the detour through words. There is not really much to say about emergent performances; they resist scientific stories of predictable mechanisms lurking behind the scenes of the visible.

2   Conventional psychiatry is socially and technically asymmetric. Doctors make assessments and prescribe treatments to people who are literally patients; the patient's agency goes unrecognized (except as a problem). This hangs together with the detour through words and the consequent asymmetry in technical expertise that accretes around it. Antipsychiatry was, in contrast, symmetric.

The antipsychiatrists did not issue diagnoses or order treatments; they did not act as experts. Instead, the agency, the performance, of the patients was integral to the practice of antipsychiatry.

3 Conventional psychiatry imposes a universal one-step structure on the dance of agency. The way to treat mental problems just is electroshock, or drugs, or whatever. This scientistic universalism is, of course, a standard trope of Western biomedicine, reinforced by the norms of double-blind testing and "evidence-based medicine." The goal here is to eradicate in advance all traces of situatedness and emergence. Either drugs work in a linear, causal, and predictable fashion or they don't. Situatedness and emergence, on the other hand, were integral to antipsychiatry – finding out what works or not on this occasion with this person or that. Laing taking his clothes off on this occasion, but doing something else on another.

4 Conventional psychiatry also imposes a norm on sufferers. The object is to return them to a normal mental state, defined as some functioning version of the modern worker, shall we say. To be cured is to be able to hold down a job, or to carry on a conversation with someone like me. Again, anti-psychiatry was not like that, and this is a difference that deserves some elaboration.

Although it is hard to imagine a science of antipsychiatry, it was hardly bereft of ideas. The symmetry of its practice hung together with the idea that the modern self is not a norm we should admire and seek to impose on others. It is, instead, a functional requirement of modern capitalism and militarism, historical formations that look even less admirable today than they did back in the 1960s, if that is possible. The modern self is the product of certain disciplines (including conventional psychiatry) that seek to shape and restrict, normalize, the human potential (this is where we could bring in the work of Michel Foucault – another great writer who was very serious about performative experimentation but wrote almost nothing about it; see the collected interviews, Foucault 1996). Far from attempting any sort of normalization, then, antipsychiatry aimed to undermine these disciplines and selves and to open up new spaces and foster the emergence of new sorts of selves, new kinds of people. At Kingsley Hall the selves of the therapists were deliberately and symmetrically as much at stake and liable to transformation in this process as those of the mad. And here I would say that antipsychiatry staged a special form of the dance of agency. My idea is that, as I said, we are entrained in these dances all the time whether we like it or not, but, in fact, they typically become routinized, at work, in prison, in love; they often stabilize selves. Although it sounds cynical to say this, the mad therefore had a special place in antipsychiatry as the keepers of the flame, in keeping dances of agency alive. Just because madness and unpredictability go together, Kingsley Hall was just the place to continually jolt members of the Philadelphia Association into altered states.

Here the cognitive Laing reappears. His 1967 book, *The Politics of Experience*, does a wonderful job of problematizing the modern self and conjuring up mystical worlds of horror, wonder, and ecstasy for nonmodern selves to inhabit and explore. (The account of Jesse Watkins's "ten-day voyage" is what I still remember from first reading Laing.) What can we say about this? Evidently, this discursive component of antipsychiatry was not a science in the same way as neuropharmacology is a science. It certainly takes us away from performance into the world of words, and yet, as a simple reminder that the self is not given, that we can be otherwise, it sends us straight back there as an incitement to performative experimentation. And this idea of other selves and other worlds has a long history – arriving with Laing via Gregory Bateson and Bateson's interaction before that with Alan Watts, Zen Buddhism, and koans, performative contradictions, as the path to Eastern Enlightenment (Pickering, 2010). Yet again we have left modernity behind, now at the discursive level. And it is worth remembering that the one thing that Eastern and mystical traditions agree on is the worthlessness of words and everyday cognition as incapable of grasping the mystery of being. In 1970, Laing left London to meditate in India and Sri Lanka – something that I have again found it impossible to find out much more about.

·

This, then, is my overall conclusion. There are different ways of staging this omnipresent dance of agency, and the specialness of antipsychiatry lay in its foregrounding the dance as method – in contrast to conventional approaches such as psychoanalysis, ECT, or drugs, which in different ways obscure it. The remarks on the self suggest that anti-psychiatry has much in common with other performative ways of destabilizing the modern self, including psychedelic drugs and meditation. If you think that neoliberalism and disciplined modern selves hang together, then this is another angle on the political attractiveness of antipsychiatry.

·

I can finish by coming at antipsychiatry from a different angle. My experience over the last few years has been frustrating. I have spoken not only at all sorts of workshops and conferences on all sorts of things – on antipsychiatry – but also at a conference on biologically inspired robotics, at several art galleries and shows, a couple of workshops on organizations and management, at a center for the study of complex systems, and at a conference on Chinese medicine, as well as various straight meetings in my own fields, science and technology studies and social theory. And what strikes me, even when talking to people I like who are doing things I consider important, is how narrow-minded they are, how their vision is fixed to the ground of their own specific field. I sometimes feel like screaming, "Can't you see how it all fits together?" In an interview with BBC TV in February 1968 David Cooper says that the aim of the AntiUniversity of London is the "breaking open or explosion of all boxes" (antihistory.org/tagged/David-Cooper). As Jeff Nuttall (1968) noted at the time, the counterculture was great at exploding things but not great at all at building anything constructive in the wreckage. I think it is time to try.

We could start by remembering that anti-psychiatry was not an isolated phenomenon. It, like Laing himself, was central to the counterculture of the 1960s.

This is something to be celebrated, not disavowed. The counterculture, too, dreamed of explorations of consciousness and the emergence of new selves and forms of life in performative experimentation: try it and see.

The high point of countercultural politics was the Dialectics of Liberation conference at the Roundhouse in London sponsored (like the AntiUniversity) by the Institute of Phenomenological Studies – a spin-off from the Philadelphia Association – in 1967, the Summer of Love. Cooper and Laing both spoke on revolutionary themes at the Dialectics conference, Laing (1968) about a sort of meso-revolution at the level of specific institutions which he imagined spreading outward from places such as Kingsley Hall (an idea first articulated by his fellow Scotsman Alexander Trocchi in his sigma project – which I would like to resurrect, in fact; Pickering, in press). But Gregory Bateson (1968) was also on the bill and he chose not to talk about his theory of schizophrenia but about his later concerns with the environment. And it interests me a lot that what he had to say about the environment was a more or less exact translation of his thoughts on madness. This psychiatry/environmental studies connection is an example of the sort of anti-disciplinary bridging that I think we need much more of.

How does this go? Following Bateson, we could see both people and nature as emergent entities that will always surprise us. We cannot, therefore, control either of them. We can, of course, act as though we are in control, and we usually do. Families normalize each other; farmers eradicate pests with DDT. Sometimes this works; sometimes it doesn't. Schizophrenia and Rachel Carson's *Silent Spring* (1962) are the parallel dark sides of modern selves and industrial agriculture. Antipsychiatry was the other way to go on in the field of mental health, refusing normalization and letting dances of agency propagate without stamping a modern form upon them. Typically, Bateson himself never thought about alternative practices in respect of the environment, falling instead into talk about epistemology, knowledge and his mysterious "pattern that connects." But one can continue the story for him. Today's counterpart to antipsychiatry is called adaptive environmental management, a performative experimental approach to nature that aims to find out what nature wants to do before acting irrevocably on it – staging experimental floods on the Colorado River, for example, to see how the river and its ecosystem will respond to different initiatives (Asplen, 2008; Pickering, 2013) – a dance of agency just like Mary Barnes and Joe Berke's, trying things out to see what would happen. So we do not necessarily have to see antipsychiatry as being an isolated thing in itself and only about people, the sane and the mad. We can see it as an instance of something much more general, a nonmodern paradigm, I would call it, that can be played out in all sorts of fields and that has as much to do with nonhuman nature as with human selves. *Silent Spring* as the madness of the cornfields, madness as the Hurricane Katrina of the soul.[5]

What is the point here? It is that it is fine to think back to Laing and antipsychiatry with an eye to renewing those initiatives and taking them further. I am all in favor of it. But it would be even finer to widen the frame to include these adaptive engineers I just mentioned, as well as strange artists I know who are more interested in performance than representation, weird management types, complexity theorists, Chinese doctors, bonsai enthusiasts . . . this would be my version of Trocchi's sigma project. If only I could persuade you all to see yourselves as doing the same sort of nonmodern thing together – orbiting around emergence and performative dances of agency, putting the detour through language in its place. Then we could seriously set about changing the world and not just psychiatry, about liberation and revolution and making a future we could be optimistic about, the sort of future we had in the 1960s but somehow can no longer even imagine. If I could turn you on, to quote the last sentence of *Politics of Experience* . . .

Acknowledgments

I thank Steve Gans and Leon Redler for comments on an earlier draft, especially Leon for his extensive and thoughtful responses. This work was supported in part by a National Research Foundation of Korea Grant funded by the Korean Government (NRF-2013S1A3A2053087).

Notes

'R. D. Laing in the 21st Century,' symposium, Wagner College, Staten Island, New York, 25–27 October 2013.

1 What follows draws on a much longer study of Laing and Gregory Bateson in Pickering (2010, Chap. 5), which includes extensive documentation and places their work in the wider context of the history of cybernetics.
2 The exception that proves the rule is Laing (1972).
3 The quote continues: "Laing did not write anything about his therapeutic practice, and . . . did not seek to build his reputation around case studies . . . Laing's own accounts and the anecdotes that float around show him as unorthodox in his approach, to say the least . . . anything could happen" (Kotowicz, 1997, 75).
4 See also the story of Jerome at the Portland Road community in the early 1970s in Thompson (1997).
5 "[I]f Lake Erie is driven insane, its insanity is incorporated in the larger system of *your* thought and experience" (Bateson 2000 [1972], 492).

References

Asplen, L. (2008) 'Going with the Flow: Living the Mangle in Environmental Management Practice,' in A. Pickering and K. Guzik (eds.), *The Mangle in Practice: Science, Society and Becoming* (Durham, NC: Duke University Press), pp. 163–84.
Barnes, M. and J. Berke (1971) *Two Accounts of a Journey Through Madness* (New York: Harcourt Brace Jovanovich).
Bateson, G. (1968) 'Conscious Purpose Versus Nature,' in D. Cooper (ed.), *To Free a Generation: The Dialectics of Liberation* (New York: Collier), pp. 34–49.
Bateson, G. (2000 [1972]) *Steps to an Ecology of Mind* (Chicago: University of Chicago Press, 2nd ed.).
Burns, D. (2002) *The David Burns Manuscript.* Unpublished; available at laingsociety.org/colloquia/thercommuns/dburns1.htm#cit

Cameron, J. L., R. D. Laing, and A. McGhie (1955) 'Patient and Nurse: Effects of Environmental Change in the Care of Chronic Schizophrenics,' *Lancet, 266* (31 Dec 1955), 1384–86.

Carson, R. (1962) *Silent Spring* (New York: Houghton Mifflin).

Cooper, D. (1967) *Psychiatry and Anti-Psychiatry* (London: Tavistock Institute; reprinted by Paladin, 1970).

Foucault, M. (1996) *Foucault Live* (Interviews 1961–1984) (New York: Semiotext(e)).

Kotowicz, Z. (1997) *R. D. Laing and the Paths of Anti-Psychiatry* (London: Routledge).

Laing, A. (1994) *R. D. Laing: A Biography* (New York: Thunder's Mouth Press).

Laing, R. D. (1967) *The Politics of Experience* (New York: Pantheon).

Laing, R. D. (1968) 'The Obvious,' in D. Cooper (ed.), *To Free a Generation: The Dialectics of Liberation* (New York: Collier), pp. 13–33.

Laing, R. D. (1972) 'Metanoia: Some Experiences at Kingsley Hall, London,' in H. Ruitenbeek (ed.), *Going Crazy: The Radical Therapy of R. D. Laing and Others* (New York: Bantam), pp. 11–21. Reprinted from *Recherches*, December 1968.

Nuttall, J. (1968) *Bomb Culture* (New York: Delacorte Press).

Pickering, A. (1995) *The Mangle of Practice: Time, Agency, and Science* (Chicago: University of Chicago Press).

Pickering, A. (2008) 'Against Human Exceptionalism,' paper presented at a workshop on 'What Does It Mean to Be Human?' University of Exeter, 25 January 2008. http://hdl.handle.net/10036/18873

Pickering. A. (2010) *The Cybernetic Brain: Sketches of Another Future* (Chicago: University of Chicago Press).

Pickering, A. (2011) 'Ontological Politics: Realism and Agency in Science, Technology and Art,' *Insights, 4.* www.dur.ac.uk/resources/ias/insights/Pickering30Jan.pdf

Pickering, A. (2013) 'Being in an Environment: A Performative Perspective,' *Natures Sciences Sociétés, 21.* http://dx.doi.org/10.1051/nss/2013067

Pickering, A. (In press) 'Neo-sigma: Art, Agency and Revolution,' in M. Søndergaard (ed.), *Cybernetics Revisited,* special issue of *Leonardo Electronic Almanac.* www.leoalmanac.org

Thompson, M. (1997) 'The Fidelity to Experience in R. D. Laing's Treatment Philosophy,' *Contemporary Psychoanalysis, 33*(4), pp. 595–614.

6

LAING'S *THE DIVIDED SELF* AND *THE POLITICS OF EXPERIENCE*

Then and now

Douglas Kirsner, PhD

The Divided Self and *The Politics of Experience* are two very different books. The first is a careful, clinical existential study of schizophrenia whereas the second is an impassioned condemnation of the way modern society has thwarted and violated human experience. Laing brought the idea of politics to experience, and as well as to relationships, the family and other interconnected social contexts. But both books, which I want to revisit, show very important similarities that illuminate central features of Laing's existential quest.

The Divided Self (Laing, 1965) was a study of schizoid and schizophrenic people; its basic purpose, Laing claimed, was "to make madness, and the process of going mad, comprehensible". He was also attempting to offer an existential account of some forms of madness. But he was not attempting to present a comprehensive theory of schizophrenia, nor to explore constitutional and organic aspects (Laing, 1965, p. 9).

The Politics of Experience (Laing, 1967) represents a very different phase in Laing's development than *The Divided Self*, one which I believe developed during the 1960s and ended after his return to London from a "sabbatical" in Ceylon in the early 1970s.

This book crystallized some central ideas and deeply impressed itself upon the minds of a generation. It sold six million copies in the US alone. It was poetic, possessing some of the rhetorical resonances of Alan Ginsberg's *Howl* from a decade earlier but probably made slightly more sense!

The publication of *The Divided Self* in 1960 was an important moment in the history of psychiatry. While there had been some previous discussions on the understanding of psychotics, Laing's book was a pioneering work in systematically trying to understand where the patient was "at". During the 1950s, when Laing was working in back wards, and later at the Tavistock Clinic, many psychiatrists accepted that the speech of neurosis and not psychosis was potentially intelligible.

Freud insisted that neurosis was intelligible, that dreams, slips and symptoms were disguised expressions of human subjectivity, which could be interpreted using free association. Laing did for the psychotic what Freud did for the neurotic. He attempted to listen to psychotic patients and to treat their speech and actions as potentially understandable and meaningful. Psychotics for Laing were not beyond all reason; like other human beings psychotics could be seen as agents whose experience could be understood as meaningful.

Psychosis is, as Laing puts it in *The Divided Self,* the product of a disjunction: "sanity or psychosis is tested by the degree of conjunction or disjunction between two persons where the one is sane by common consent. The critical test of whether or not a patient is psychotic is a lack of congruity, an incongruity, a clash, between him and me" (Laing, 1965, p. 36).

Psychosis always involves problems of communication. "Schizophrenia", Laing told me in 1980, "is the name a psychiatrist gives for somebody who can't understand" (Kirsner, 2013, p. 370). Never having found difficulty in listening to schizophrenics, Laing could not resonate with the remark by Eugen Bleuler, the Swiss psychiatrist who first used the term *schizophrenia*, that when all was said and done schizophrenics were stranger to him than the birds in his garden (Laing, 1965, p. 24). For Laing, such a lack of understanding of the world of the psychotic was not so much given as constructed. Throughout his life Laing constantly challenged the dichotomy in the classic formulation by the German psychiatrist and philosopher Karl Jaspers in his *General Psychopathology* about the "ununderstandability" of psychotic phenomena which manifested an "abyss of difference" between sane and psychotic experience (see Kirsner, 1990). In *The Divided Self* Laing understood the thoughts and actions of psychotics to be expressions of human subjectivity, not simply emanations of psychobiological processes. Seen in context and from the point of view of the patient as agent, madness could be understood as resulting from choices within psychosocial and biological parameters.

Our fundamental assumptions about the world determine many of our beliefs and actions. A prevalent modem assumption is that despite our feelings to the contrary, we are in reality complex machines or even computers; such an assumption has major consequences for our view of what neurosis and madness are and how they should be treated. The psychiatrist may collude with the schizophrenic in assuming that he or she is primarily a machine. For Laing, "one's relationship to an organism is different from one's relationship to a person . . . one's theory of the other as organism is remote from one's theory of the other as person" (Laing, 1965, p. 21). But in Laing's view diagnosis is literally "seeing through", both looking at the categories that we *see* through and seeing *through* what appears so concrete. The standpoint one adopts conditions what one sees, whether we attribute agency or mechanical processes to ourselves or to patients. For Laing, attributions of autism, and lack of affect and relationship, applied at least as much to those doing the diagnosing as those diagnosed. In Laing's view the scientific, objective "look" stands opposed to the empathic approach. One cannot move into an empathic mode while retaining a view of the patient as an organism. "To try to find understanding within that way of looking", Laing once told me, "is like trying to buy a camel in a donkey market".

Laing emphasized the importance of the point of view of the observer who partly determined the observational field: "The standard psychiatric patient is a function of the standard psychiatrist and the standard mental hospital" (1965, p. 24). In his 1964 preface to *The Divided Self*, Laing lamented that he had written "too much about Them and not enough about Us" (Laing, 1965, p. 11). Much of his later work would rectify this flaw; he systematically concentrated on contexts and meta-contexts in his project to render mental illness more intelligible.

Laing was profoundly interested in investigating patients' experiences of inter-personal relationships, familial, social and psychological situations. In a real sense, his work tried to be a living phenomenology. The asylum communities he was responsible for setting up in London from the late 1960s took the primacy of experience of the often psychotic residents as their basic ground. By having their experience taken seriously and not invalidated, the resident patients could feel listened to. At least that was the idea.

The Divided Self was the first major work in existential psychoanalysis to make a mark on the English-speaking world. The existential psychoanalytic collection *Existence*, edited by May, Angel, and Ellenberger (1958), with its complex Heideggerian focus, appeared just two years earlier, but its influence did not extend beyond a limited number of psychotherapists and academics. In contrast *The Divided Self* became popular, resonating with a far wider audience. Although *The Divided Self* undoubtedly is indebted to object relations theory, particularly that of D. W. Winnicott, Laing's primary position owed much to the philosophy of Sartre. For Laing, Sartre's early work provided what he termed a "gate-opener to the tradition that Sartre espoused, Hegel, Husserl and Heidegger" (Charlesworth, 1975, p. 49). He went on to devour the work of many other philosophers, including Merleau-Ponty, Buber, Foucault and Levi-Strauss.

But what grabbed Laing was Sartre's basic tenet of the ineluctable freedom and agency of all human beings. For Sartre, Human beings are characterized by freedom and agency, no matter how much we attempt to escape this situation or deny it. Sartre coined the term *mauvaise foi* (self-deception) for our efforts to escape our responsibility as free agents by treating ourselves or others as things (Sartre, 1943/1966). Given freedom as his point of departure, for Sartre through Laing "mental illness" can be seen as a way out: perhaps, as Laing put it, an attempt to live in an otherwise unlivable situation. No matter how alienated they may be, patients like all other humans always exercise some degree of choice. The task of existential psychoanalysis is to explore how patients' original and subsequent choices have contributed to their present predicaments and self-deceptions. Sartre's ideas in *Being and Nothingness* provided the prism through which Laing later read and understood Hegel and Husserl. Laing and David Cooper summarized Sartre's *Problem of Method* and *Critique of Dialectical Reason* (1960) in their *Reason and Violence* (1964).

The Divided Self was Sartrean existentialism blended with object relations theory with the unconscious-lite. Like Sartre, Laing rejects at least a received mechanistic view of the Freudian unconscious. The Freudian concept of "the unconscious" is only mentioned in *The Divided Self* to disagree with its application to a patient's basic existential position of wanting to achieve "ontological security" (Laing, 1965, pp. 56–57). Nevertheless, Laing like Sartre respected Freud's inspiration. For Laing the confrontation with the "terrors" had distorted and ossified the psychoanalytic vision. According to Laing, Freud was "the greatest psychopathologist", a "hero" who "descended to the 'Underworld' and met there stark terrors". For Laing, Freud carried with him his theory as a Medusa's head, which "turned these terrors to stone' (Laing, 1965, p. 25). However, Laing's disagreements with Freud were like disagreements between close friends. I remember Laing lecturing on Freud's *Introductory Lectures on Psychoanalysis*, providing a close reading and appreciation of Freud's basic thrust and insights.

Laing's important concepts of "ontological security" and "ontological insecurity" in *The Divided Self* (Laing, 1965, pp. 39–61) are about our "at-homeness" in the world. The ontologically secure person feels his or her life as "real, alive, whole[,] as differentiated from the rest of the world in ordinary circumstances so clearly that his identity and autonomy are never in question" (Laing, 1965, p. 41). This is not the case for the ontologically insecure person who in ordinary circumstances "may feel more unreal than real; in a literal sense, more dead than alive; precariously differentiated from the rest of the world, so that his identity and autonomy are always in question" (Laing, 1965, p. 42).

Laing's discussions of the "true self" and "false self systems" (not one but a number of false selves) owed much to object relations theory, in particular to the work of D. W. Winnicott with whom Laing worked. According to Laing, the schizophrenic's vulnerable true self does not feel it is participating in the activities of the false self systems that mask it (Laing, 1965, p. 74). Laing's false self systems or personas can be understood as cases of Sartrean self-deception. In fact, Laing highlighted the importance of understanding truth, deception and mystification in the world of the schizophrenic. As I've already suggested, listening and aspiring to discovering the patient's truth was crucial for Laing, as it was, of course, for Freud.

The Divided Self is structured around ideas such as anxiety, implosion, petrification, engulfment, ontological security, reality, dread, being at home, alienation, agency and responsibility. These existential concepts focus on the vagaries of the relationship between freedom and the self, and form part of a phenomenology of mental illness in which interactions between self and others affect the very constitution and experience of the "self" and "reality". More important, the psychotic is understood in terms of attempts to solve existential problems through the use of the person's ineluctable freedom and subjectivity. The hysteric's dissociations are for Laing best described as Sartre's concept of "self-deception". Going to extremes in generalizing as was too often his wont, Laing sees much of schizophrenia as consciously intentional, as "simply nonsense, red-herring speech, prolonged filibustering to throw dangerous people off the scent, to create boredom and futility in others. The schizophrenic is often making a fool of himself or herself and the doctor. He or she is playing at being mad to avoid at all costs the possibility of being held responsible for a single coherent idea, or intention" (Laing, 1965, p. 164).

Even in this early work Laing takes note of the family's role in the occurrence of schizophrenia. The mother and the family may "impede rather than facilitate the child's capacity to participate in a real shared world, as self with other". For Laing, "schizophrenia is a possible outcome of a more than usual difficulty in being a whole person with the other, and with not sharing the common-sense (i.e., the community sense) way of experiencing oneself in the world" (Laing, 1965, p. 189). The role of the social context in which schizophrenia takes place forms the axis of Laing's concerns throughout his career.

The relation to embodiment is for Laing the hallmark of understanding a divided self. According to Laing, for schizophrenics "the body is felt more as one object among other objects in the world than as the core of the individual's own being. Instead of being the core of his true self, the body is felt as the core of a false self, which a detached, disembodied, inner, 'true' self looks on at with tenderness, amusement, or hatred as the case may be" (1965, p. 65). In normality and neurosis, according to Laing, the basic distinction is between one's self and one's own body, on one hand, and other people, on the other, as outside. However, schizophrenics see their selves as being totally separate from the cluster of other people and their own bodies, which are seen to be on the same plane (1965, p. 82).

The Divided Self is a skeptical book that does not so much provide answers as stimulate more questions and challenges. In the light of our understanding of biological aspects, Laing overrated the magnitude of the patient's choices in schizophrenia. By challenging the role of unconscious factors as well as organic ones, he was left with little alternative. It was a case of testing the limits of the intelligibility of human experience that even schizophrenics can be seen as agents and not as only being victim to organic processes.

The Divided Self was a radical book when it appeared in 1960. It remains a remarkable one. It is still refreshing in its closeness to schizophrenic experience and in its attempts to find at least part of an explanation in terms of human agency. *The Divided Self* remains a powerful reminder of the advantages of a sensibility that adopts an existential, psychodynamic point of departure that tests the limits of the full significance of human agency instead of denying it.

I now turn to *The Politics of Experience*, which arguably became the cult book of the 1960s. It chimed in with the antiestablishment and countercultural concerns of many younger people. A much maligned and misinterpreted book, it was far more complex and sophisticated than a first reading might reveal. Laing took things to extremes in *The Politics of Experience*, and breakdown was only sometimes breakthrough; the mad were not always, or even often, more sane than "normal" people.

Although published in 1967 *The Politics of Experience* represents the development of Laing's views between 1962 and 1967. Here, Laing focuses on the central development of the concept of experience with chapter headings: "Persons and Experience", "The Psychotherapeutic Experience", "The Mystification of Experience", "Schizophrenic Experience", "Transcendental Experience" and a ten-day experiential voyage. Laing, like his fellow Scott, David Hume was a profound skeptic, fundamentally questioning given established ways of thinking, moving from physical and intrapersonal "reality" to interpersonal space as the given ground of experience.

I take Laing's quest to be for an abiding rationality, which starts with human experience, especially aberrant experience, in a quest to understand the universe. As I argued in *The Schizoid World of Jean-Paul Sartre and R. D. Laing* (Kirsner, 2003), Laing worked through contexts, meta-contexts, meta-meta-contexts, and so on: from the self, through self and other, to the family system to the total social world system and through to a cosmology which would possibly make sense of that. Laing's later works should be seen in the context of this project.

According to Laing, *The Divided Self* described the split between experience and behavior, an issue that became theoretically central in *The Politics of Experience*. But in Heidegger's phrase cited by Laing (1967, p. 46), the dreadful has already happened. The myriad fragmentations of experience and behavior mean that we cannot reconstitute a unity, the inner seems so inexorably split from the outer that people seriously argue that the inner world does not exist even though it is this inner world that gives substance to the outer. Taking place in a condition of alienation, psychotherapy, which involves a research for being human, is an honest attempt to start or even end with the absence of relationship (Laing, 1967, pp. 48–49).

The Politics of Experience is nothing if not dramatic. The introduction describes our setting in the very New Left terms of the time:

> There is little conjunction of truth and social "reality". Around us are pseudoevents, to which we adjust with a false consciousness adapted to see these events as true and real, and even as beautiful. In the society of men the truth resides now less in what things are than in what they are not. Our social realities are so ugly if seen in the light of exiled truth, and beauty is almost no longer possible if it is not a lie. We are still half alive, living in the often fibrillating heartland of a senescent capitalism.
>
> *(Laing, 1967, p. 11)*

In this setting it is "the requirement of the present" to "provide a thoroughly self-conscious and self-critical human account of man" (Laing, 1967, p. 11). But while our starting point is always our "alienation", for Laing, "we are all murderers and prostitutes", here alluding to Dostoevsky's *Crime and Punishment* without saying so. Humanity was, he said, "estranged from its authentic possibilities" (1967, p. 11).

The introduction to *The Politics of Experience* certainly gives credibility to some of the views of Laing as a countercultural, New Left political radical who added personal and transcendental experience to a location within social and political categories. For Laing our alienation forms the foundation of any investigation of the sanity of common sense or the madness of madmen. As "crazed and bemused creatures" we can barely glimpse our true selves and are strangers to each other.

In *The Politics of Experience* Laing closely linked the idea of the false self or mask with the New Left and Marxist "false consciousness" of the social totality. Combining Marxism and existentialism Laing maintains that our alienation is the social product of the violence of human beings on one another. This was excessive language even for that time, making generalizations about whole cultures by placing all-encompassing, collective abstract nouns as the subjects of emotive sentences.

Rhetorical flurries sit alongside profound insights throughout. In fact, *The Politics of Experience* is in many ways a work of rhetoric, enjoining us to question our categories. Strings of emotional assertion upon generalization on assertion struck the mood of the times among "us", if not among "them".

Laing begins the chapter "Persons and Experience" with the proposition that we experience only each other's behavior and that the task of social phenomenology is to relate my experience of the other's behavior with the other's experience of my behavior as inter-experience. Once the unbridgeable divide is made between experience and behavior, it becomes clear that experience must be an intrinsically private event.

Laing claims following Sartre that violence dictates so many interpersonal experiences and that attributions of sanity and madness are used in promoting this agenda. Thus, for Laing we are inherently alienated with levels and varieties of social alienation heaped upon us still further.

I understand Laing's point is that we should not *presume* that we know what the other person is experiencing, certainly not without asking him or her, that we should not equate real categories of sanity and madness with the way people behave socially. Laing wants us to adopt an individual sensibility for every person as unique; it is an approach toward another person that brackets out assumed knowledge of him or her.

For Laing, "experience is the *only* evidence". While our experiences of each other are not "inside" our physical bodies, nonetheless our experiences are invisible to each other. While I do not experience your experience, I do experience you as experiencing, infer from my experience of your experiences of my experience, and so on. Laing maintains that the distinctions between "inner" and "outer" make assumptions that stand in the way of our making sense of the data of inter-experience. We often attempt to escape from the subjective, from being a person, attempting to eliminate experience, akin to Sartre's self-deception.

Yet the radical subjectivity assumed in the experience–behavior dichotomy makes togetherness almost impossible. Perhaps we experience others more than just as their behavior, which seems defined as not what is experienced and could be mechanistic. We are, for Laing, "invisible men" who cannot see each other. This sounds to me another form of Cartesianism.

Laing claims that Freud's major contribution was his "*demonstration* that the *ordinary* person is a shriveled, desiccated fragment of what a person can be" (Laing, 1967, p. 22). We have forgotten our dreams, our phantasies, deny the inner world, all of which "represents a devastation of our experience" (Laing, 1967, p. 23), based on the divorce of experience from behavior). I am sure that Freud would not have agreed; Freud's view was tragic, not romantic. For Freud, civilization was inherently flawed in its Mephistophelean pact that exchanged happiness for a degree of security and sublimation for love, all under the co-reign of the death drive. The very early Freud thought that the aim of analysis was "to transform hysterical misery into common unhappiness" and later argued with Einstein about whether human aggression was innate and was not socially produced.

But for Laing, so-called normality is the product of repression, denial and so on, which are destructive to our experience, estranging us from the structure of being. "The condition of alienation, of being asleep, of being unconscious, of being out of one's mind, is the condition of the normal man" (Laing, 1967, p. 24). Now, since "normal men have killed perhaps 100,000,000 of their fellow normal men in the past fifty years" (Laing, 1967, p. 24), the relation between normality and violence demands investigation together with the relation between sanity, madness and normality. Since our behavior is a function of our experience, if our experience is destroyed, our behavior will be destructive. As was so common in the 1960s, Laing takes for granted the common radical 1960s assumption that we live in "a world where the normal condition is one of alienation" and that therefore "most personal action must be destructive both of one's own experience and of that of the other" (Laing, 1967, p. 29).

According to Laing, the only way I can act is on our own or on the other's experience. In so doing I can confirm or encourage or deny or discourage my or his or her experience. I can dissociate myself from my own action through defense mechanisms I use on my experience that devastates it. Importantly, another can invalidate my experience by saying it is unimportant, can change its modality from memory to imagination and invalidate its content. This Laing does via the originally Marxist concept of "mystification" (Laing, 1967, pp. 28–31).

If we strip away the social "things" and reveal who we "really" are, Laing contends that there is nothing between us. Laing shares a romantic vision of the real self or nothingness below the veneer, after the diagnosis of mystifications has revealed how ordinary social life is so extraordinarily oppressive. In *The Politics of Experience* Laing himself invalidates and deprecates ordinary experience as was usual in the "Little Boxes" era during which only the lucky few could manage to escape the comfortable alienation a one dimensional society had bought for and from them.

During the early 1970s after his return from Ceylon, Laing began to move away from such extremes. But for the Laing of *The Politics of Experience* the creative person was in touch with his or her nonbeing and to that extent estranged from the pseudo-wants, pseudo-values and pseudo-realities of the endemic delusion of life and death and give us "the acts of creation that we despise and crave" (Laing, 1967, p. 37). Our fundamental nonbeing is the creative source to be recognized and tapped. But in our state of alienation, creation "arises from despair and ends in failure". Here Laing seems to hold to a transcendental, "trippy" view of reality: The creative person who has trodden the path to the end of time and space "does not know that where it all ends, there it all begins" (Laing, 1967, p. 38).

Laing believes that the mystification of experience is ubiquitous in the contemporary world. Normality is achieved when by the age of fifteen a human being is a "half crazed creature, more or less adjusted to a mad world" (Laing, 1967, p. 50). This "mad world" is characterized by the reign of violence masquerading as love, where violence constrains freedom with a lack of concern. The devastation of experience takes place through violence by the world and by ourselves on ourselves (Laing, 1967, pp. 50–51). In fact, "only by the most outrageous violation of ourselves have we achieved our capacity to live in relative adjustment to a civilization apparently driven to its own destruction" (Laing, 1967, p. 64).

The Politics of Experience went well beyond *The Divided Self.* For Laing, the schizophrenic may find himself or herself on a journey within the lost inner realm, a voyage that just might be part of a natural healing process. Perhaps, Laing suggests, we should accord the schizophrenic who has come back to us no less respect than returning explorers were in the Renaissance. Laing believes that future generations will view our present age as an age of darkness and that schizophrenia was a way that some ordinary people had of seeing the light break through (Laing, 1967, p. 107). Although this far-out and far-fetched position, again more poetry than prose, is about the nature of experiencing, not illness.

I think that Laing's approach to schizophrenia should be viewed in terms of his focus on the importance of looking at the invalidation and loss of a whole realm of experience of the inner world.

For Laing, violence has been so successful in seeming to take this realm from the rest of us that schizophrenia could be seen as a last-ditch way we have of encountering this lost world. Whether any transcendental experience is mad or mystical, it is testament to the importance of inner experience that has been devastated by the outer but that is so essential to a sane, whole way of living.

Freud thought that slips of the tongue and other marginalia of the psychopathology of everyday life could provide us with important discoveries about the nature of the human mind. I think that for Laing schizophrenia plays a similar role in providing a way into understanding the lost world of human experiencing. I think one of the reasons that Laing so often felt he had been misunderstood is that his project was far larger than understanding schizophrenia. It is as though Freud were recognized only for his concept of Freudian slips instead of Freudian slips being seen as a waystation toward an end point of the theory of neurosis and the unconscious. I think Laing's end point is what he sees as the lack of a world of valid experience as the problem of our age. Laing starts with schizophrenia the way Freud started with dream interpretation and slips of the tongue.

In his 1964 preface to the Pelican Edition of *The Divided Self,* Laing wrote,

> Freud insisted that our civilization is a repressive one. There is a conflict between the demands of conformity and the demands of our instinctive

energies, explicitly sexual Freud could see no easy resolution of this antago-
nism, and he came to believe that in our time the possibility of simple natural love between human beings had already been abolished.

(Laing, 1965, p. 10)

In his 1980 interview with me, Laing reminded me of this passage from Freud's
Civilization and its Discontents:

> Among the works of the sensitive English writer, John Galsworthy . . . there
> is a short story of which I early formed a high opinion. It is called "The
> Apple-Tree" and it brings home to us how the life of present day civilized
> people leaves no room for the simple natural love of two human beings.
>
> *(Freud, 1930, p. 105)*

Although Laing followed Sartre in so much, I think his view of human nature,
certainly as expressed in *The Politics of Experience*, is more romantic as in Rousseau's "man is born free but everywhere he is in chains" and is based on one of the
British object relations school's views that destructiveness derives principally from
frustration. We are inherently and naturally good if only the world would leave
us alone. Schizophrenics might be in a better state if only psychiatrists would not
interfere with them.

Although *The Politics of Experience* is such a 1960s' book, its sensibility and
preoccupations with the value and validation of experience in its social context
put *The Politics of Experience* at the heart of Laing's project, making it a fascinating
continuation of *The Divided Self* as well as making *The Divided Self* more intelligible in broader terms.

The Divided Self not only humanized patients with a major mental illness, but
it mentalized them, to comprehend their behavior as persons, as agents whose
intentions and actions have potential meaning. Peter Fonagy's (Fonagy, Gergely,
Jurist, & Target, 2002) concept of "mentalization" involves our ability to understand others' behavior as the product of their mental state rather than just a physical state. This activity is goal-directed behavior, the result of human intention
and agency. It involves the concept that we all have minds that are active. Laing
didn't say that schizophrenic speech was intelligible but that it was more intelligible using social phenomenology than had been assumed and that, moreover,
psychiatry should not itself be autistic. Behavior and language are understandable
in the social context of self and others. It was a major development in existential
psychoanalysis that was a profound humanism, a human science set on human
foundations.

I don't think *The Politics of Experience* fares nearly so well. It expresses some
important truths alongside half-truths. Some of the ideas shared their fate with
the New Left while others have been taken aboard in many arenas. These include
the idea that there is a politics to the way we experience ourselves, each other and
the world that reaches even into the inner private world of experience. There is a

politics to therapy, and the related issues of validation and invalidation of experience and to the ascription of "us" and "them". If *The Divided Self* was too little about "us", the authorities, the mental health professionals, and too much about "them", the patients, I think *The Politics of Experience* goes way too far the other way in so easily and comfortably demonizing "them", the bad authorities, while romanticizing "us", the good but impotent, violated victims. It so caught the zeitgeist that it got caught up in its net.

Having written *The Divided Self* so early in his professional life before the age of 30, Laing was faced with the problem of whether and how to better it.

Although Laing did not succeed in terms of another such brilliant individual work, his general project, journey and spirit of attempting to provide an existential account and social phenomenology of experience in the systemic levels of the human context that spanned the next 30 years following the publication of *The Divided Self* remains both a model and inspiration for philosophy and psychology for this century.

References

Charlesworth, M. (1975). *The existentialists and Jean-Paul Sartre.* St. Lucia: University of Queensland Press.

Fonagy, P., Gergely, G., Jurist, E., & Target, M. (2002). *Affect regulation, mentalization, and the development of the self.* New York: Other Press.

Freud, S. (1961). *Civilization and its discontents.* In J. Strachey, Ed. & Trans., *The standard edition of the complete psychological works of Sigmund Freud,* Vol. 21, pp. 64–145. London: Hogarth Press. (Original work published 1930).

Kirsner, D. (1990). Across an abyss: Laing, Jaspers and Sartre. *Journal of the British Society for Phenomenology,* 21: 209–216.

Kirsner, D. (2003). *The schizoid world of Jean-Paul Sartre and R. D. Laing.* New York: Other Press.

Kirsner, D. (2013). 'Human all too human': Interview with R. D. Laing. *Psychoanalytic Review,* 100: 361–372.

Laing, R. D. & Cooper, D. G. (1964). *Reason and violence: A decade of Sartre's philosophy 1950–1960.* London: Tavistock Publications.

Laing, R. D. (1965). *The divided self.* Harmondsworth: Penguin.

Laing, R. D. (1967). *The politics of experience and the bird of paradise.* New York: Pantheon Books.

May, R., Angel, E. & Ellenberger, H., Eds. (1958). *Existence.* New York: Basic Books.

Sartre, J.-P. (1966). *Being and nothingness.* H. E. Barnes, Trans. New York: Washington Square Press. (Original work published 1943.)

7

R. D. LAING

Premature postmodern psychoanalyst

Martin A. Schulman, PhD

Introduction

Let me begin by explaining the title of my presentation. Before the U.S. entered World War II, and the struggle against fascism became respectable, those American volunteers who attempted to stop fascism by fighting in the Spanish civil war were labeled premature antifascists. I am here applying the term *premature* (*prescient* might be preferable to Laing).

My claim is that Laing, particularly the early Laing, had the roots of intersubjectivity, two-person psychology, and the clinical aspects of postmodern psychoanalysis within his writings. Unfortunately psychoanalysts, whether mainstream or modifiers, tend to often ignore the historical antecedents of contemporary ideas, particularly if they come from ex-communicants such as Jung, Fromm or, in this case, Laing. "The fetish of creativity" is such that analysts operate as if new ideas come into being full blown from their thighs or computers. In fact we find that Greenberg and Mitchell in their 1983 "manifesto", declaring the "birth of relational psychoanalysis", do not mention Laing in the body of their text and have only one bibliographical reference to him: *Sanity, Madness and the Family*, coauthored with Aaron Esterson (1964).

An autobiographical note is perhaps in order. My exposure to Laing came as part of the counterculture of the 1960s. He was a voice of humanity in a rather sterile clinical climate. Just as I believe that the roots of a new society are created in the forms the struggle to create that society takes, I also believe that authoritarian mechanistic therapy cannot lead to an enhancement of our humanness. I used his *Interpersonal Perception Method*, an underappreciated tool, as one of the scales in my doctoral dissertation, perhaps the first time Laing successfully crept into the halls of conventional academia. The theoretical framework of my dissertation was that of symbolic interactionism (Mead and Cooley) with a touch of Soviet psychology (Luria and Vygotsky) and a tad of Sullivan. The step to Laing wasn't too great since I saw him, then as now, belonging to the interpersonal perspective, with the caveat that his work was grounded in solid European philosophy, such as that of Dilthey, Sartre, and Buber, rather than the shallowness of the American empirical tradition.

While my interests and further training shifted toward psychoanalysis, I still have an affinity for the "Laing of my youth" and I think this has affected the way I work and relate to patients. While I am not a postmodernist, an intersubjectivist or a relational psychoanalyst (early Freud is more to my liking) I think the time is ripe to place Laing in the forefront of historical antecedents to these "tendencies". I am not making the claim that Laing was a philosophical postmodernist, since unlike philosophical postmodernism, with its nihilistic tendencies, his was more of an existential phenomenologist. He accepted the self, the unconscious, and particularly authenticity. For example, in 1969 Laing stated that "[t]o be 'authentic' is to be true to oneself, to be what one is. To be 'inauthentic' is to not be oneself, to be false to oneself: to be not as one appears to be, to be counterfeit" (1969/1971, pp. 108–109). Authenticity, becoming the desired end result of treatment, in many ways led Laing to set the basis for a pragmatic clinical postmodern psychoanalysis. He represented a movement and application in the clinical realm from, in Buberian terms, an I–It paradigm to an I–Thou one (Buber, 1923/1937).

Modernism

Postmodern thinking, at least with regard to psychoanalysis, is not easy to define. I'll try nevertheless, but first for modernism, what seems inherent, to the various definitions of modernism is the attempt to demystify, clarify and reveal. The advocacy of reason, rationality, universal moral truths and linear historical progress, all culminating in the ideals of emancipation and enlightenment are integral to this perspective. This is counterposed to irrationality and superstition, the forces in opposition to which modernism arose.

Jameson (1991) also posits that "depth" is an ingredient of modernist thinking and can be seen in dichotomous categories or binary opposites such as true and false consciousness as witnessed in the writings of the Marxists, essence and appearance (Hegel), good and bad faith (the existentialist paradigm), true and false selves à la Winnicott and latent and manifest content and primary and secondary process as developed by Freud.

Within this frame, Freudian psychoanalysis can be seen as representative of modernism with regard to its understanding that reason needs to struggle with the resistance to understanding and to emancipation, both clinically as well as societally. Freudian psychoanalysis can also be viewed as attempting to apply the domain of reason to the emotions and those aspects of irrationality that, as Rustin (2001) posits, "were not readily comprehensible within rationalistic categories" (p. 12). Indeed as Fenichel (1933/1941) in his red books points out, "[t]he subject matter, not the method of psychoanalysis is irrational" (pp. 12–13).

Understanding through insight, not just cognitive but having the attached affect, and rendered via interpretations, follows from this as does the need to differentiate psychoanalysis from its historical irrational antecedent; suggestion. Freud's (1933) famous aphorism "where Id was, there shall ego be" (p. 112) highlights this striving for the triumph, without any expectation of success, of rationality. This same "where id was, ego shall be", or "wo es war, zoll ich sein", can also be translated as "where it was, I shall become", a teleological perspective parallel to Laing's search for authenticity. Thus, for Freud and for contemporary Freudian based psychoanalysis, the triumph of rationality, the belief that the irrational can be understood rationally and that the technique of psychoanalysis as a scientific endeavor has been a hallmark of its historical development.

Postmodernism

With regard to the postmodern trend in psychoanalysis, definitions are even more vague. I see the following factors as integral to the postmodern perspective: the outright rejection of the concepts of objectivity, historical reality, truth, analytic neutrality and biological underpinnings to psychic elaboration, essentialism and universalism.

Clinically, the stance includes the dicta that both patient and analyst create an interactive system that affects both of them; along with this, meaning is co-created and not absolute, each analytic dyad is unique and therefore absolute technique cannot exist, and the analytic experience is an interaction of the subjective worlds of the participants.

The differences can be delineated as following the gradients of transference replaced by countertransference as the main source of psychic data: countertransference as feeling replaced by countertransference as enactment and countertransference, in turn, replaced by co-creation as the dynamic within the consulting room; thus, a two-person psychology replacing a so called one-person model, objectivity and neutrality replaced by subjectivity, the interpersonal or the intersubjective replacing the intrapsychic, the here and now replacing the past, insight replaced by intersubjectivity, truth and distortion replaced by perspectivism, interpretive content replaced by process and, what has all too often been overlooked, cognition being replaced or superseded by affectivity.

This in many ways, has become the modal model, at least in the United States. As Mills (2005) states,

> Psychoanalysis today is largely a psychology of consciousness: post- and neo-Freudians form a marginalized community within North America in comparison to contemporary relational and intersubjective theorists who emphasize the phenomenology of lived conscious experience, affective attunement, social construction, and interpersonal recognition over the role of insight and interpretation.
>
> *(p. ix)*

Benjamin (1990) posits that "[w]hat these approaches share is the belief that the human mind is interactive rather than monadic, that the psychoanalytic process should be understood as occurring between subjects rather than within the individual" (p. 33). And we find H. Greenberg and Mitchell (1983) stating that for the relational model analyst, the psychoanalytic situation is inherently dyadic; events within the analysis are not understood as preset and unfolding from within the dynamic structures of the patient's neurosis. Rather, they are created in the interaction between the patient and the analyst (p. 389).

We can posit the key concepts of postmodern psychoanalysis as: co-creation, two person psychology, intersubjectivity, perspectivism, affectivity, interpersonalism, subjectivity, antiauthoritarianism, contextualism and experience over interpretation. Since everyone here is familiar with the body of Laing's work, I think you can see where I'm going.

Laingian contributions

At the heart of *The Divided Self* we find the outright rejection of the idea that "objectivity" has greater salience than subjective knowledge. Along with the denial that there is a neutrality to the therapeutic context emphasis is placed on the observer's presence in the situation. Laing states in regard to schizophrenia (and we can extrapolate to all diagnoses being an infringement on our "neutrality") that "the psychiatrist adopting his clinical stance in the presence of the pre-diagnosed person, whom he is already looking at and listening to as a patient, has too often come to believe that he is in the presence of the 'fact' of "schizophrenia" (Laing & Esterson, 1964, p. 18). He acts "as if" its existence were an established fact. He then has to discover its "cause" or multiple "aetiological factors", to assess its "prognosis", and to treat its course. The heart of the "illness", all that is the outcome of process, then resides outside the agency of the person. That is, the illness, or the process, is taken to be a "fact" that the person is subject to, or undergoes, whether it is supposed to be genetic, constitutional, endogenous, exogenous, organic or psychological, or some mixture of them all. This, we submit, is a mistaken starting point.

Furthermore,

> [i]t is unfortunate that personal and subjective are words so abused as to have no power to convey any genuine act of seeing the other as person (if we mean this we have to revert to "objective") but imply immediately that one is merging one's own feelings and attitudes into one's study of the other in such a way as to distort our perception of him. In contrast to the reputable "objective" or "scientific", we have the disreputable "subjective", "intuitive", or, worst of all, "mystical." It is interesting, for example, that one frequently encounters "merely" before subjective, whereas it is almost inconceivable to speak of anyone being "merely" objective.
>
> *(Laing, 1960, pp. 24–25)*

Therefore, general laws and truths do not exist; instead, there exist unique, personalized contextualized "truths". This leads to a rejection of the belief that theories mirror reality, and we are left with the supposition that our experience is always filtered through interpretative schemes à la Rorty (1989). Stern (1997), from the interpersonalist postmodern tendency and influenced by Gadamer, concurs and claims that what we experience is our interpretation of reality, not reality as such (p. 181).

Between the known and the object-to-be-known, there always exists some mediator or intervening variable such as narrative, construct and, particularly, language, preventing the direct knowing of reality. These intervening variables always distort the experience of the "object to be known", making all knowledge subjective or at least relative. As Laing (1966) says, "[o]ur experience of another entails a particular interpretation of his behavior. To feel loved is to perceive and interpret, that is, to experience, the actions of the other as loving . . . [Hence,] in order for the other's behavior to become part of self's experience, self must perceive it. The very act of perception [and hence experience] entails interpretation" (pp. 10–11).

Objectivity is one of the hallmarks of the "natural sciences." However, what these sciences cannot investigate according to Laing (1982) are "love and hate, joy and sorrow, misery and happiness, pleasure and pain, right and wrong, purpose, meaning, hope, courage, despair, God, heaven and hell, damnation, enlightenment, wisdom, compassion, evil, envy, malice, generosity, camaraderie and everything, in fact, that makes life worth living" (p. 18). To use a natural science paradigm to study people can therefore only lead to false knowledge. Thus, the subject matter for the study of people requires its own methodology.

What emerges as that methodology is intersubjectivity, or what Laing preferred to label "existential." However, and this is a major however, as Thompson (2005) points out, Laing's intersubjectivity, grounded in Husserl, Buber, Sartre and Heidegger, is quite different from the "intersubjectivity" of relational analysts where the philosophical basis is a rather shoddy pastiche. *The Divided Self* mind you, was published in 1960, twenty-three years before Greenberg and Mitchell's salvo against Freudian modernistic drive psychology and the formal advent of relational postmodern psychoanalysis.

We can see Laing taking this a step further in a later manifestation of the penultimate in intersubjectivity: *Knots* (1970). The implications of this shift to intersubjectivity permeate the entire psychoanalytic project. As he stated (1967), "Over one hundred years ago Feuerbach effected a pivotal step in philosophy. He discovered that philosophy had been exclusively orientated around "I". No one had realized that the "you" is as primary as the I" (p. 4).

Baranger (2012) states that psychoanalysis is now no longer

> an evolution of patients and their history from birth, but that it requires a study of the evolution of psychoanalysis itself and its changes: from an individual study of a subject's pathology by a therapist, to the study and

understanding of the analyst–patient relationship, its vicissitudes, and its possible results. The object of investigation is now the pair formed by analysand and analyst, its evolution as a couple, with difficulties and possible contributions to understanding the consulting patient, who is still the justification (pretext) of the psychoanalytic encounter. This study is far more complex than mere psychoanalysis of an individual, and brings to light many new questions.

(p.132)

Intersubjectivity

We also see in early Laing (1960) the importance and necessity of contextualization for understanding behavior: "any theory that begins with man or a part of man abstracted from his relation with the other in his world" will necessarily fail to understand the workings of the human psyche (p. 19). In *The Self and Others* Laing (1961) writes that

we cannot give an undistorted account of 'a person' without giving an account of his relation with others. Even an account of one person cannot afford to forget that each person is always acting upon others and acted upon by others. The others are there also. No one acts or experiences in a vacuum.

(pp. 81–82)

In fact, he goes further than most postmodern theorists in positing multiple meta-contexts rather than a universalism. He said in 1967 at The Dialectics of Liberation Conference that "[a] fundamental lesson that almost all social scientists have learned is that the intelligibility of social events requires they be seen in a context that extends both spatially and in time. The fabric of sociality is an interlaced set of contexts interlaced with meta contexts" (Laing 1968, p. 15). Thus, we can go from dyad to group to subculture to culture to society or in reverse. One must, however, entertain the question that if all is contextualized, then perhaps contextualism becomes a universal.

The positing of intersubjectivity as the communicative mode in treatment, along with the stress on contextualism leads to a denial of a universalism in doing treatment. While Freud never wrote a manual on how to do psychoanalysis, his *Recommendation* papers have been treated as holy writ, with deviations seen as anti-analytic. Laing also never developed a technique book, not believing that there was a Laingian psychoanalysis and, in postmodern terms, saw each therapeutic encounter as unique. Being trained at the battleground of the British Psychoanalytic, little wonder that sectarian fights and dictas on the one and only way to do treatment was a trap he wasn't going to get caught in. He says in his interview with Mullan (1995) when asked what patients got when seeing him in treatment, simply "They got Laing. . . . They've had my company and attention, my engagement on their behalf. As a matter of honor they've had my attention and I've put myself at their service and of their life and addressed myself as best I could to what's troubling them" (Mullan, 1995, p. 329). Can there be a more definitive statement against a template or formulistic univer-salist view of treatment? Nor can there be a stronger statement showing the presence of the analyst is not a simple reflective mirror but an integral part of a dyadic relationship. This can be further witnessed in Laing's (1967) stating that "[p]sychotherapy must remain an obstinate attempt of two people to recover the wholeness of being human through the relationship between them" (p. 53). *Obstinate* implies that from both parties in the dyad there will be some forces fighting against recovering that wholeness, what I would call from my Freud-ian framework: "resistance". This resistance can be foundational. In an earlier paper, I said,

> Laing (1960) posits the following: to relate as one human being to another requires a relatively firm sense of one's autonomous identity. If this is not present, each relationship tends to threaten the person with the loss of identity. Relatedness is thus often filled with the dread of the loss of both autonomy as well as identity. Therefore what Laing calls engulfment can be experienced as a risk in being understood, in being loved, or simply in being acknowledged.
>
> *(pp. 299–300)*

Thus, empathic attunement and not just empathic failure can lead to isolation and aggression. Clinically, to let the patient "be" is to appreciate the true otherness of the other, the non-imposition and non-destruction of the other by the imposi-tion of one's self on them.

Unlike, so many relational analysts, Laing does not simplify the concept of relating in some Pollyanna manner nor see it as a simple panacea for all human dynamics. It is an operational dynamic and as such fraught with complexity, nuance and ambiguity.

He goes on to write, "In a science of persons, I shall state as axiomatic that: behaviour is a function of experience; and both experience and behaviour are always in relation to someone or something other than self" (Laing, 1967, p. 21). The two-person nature of treatment was spelled out clearly by Laing when he wrote that "[t]he behavior of the patient is to some extent a function of the behav-ior of the psychiatrist in the same behavioral field" (1960, p. 28). It can be asked whether this is significantly different from Lyotard's statement that

> [a] self does not amount to much, but no self is an island; each exists in a fabric of relations that is now more complex and mobile than ever before. Young or old, man or woman, rich or poor; a person is always located at "nodal points" of specific communication circuits, however tiny these may be. . . . The atoms [of society; that is to say, people] are placed at the cross-roads of pragmatic relationships, but they are also displaced by the messages

that traverse them, in perpetual motion. Each language partner, when a "move" pertaining to him is made, "undergoes a 'displacement,' an alteration of some kind that not only affects him in his capacity as addressee and referent, but also as sender."

(1979/1997, pp. 15–16)

Thus, treatment is a process of mutual interaction and influence, where the analyst is anything but the so-called objective neutral ideal of the so-called Freudian model as interpreted by American ego psychologists, but operates in line with postmodern thinking, as well as the actual way Freud and his early followers worked.

This is mirrored in Greenberg and Mitchell's 1983 opus, once again without lineage attribution to Laing or to Jung: "For the relational model analyst the psychoanalytic situation is inherently dyadic; events within the analysis are not understood as preset and unfolding from within the dynamic structures of the patient's neurosis. Rather, they are created in the interaction between the patient and the analyst" (p. 389).

Neutrality

Neutrality, has often been considered one of the mainstays of the classical position, even though Freud (1958b) mentions the term only once in his transference love paper positing it as a suggestion to avoid the ubiquitous counter-transferences that hallmark the analytic process:

> Since we demand strict truthfulness from our patients, we jeopardize our whole authority if we let ourselves be caught out by them in a departure from the truth. Besides, the experiment of letting oneself go a little way in tender feelings for the patient is not altogether without danger. Our control over ourselves is not so complete that we may not suddenly one day go further than we have intended. *In my opinion, therefore, we ought not to give up the neutrality towards the patient, which we have acquired through keeping the counter-transference in check.*
>
> *(p. 164, emphasis added)*

It should be noted that here Freud uses the German word *Indifferenz*, which while accepted in translation as "neutrality" might have subtly different connotations from the word *Neutralitat*. It should also be noted that his use of the term is in relation to the erotization of the treatment and nowhere does it infer that the analyst should be cold, remote, distant, and so on. Nor I may add, does it infer that human warmth, tact. and concern are precluded from the "analytic attitude". In fact the question arises as to whether "neutrality" is a recommendation of technique, or rather an attitude and ethical stance that is necessary, or at least so Freud felt, for successful analytic work.

Laing, once again predating postmodern psychoanalysts denies that this definition of neutrality can exist, even in the limited nature Freud envisioned. He states
in *The Divided Self* (1960) that

> [t]he clinical psychiatrist, wishing to be more "scientific" or "objective"
> may propose to confine himself to the "objectively" observable behavior of
> the patient before him. The simplest reply to this is that it is impossible. To
> see "signs" of "disease" is not to see neutrally . . . We cannot help but see the
> person in one way or other and place our constructions or interpretations on
> "his" behavior as soon as we are in a relationship with him.
>
> *(p. 31)*

In essence to see the other as anything other than a fellow human being is a devia-
tion from that "ideal fiction" of neutrality. He points out how difficult it is to be
truly neutral, and this differentiates him from those postmodern psychoanalysts
who say that since the ideal cannot be attained, discard the concept. I also see this
as saying that to diagnose is, by definition, not to be neutral and to negate the
person in favor of some preordained intellectualized category that biases the way
we hear and relate to the "other". As Thompson says,

> Laing not only embraced Freud's insistence on fidelity to the fundamental
> rule (that patients should endeavor to be as honest as they are able), but also
> endorsed its correlate, the analyst's neutrality, even more emphatically. In
> Laing's assessment, this technical principle, in spite of the current tide of
> opinion against it, meant nothing more onerous than to be unequivocally
> open-minded toward the person one happens to be treating, no matter how
> trying or difficult a given patient may be.
>
> *(2000, p. 491)*

Renik (1993) dismisses neutrality as a possibility in that "since we are constantly
acting in the analytic situation on the basis of personal motivations of which we
cannot be aware until after the fact, our technique, listening included, is inescap-
ably subjective" (p. 414). Hutsebaut (2001) states that "[a]s of the moment that the
analyst intervenes interpretatively, thus giving prejudice to one interpretive line
over another, he/she departs from a strictly neutral position and imposes his/her
personal vision on the material" (p. 68).

By dismissing the concept due to its lack of "purity" the door is opened for a
nihilism based on the individuality of each analyst as to positions taken in regard
to each analysand. Disregarding the "personal motivations" Renik mentions, since
the ontological identity of the individual is a modernist myth – but perhaps that
applies only to patients and not to analysts, we are left with a confusion of desir-
ability with actuality. Neutrality does not mean, nor has it even implied, the
absence of values, standards, feelings or morality on the part of the analyst – it has
simply meant the necessity to contain these as much as possible and let the patient

set the tone and direction of the treatment. It would seem that this definition is one Laing could easily live with.

Personology

Many intersubjective and relational analysts, while attacking the absence of the person in ego psychological theory as well as object relations theory, repeat the omission of the living, breathing person. For Laing the person is central. As Frederickson (2005) astutely points out,

> [i]n brief, some intersubjective and relational theorists, pose a problem for relationality: the absence of the person. They mistakenly prioritize what we know (epistemology) over who we are (ontology). They conflate subjectivity with the subject. They mistake the logic of inference for the logic of causality. Contexts and relational fields, not the quality of personhood, have laid claim to the ontological content of human existence. As a result, we end up at times with an intersubjective theory without a subject, and an interpersonal theory without a person.
>
> *(p. 92)*

We find Stolorow (1988) talking about "reciprocally interacting subjectivities" (p. 178), while Mitchell (1988) points out that " mind is fundamentally dyadic and interactive; above all else, mind seeks contact, engagement with other minds" (pp. 3–4).

Laing certainly serves as a corrective, where the person is not an epiphenomenal addition to a mystical connectedness between participants. Reification and mechanization are repellant to the existentialism in which Laing's writings are grounded.

> We are not concerned with the interaction of two objects, nor with their transactions within a dyadic system; we are not concerned with the communication patterns within a system comprising two computer-like subsystems that receive and process input and emit outgoing signals. Our concern is with two origins of experience in relation.
>
> *(Laing, 1967 p. 45)*

Also, "[t]o say that my experience is intrapsychic is to presuppose that there is a psyche that my experience is in. My psyche is my experience. My experience is my psyche" (p. 21). In that sense he is the ultimate "personologist" with human experience at the center. If one's experience is one's psyche and one of the aims of treatment is to expand one's experience to the fullest, then to bring into experience or in my terms "make the unconscious conscious" fits with the original Freudian project. As Laing further stated in 1967,

> The other person's behaviour is an experience of mine. My behaviour is an experience of the other. The task of social phenomenology is to relate my

experience of the other's behaviour to the other's experience of my behaviour. Its study is the relation between experience and experience: its true field is inter-experience.

(p. 15)

We can define phenomenology as that vista which is preoccupied with the character of subjective processes. Inherent in this is the suspension of beliefs of truths of any kind and the supremacy of experiences for themselves. For Sartre, for whom Laing had a definite affinity, it also entails that each individual must choose what he or she is to be, in line with total involvement. The therapeutic implications as specified by Laing seem to predate the relational and postmodern view of treatment. For example, Laing (1960) affirms that "[e]xistential phenomenology becomes the attempt to reconstruct the patient's way of being himself in his world, although in the therapeutic relationship, the focus may be in the patient's way of being with me" (p. 25). Once again this was decades before Mitchell (1993) defined the goal of treatment as "not clear understanding but the ability to generate experience felt as real, important and distinctively one's own" (p. 32). Experience, which is different from understanding and from interpreting, is at the heart of Laing's work as it is with postmodern therapists. But here too, no attribution to Laing is cited.

Laing goes on to say, "Psychotherapy is an activity in which that aspect of the patient's being, his relatedness to others, is used for therapeutic ends" (1960, p. 26). Furthermore, the psychotherapeutic relationship is therefore a research.

> A search, constantly reasserted and reconstituted, for what we have all lost and whose loss some can perhaps endure a little more easily than others, as some people can stand lack of oxygen better than others, and this research is validated by the shared experience of experience regained in and through the therapeutic relationship in the here and now.
>
> *(Laing, 1960, p. 126)*

Relatedness, not drive-conflict and not object relations in the intrapsychic sense, becomes the focus of the treatment. It is an interactive or two-person encounter.

Two-person psychology

As far as the two-person system and the antiauthoritarianism that deny that the analyst "knows" while the patient is to be informed of, we see Laing stating as early as 1960 in taking a position of the exploration of mutual subjectivities that

> one has to be able to orient oneself as a person in the other's scheme of things rather than only to see the other as an object in one's own world, i.e. within the total system of one's own reference. One must be able to effect this reorientation without prejudging who is right and who is wrong.
>
> *(p. 25)*

As Charlesworth said, and it is hard to be more definitive than this

> [t]here are therapists – whether they're Freudian or Jungians, or whether they call themselves one thing or another, or simply psychotherapists – who don't treat people as objects and as things, and who don't feel it is their job to impose their numbers and their scenarios and their values on the patient, but rather see therapy as a reciprocal undertaking and just don't have that impulse to depersonalize and reify the patient.
>
> *(Charlesworth, 1993, 32)*

This is not only the so-called spirit of post-postmodern psychoanalysis but in tune with Freud, who stated,

> We refused most emphatically to turn a patient who puts himself into our hands in search of help into our private property, to decide his fate for him, to force our own ideals upon him, and with the pride of a Creator to form him in our own image and see that it is good. I still adhere to this refusal, and I think that this is the proper place for the medical discretion which we have had to ignore in other connections.
>
> *(1955, p. 164)*

This does not mean interpretations are not part of the analytic encounter but seem secondary to the relatedness. Thompson (1996) states, "It seemed to Laing that most analysts had become so taken with the complicated nature of unconscious phantasy and its interpretation that they had forgot how to be real with their patients when it was indicated" (p. 845). Mutuality and being real do not mean for Laing a disclosure of his inner world, fantasies and so on as it does for many relational postmodernists. This would be seen as an imposition on the "other" and a setting of the agenda.

According to Thompson, "Although valued interpretations and employed them in his practice, he believed that the psychoanalyst's principal task is to validate our patients' experience. The goal of therapy should be to help others find their way to the ground of their experience, through their relationship with their therapist" (p. 845). If validating our patients experience is the principle therapeutic task, then one can assume that that validation did not occur in the past, either in primal relationships within the family or other interpersonal encounters. If that is true, then therapy becomes a "corrective emotional experience" without the false manipulative quality that characterizes Alexander's work. For example, Alexander (1956) states,

> Knowledge of the early interpersonal attitudes which contributed to a patient's neurosis can help the analyst to assume intentionally a kind of attitude which is conducive to provoking the kind of emotional experience in the patient which is suited to undo the pathogenic effect of the original parental attitude.
>
> *(p. 92)*

Greenberg (1986) mirrors this when he states and advocates rather than simply validates that "[t]he analytic behaviors which implement the goal of optimal tension between old and new necessarily vary with the openness to new experience of a particular patient's internal object world" (p. 142). Therefore, with a patient with a closed world of object relations, the analysts would have to be more active and assertive, while with a patient with a more open one, silence and relative anonymity would be called for. There is thus a shifting neutrality based on the transference of the patient. I strongly believe Laing would see the above statements as indicative of the inauthenticity that he sees characterizing so much of psychoanalysis.

Perspectivism

This brings us to the question of perspectivism, as opposed to absolute truth and Laing's most noted statement, from *The Politics of Experience*, often misinterpreted to make him an advocate of psychosis: "madness need not be all breakdown. It may also be breakthrough. It may be liberation and renewal as well as enslavement and existential death" (1967, p. 87). As an aside, we find Freud (1907) in the Gradiva paper discussing hallucinations as attempts to recathect the world, and Jung (1956) asserting that psychosis and other psychological problems were not merely difficulties to be overcome or repressed but that they represented opportunities for growth and maturation, whereby parts of the unconscious could be integrated into our psyche. Therefore, Laing's perspectivist statement can be seen as within the mainstream of psychodynamic thinking and not the "off the wall" way it was received within the conventional therapeutic community.

In rejecting objectivity for an understanding of persons, Laing is claiming that other perspectives have equal if not greater validity. These alternatives serve to counter illness interpretations by positing creative and even theological/spiritual interpretations. This is in direct antithesis to the modernist view that truth indeed exists and that general laws and truths may be arrived at by reason, science and technology, making progress a possibility.

Freud (1933) was clear as to the "truth-seeking" nature of psychoanalysis: there was a clear correspondence to reality: "Its endeavor (scientific thinking) is to arrive at correspondence with reality – that is to say, with what exists outside us and independently of us and, as experience has taught us, is decisive for the fulfillment or disappointment of our wishes. The correspondence with the real external world we call 'truth'" (p. 170). Also according to Sterba (1982), Freud was heard to say, "During my whole life I have endeavored to uncover truths. I had no other intention and everything else was completely a matter of indifference to me. My single motive was the love of truth" (p. 115).

Some would see the following statement of Freud's (1915) indicating that "truth" is positioned at the heart of the analytic method:

> My objection to this expedient [i.e., the use of trickery] is that psychoana-
> lytic treatment is founded on truthfulness. In this fact lies a great part of its

educative effect and its ethical value . . . Since we demand strict truthfulness from our patients, we jeopardize our whole authority if we let ourselves be caught out by them in a departure from the truth.

(p. 164)

For postmodernism, general laws and truths do not exist, as witnessed by the following statement of Orange's (1995):

Perspectival realism recognizes that the only truth or reality to which psychoanalysis provides access is the subjective organization of experience understood in an inter-subjective context. . . . A subjective organization of experience is one perspective on a larger reality. We never fully attain or know this reality, but we continually approach, apprehend, articulate.

(p. 62)

Mitchell (1993), while not as phenomenologically grounded as Orange, writes, "But psychoanalysis can no longer be a science in the way Freud thought about science. It is now a science that yields multiple truths, changing truths, truths that are embedded in the particular interactive context of the analytic relationship" (p. 50). Stolorow (1998) goes even further by claiming that "objective reality is unknowable by the psychoanalytic method, which investigates only subjective reality . . . there are no neutral or objective analysts, no immaculate perceptions, no God's-eye views of anything" (p. 425). Spence (2001) sums this position up by stating,

The postmodern position[,] by contrast, is inclined to believe that our observations are always rooted in a particular intersection of time and space; accordingly, there may be no such thing as 'objectivism' (e.g. scientism)[,] value-free languages (e.g. positivism)[,] metaphysical reduction (e.g. natural laws) and so-called "Archimedean" points of reference (e.g. observables).

(p. 452)

This broaches a fundamental question for all clinicians, that goes beyond Freud's (1912) positing of an evenly hovering attention. Do we focus on the pathology, as those who believe in diagnosis do? Do we focus on the growth potential and strengths of the patient? Or, in line with Laing, is our function to be able to empathically attune (my words, not Laing's) to the full experience of the other in our consulting room. Which "perspective" we adopt will naturally determine our contribution to the course of the therapeutic encounter.

While Laing's perspectivism is in line with postmodern thinking we find something else present in regard to truth. Laing emphasizes the dialectic between truth and falsehood and how the conflict between them accounts for a basic split in the self that leads to the forms of human suffering for which people enter treatment. If life is rooted in experience and experience engenders suffering, then we may attempt to reduce that suffering by deceiving ourselves and adopting "false truths" that are syntonic to us, resulting in a further split within ourselves. If the words *authenticity* and *truth* are used interchangeably we see him accounting for that which, as a Freudian, I call defense mechanisms, and the legitimacy of the concept of "self" is a modernist slant on development and certainly a position that differentiates his thinking from postmodernists.

We all too often find, as much as relationalists bemoan the "authoritarianism" of the classical model, an imposition of their model on the patient. For example, Aron, (1991) states, "In the clinical situation I often ask patients to describe anything that they have observed or noticed about me that may shed light on aspects of our relationship" (p. 252), or "I find that it is critical for me to ask the question with the genuine belief that I may find out something about myself that I did not previously recognize" (p. 252), or "I encourage patients to tell me anything that they have observed and insist that there must have been some basis in my behavior for their conclusions. I often ask patients to speculate or fantasize about what is going on inside of me, and in particular I focus on what patients have noticed about my internal conflicts. I assume that the patient may very well have noticed my anger, jealousy, excitement, or whatever before I recognize it in myself" (p. 252).

And finally, "It is often useful to ask patients directly what they have noticed about the analyst, what they think the analyst is feeling or doing, what they think is going on in the analyst or with what conflict they think the analyst is struggling" (p. 262). Can you imagine Laing imposing himself on the other's space in such a manner?

Conclusion

Where does this leave us? I think the evidence is clear that Laing was a precursor of the postmodern psychoanalytic tendency, if not as theory, certainly as practice. His emphasis on experience, therapeutic mutuality, perspectivism, contextualism, the uniqueness of each therapeutic encounter, phenomenology and intersubjectivity all philosophically grounded, places him in the forefront of non-drive-based interpersonalist psychoanalysts. His acceptance of the unconscious, albeit idiosyncratically defined, the use of interpretation, of neutrality, of authenticity and of the concept of self along with an appreciation of Freud's contributions differentiates him from contemporary postmodern psychoanalysts.

I also think, and here it is naturally speculative, that Laing would be critical of the American post-modern tendency for several reasons. He might find its philosophical underpinnings overly simplified and scattered at best, particularly in its ignoring existentialist writings. He might see the total dismissal of Freud as intellectually dishonest since while having strong disagreements with Freud he never denied his genius or his intellectual importance. He might posit the postmodern use of relatedness as typically American in that it did not deal with the complexity and underside of the concept. He might indeed see it as too focused on inauthenticity: a false niceness, compassion and connectedness passing for its opposite. Remember, part of his distaste for Rogers was the latter's claim that he personally never experienced evil within himself. Thompson (1996), without putting words into Laing's mouth, but mirroring his thoughts about humans, says that "[h]uman beings are devious and dishonest creatures who, without thinking, violate and betray one another as a matter of course" (p. 835). Laing might find its negation of authenticity to be a severe shortcoming, and abridgment of therapeutic goals, and he might see its denial of a historical lineage for its ideas as poor scholarship.

While Laing and the postmodernists have arrived at similar critiques of Freudian-based psychoanalysis the contexts are different. For Laing, European philosophy is integral to his concept of psychiatry and treatment. Add to this the pettiness of the British Psychoanalytic Society, Laing's difficulties during his training and the anti-philosophical bias of organized psychoanalysis and we see the roots of his moving toward his own vision of therapy.

To comprehend American postmodern psychoanalysis one has to understand the context of the historical development of psychoanalysis in the United States. For indeed, relationalism is a movement, with its own journal *Psychoanalytic Dialogues*, its own training ground (including its birthplace, the New York University Postdoctoral Program in Psychotherapy and Psychoanalysis) and its nascent international organization, the International Association for Relational Psychoanalysis and Psychotherapy. It has become a political movement. The first point is that the origins of relationalism are in the interpersonalist psychoanalysis of Sullivan. This was housed in the William Alanson White Institute in New York and the Washington School. They never were accepted by the organizational mainstream (the American Psychoanalytic Association) and were not only discounted as analysts but also ostracized and at one point sued to not be able to use the title "psychoanalysts". Resentment of oppression does linger, as history shows us. The second point is that the leadership of the relational/postmodern movement in psychoanalysis, with a few notable exceptions such as Renik, and Ogden, tend to come from specializations other than medicine, that is, Mitchell, Aron, Stolorow, Benjamin, Altman, Harris, Hoffman, Bromberg, Davis and Spezzano, among others, the majority of whom have advanced degrees in psychology. They, therefore, were, until recently, ineligible for full training in the constituent organizations of the American Psychoanalytic Association, or even membership in the Association. This entails a second form of discrimination added to the exclusion of interpersonalists, one that was only settled by legal means rather than by collegiality.

It should be noted that the "base of operations" for the relationalists is not the American nor the International Psychoanalytical Association but in line with their degrees, Division 39 – The Division of Psychoanalysis – of the American Psychological Association, where they are the most influential grouping.

A third factor is speculative, but worth considering. Many of the "leaders" of the relational movement had their organizational teeth cut during the 1960s. This was a time where antiauthority as well as antiauthoritarian stances and struggles were the zeitgeist. This "battle" with the advocacy of "two-person psychology" and a seemingly more egalitarian view of the analytic encounter is also the hallmark of the postmodern/relationalists.

While these sociological variables may be operative, a fourth factor, a psychological one, can also be posited, namely, the generational struggle (Oedipal conflict, to be exact) between the establishment parents as represented by the American Psychoanalytic Association and the "upstarts" who desire to supersede them. While narcissism and power highlight most political movements we should not forget the unconscious factors that appear not only in the clinical setting but also in the dynamics of group relations and conflicts. While Laing and the postmodernists might arrive at similar clinical positions, the motives are different and the resultant gestalt certainly differs. This, however, is the topic for a subsequent paper.

References

Alexander, F. (1956) *Psychoanalysis and psychotherapy: Developments in theory, technique and training.* New York: Norton.

Aron, L. (1991) The patient's experience of the analyst's subjectivity. *Psychoanalytic Dialogues,* 1, 29–51.

Baranger, M. (2012) The intrapsychic and the intersubjective in contemporary psychoanalysis. *International Forum of Psychoanalysis,* 21(3–4), 130–135.

Benjamin, J. (1990) Reorganization and restructuring. *Psychoanalytic Psychology,* 7 (suppl.), 33–47.

Buber, M. (1923/1937) *I and thou* (Trans., R. G. Smith). Edinburgh, Scotland: T. and T. Clark.

Charlesworth, M. (1993) Sartre, Laing, and Freud. In K. Hoeller (Ed.), *Sartre and psychology.* Princeton, NJ: Humanities Press.

Fenichel, O. (1941) *Problems of psychoanalytic technique* (M. Brunswik, Trans.) New York: The Psychoanalytic Quarterly Inc. (Original work published 1933)

Frederickson, J. (2005) The problem of relationality. In J. Mills (Ed.), *Relational and intersubjecive perspectives in psychoanalysis: A critique.* Lanham, MD: Jason Aronson.

Freud, S. (1907) Delusions and dreams in Jensen's *Gradiva.* In J. Strachey (Ed. & Trans.), *The standard edition of the complete psychological works of Sigmund Freud* (Vol. 9). London: The Hogarth Press.

Freud, S. (1912) Recommendation to physicians practicing psychoanalysis. In J. Strachey (Ed. & Trans.), *The standard edition of the complete psychological works of Sigmund Freud* (Vol. 7). London: The Hogarth Press, 1958.

Freud, S. (1915) Observations on transference love. In J. Strachey (Ed. & Trans.), *The standard edition of the complete psychological works of Sigmund Freud* (Vol. 12). London: Hogarth Press, 1958.

Freud, S. (1919) Lines of advance in psycho-analytic therapy. In J. Strachey (Ed. & Trans.), *The standard edition of the complete psychological works of Sigmund Freud* (Vol. 17). London: Hogarth Press, 1955.

Freud, S. (1933) *New introductory lectures on psychoanalysis.* New York: Norton & Co. Inc.

Greenberg, H. & Mitchell, S. A. (1983) *Object relations in psychoanalytic theory.* Cambridge, MA: Harvard University Press.

Greenberg, J. (1986) Theoretical models and the analyst's neutrality. In S. Mitchell & L. Aron (Eds.), *Relational psychoanalysis: The emergence of a tradition*. Hillsdale, NJ: Analytic Press.

Hutsebaut, J. (2001) The problem of "false memories": The role of suggestion. In P. Van Haute & J. Corvelyn (Eds.), *Seduction, hypnotism, psychoanalysis*. Leuven, Belgium: Leuven University Press.

Jameson, F. (1991) *Postmodernism or, the cultural logic of late capitalism*. London: Verso.

Jung, C. G. (1956) *Two essays on analytic psychology*. New York: World Publishing.

Laing, R. D. (1960) *The divided self*. London: Tavistock.

Laing, R. D. (1961) *The Self and others*. London: Tavistock.

Laing, R. D. (1967) *The politics of experience (P.O.E) and the bird of paradise*. New York: Pantheon.

Laing, R. D. (1968) The obvious. In D. Cooper (Ed.), *The dialectics of liberation*. Harmondsworth, England: Penguin.

Laing, R. D. (1970) *Knots*. New York: Pantheon Books.

Laing, R. D. (1971) *The politics of the family and other essays*. Harmondsworth, England: Penguin Books Ltd. (Original work published 1969)

Laing, R. D. (1982) What's the matter with mind? In S. Kumar (Ed.), *The Schumacher lectures*. London. Abacus.

Laing, R. D., & Esterson, A. (1964) *Sanity, madness and the family: Vol. 1. Families of schizophrenics*. London: Tavistock.

Laing, R. D., Phillipson, H., & Lee, A. R. (1966) *Interpersonal perception: A theory and a method of research*. London: Tavistock Publications.

Lyotard, J.-F. (1997) *The postmodern condition: A report on knowledge* (G. Bennington & B. Massumi, Trans.). Minneapolis: University of Minnesota Press. (Original work published 1979)

Mills, J. (Ed.) (2005) *"Introduction" to relational and intersubjective perspectives in psychoanalysis: A critique*. Lanham, MD: Jason Aronson.

Mitchell, S. A. (1988) *Relational concepts in psychoanalysis: An integration*. Cambridge, MA: Harvard University Press.

Mitchell, S. A. (1993) *Hope and dread in psychoanalysis*. New York: Basic Books.

Mullan, B. (1995) *Mad to be normal: Conversations with R. D. Laing*. London: Free Association Books.

Orange, D. (1995) *Emotional understanding: Studies in psychoanalytic epistemology*. New York: Guilford.

Renik, O. (1993) Analytic interaction: Conceptualizing technique in light of the analyst's irreducible subjectivity. In S. Mitchell & L. Aron (Eds.), *Relational psychoanalysis: The emergence of a tradition* (pp. 407–424). Hillsdale, NJ: Analytic Press.

Rorty, R. (1989) *Contingency, irony and solidarity*. Cambridge, England: Cambridge University Press.

Rustin, M. (2001) *Reason and unreason: Psychoanalysis, science and politics*. Middletown, CT: Wesleyan University Press.

Schulman, M. (2003) R. D. Laing and existential psychoanalysis: A blast from the past. *Psychoanalytic Review*, 90(3), 293–301.

Spence, D. (2001) Case reports in a two-person world. *Psychoanalytic Psychology*, 18(3), 451–468.

Sterba, R. (1982) *Reminiscences of a Viennese psychoanalyst*. Detroit, MI: Wayne State University Press.

Stern, D. B. (1997) *Unformulated experience: From dissociation to imagination in psychoanalysis*. Hillsdale, NJ: The Analytic Press.

Stolorow, R. (1998) Clarifying the intersubjective perspective: A reply to George Frank. *Psychoanalytic Psychology*, 15(3), 424–427.

Stolorow, R., Brandchaft, B., & Atwood, G. (1988) *Psychoanalytic treatment: An intersubjecive approach*. Hillsdale, NJ: Analytic Press.

Thompson, M. G. (1996) Deception, mystification, trauma: Laing and Freud. *Psychoanalytic Review*, 83, 827–847.

Thompson, M. G. (2000) The heart of the matter: R. D. Laing's enigmatic relationship with psychoanalysis. *Psychoanalytic Review*, 87, 483–509.

Thompson, M. G. (2005) Phenomenology of intersubjectivity: A historical overview of the concept and its clinical implications. In J. Mills (Ed.), *Intersubjectivity and relational theory in psychoanalysis*. Hillsdale, NJ: Jason Aronson.

8

AWAKENING TO LOVE

R. D. Laing's phenomenological therapy

Steven Gans, PhD

To begin with I'll say how I came to be associated with Ronnie Laing and the Philadelphia Association (PA). I had trained in the phenomenological or Continental philosophical tradition at Penn State, completing my doctoral dissertation on Martin Heidegger's theory of language in 1967. Al Lingus, who would become translator of Levinas into English, joined the Penn State faculty that year and introduced me to the work of Emmanuel Levinas and his ethical critique of Heidegger. In 1972 I spent a sabbatical year with Laing and the PA, hoping to close the gap I felt between the world of ideas that I had been studying and teaching and the lived truth of these ideas, which I believed ought to be embodied in a lost art of philosophical practice for which I was searching. I thought that the messenger should become the message, yet the scholastic approach of academics did not lead to wisdom. As I saw it, academics did not radiate fulfillment, serenity, or goodness. At the PA I began to hear the music of the heart.

I returned to London in 1974 to train in phenomenological psychotherapy and become a member of a PA asylum community. In time I became a psychotherapist as well as a colleague and friend of Ronnie Laing's. Over some years we met on a regular basis for congenial afternoon conversations and evening study groups. Ronnie was a polymath, perhaps a genius, but what was most important for me about meetings with him was not merely learning from what he knew but from how he was. Only now am I able to begin to find the words to say something about the transmission of his teaching, which I call *an awakening to love*.

Albert Camus wrote in the *Myth of Sisyphus* and *The Rebel* that there are only two serious philosophical questions, suicide, and murder. I can imagine Ronnie as a university student in Glasgow reading this and thinking, Camus is wrong – there is really only one serious philosophical question, for that matter one theological, psychological, and sociological question: the question of love. Although we never spoke of it together as such, I have come to see that the underlying issue that informed all of Ronnie's theorizing and informal conversations, his leitmotif, from the beginning of his intellectual and practical career to its end, was the question of love. Although Ronnie did not leave any systematic exposition of what I will call his phenomenology of love, if one is possible, clearly his critique of academic phenomenology and orthodox psychoanalysis as well as institutional psychiatry was energized by his early and astonishing awakening to the lack of love and ethics in contemporary theory and practice. Anticipating Levinas, Laing saw from the outset that heartless knowledge could only lead to soul-destroying practice. The way out of heartless science was by getting through it on the way toward a science with heart, what Ronnie called a science of human relatedness, or a social phenomenology. For Ronnie phenomenology was not merely a theory that you applied in practice; for example, in psychotherapy, it was a way of *continual and provocative awakening from one's dogmatic and loveless slumber.* This awakening is itself therapeutic. I now attempt to engender attunement between you and Laing's *awakening to love*, which I believe is as much an urgent necessity for our time as it was for his.

Phase I

Interpersonal–phenomenological neurophysiology

At one point in his extended interview with Bob Mullan (1995) published in *Mad to Be Normal* (pp. 115–119) Ronnie recounts how his neurological clinical practice came together with his phenomenological interests, so that by the early 1950s he had already envisioned a critique of the medical model applied to psychopathology and the creation of an interpersonal neurophenomenology. For him phenomenology meant first of all pure description, in the manner of Husserl's *Ideas* (1913).

Positivistic science and medicine, like ordinary life, operates within the assumptions of the natural attitude. We take for granted that reality is objective, that it is in itself, out there, as we experience it by means of our bodily senses, coordinated by our brain and neurophysiology. We are no more aware of our consciousness and the part it plays in presenting and representing the meaning of what we experience than we are of our breathing or our heartbeat.

Just as light disappears in order to enable us to see what it illuminates, so consciousness puts itself to sleep to allow us to experience ordinary everyday life. But this "ordinariness" of life is an illusion, a trance. Husserl awakens us from this trance by insisting that the only evidence we really have for the existence of anything at all is through consciousness. He proposes that we perform a most unnatural act. He directs us to turn the spotlight of attention of our own acts of consciousness in order to explore how at each and every moment of experience we give ourselves the "things themselves," the meaning of our experience. He proposes a vast project of pure description, an intentional analysis, to document the evidence revealed when consciousness is turned on itself. His aim is to wake us up from our dogmatic slumber in order to "see" how subjective consciousness constitutes lived meaning, things *as* the things we experience.

Following Husserl, the study of subjective experience, once regarded as an impediment to objectivity, now becomes the foundation of any science attempting to be rigorous. We can no longer assume we know what we are investigating until we first examine how the thing is "given" to us, that is, the way in which it has become present and meaningful in the context of experience.

To assume, for example, that the mind and the body are separate realities is a positivistic, Cartesian assumption. Such a belief system posits a dichotomy for which there can be no experiential evidence, given the first awakening to the fact that all evidence is experiential, hence embodied. Our body is the heart and source of our mind, which is our conscious experience. But as Ronnie had observed, psychopathological texts characterized the schizoid condition precisely as a split between self and body. But was a person schizoid, or was it mainstream Western philosophy that was schizoid? Ronnie realized that as long as he conceived of psychopathological conditions in terms of the medical model, he would be presupposing the reality of the very "diseases" that he had as yet to discover or describe. In short, he would not really know what he was talking about. Unlike a toothache, which gives the feeling of pain, its sign, and the appearance of swelling, its symptom, there were no specific behaviors or experiences of so-called psychopathological conditions that lead to specific direct evidence of disorders, such as brain lesions. The reality of psychopathologies was presupposed in self-validating medical hypotheses, retrospectively "confirmed" by arbitrary clusters of signs and symptoms, behaviors, and experiences. In short, there was no phenomenological evidence for psychopathology, only the medicalization of madness. Ronnie found confirmation for his suspicions about psychopathology in Harry Stack Sullivan, who argued that there was a misalliance between neurology and psychiatry. The subject of psychiatry is disturbance in interpersonal relationships, whereas the subject of neurology is pathological lesions of the central nervous system. By 1954 Ronnie saw that what was called for was a fresh look at the subject of psychiatry from a phenomological vantage. By this time he was 26 years old.

Another aspect of phenomenology with which Ronnie was preoccupied was the problematic of intersubjectivity, especially Martin Buber's *I and Thou*. Ronnie was convinced, working in the West Scotland Neurosurgical Unit, that the neurophysiology of one person's nervous system was related to the neurophysiology of someone else's nervous system. These nervous systems were not completely isolated and separate. They were connected. There was interplay between your physiology and my physiology. Ronnie observed the way some people recovered from head injury and came out of a coma, recovering from conditions they might well have died from. He felt that this recovery was due to the attention lavished on them by the nursing staff. Still, no interpersonal neurophysiological theory existed, much less a theory from a phenomenological perspective. The text that came closest to speculation on this theme was Buber's, and Ronnie states, "I had a dream of the relationship between *I and Thou* and its relationship to neurophysiology" (Mullan, 1995, p. 115).

A relationship always exists between us in the world. When we become ill or diseased that relationship does not cease to exist; rather, it becomes more important than ever. In other words, whether or not love is present or absent in the relationship makes all the difference; it is the difference between life and death. Thus began Ronnie's perduring involvement with the "question of love" and his attempt to develop a lived and healing phenomenology of love and human relatedness. He sought to make Husserl and Buber "operational," to deploy phenomenology in a radical overhaul of psychiatric and medical theory and practice. This overhaul was to become a revolution.

Toward an ontology of human relatedness

In an unpublished manuscript titled "Reflections on the Ontology of Human Relations" (R. Laing, 1954), written in 1954 in Glasgow, Ronnie laid out a program for the founding of an interpersonal phenomenology on the basis of biblical love. Regarding this seminal youthful paper, it is instructive to note that *ontology* is a key word in *The Divided Self* (1960). Ontology is Heidegger's word for phenomenology. For Heidegger, Husserl only tackled the derivative question of phenomenology, the meaning of things. Heidegger raises the fundamental question, what does it mean to be? Consciousness only partially awakens, when we realize our own contribution in bringing the meaning of things to presence in experience. We only partially awaken, as we realize that our life world underlies natural appearance – appearances existing as if independent of consciousness. But Heidegger awakens us to our own existence. We beings (existences) *are*, in order to let things be. Phenomenology is ontology. It is awakening to the language of being. Humans, Heidegger argues, are obliged, sent, in order to own up to being. This means to be there as the world stage enabling being to play out.

Heidegger calls human beings *Da sein* – being there – and characterizes our being as "always in each case mine." This "my ownness" is instanced in each and every "I" (Levinas, 1998, pp. 15–33). It is not because I think that I am, as Descartes suggests; rather, it is because existence is happening that "I" results. Awakening to the adventure of being in the world, to our temporality and finitude, is the task of Heidegger's famous existential analysis, which is the springboard for Laing's ontological reflections. Heidegger points out that we systemically cloud over or mystify the adventure of our being unto death, hiding or sleeping in an indifferent average everydayness. We fall into mindless conventionality. We imagine we can unburden ourselves of the responsibility to be – and thus escape the inevitability of (put off indefinitely) our own death (Heidegger, 1927/1966).

In his "Reflections," Ronnie considers that the greatest casualty of our distracted and indifferent disowning of our destiny to be is our failure to realize our most fundamental potential, which is articulated in and is a summary of the biblical teaching old and new, *to love our neighbor as ourselves*. Even Heidegger himself failed, according to Ronnie, to make this truth the guiding light of his ontology. Not only Heidegger but all phenomenologists and existentialists thus far as well have missed this fundamental wisdom. They have done so because, disappointingly, phenomenology has not conducted a rigorous examination of human relatedness. As Ronnie put it, "Human relatedness is the Achilles heel of ontology" (R. Laing, 1954, p. 4).

So what does Ronnie propose as his new initiative in phenomenology? It is what I will refer to as a third phenomenological awakening, an awakening to love. It should be noted that here Ronnie anticipates the breakthrough ethics of Emanuel Levinas. Levinas breaks free of the totalizing movement of classical phenomenological thought that is egological and logocentric. He begins by recognizing the sanctity of the otherness of the other person. Both Ronnie and Levinas draw their inspiration from biblical sources. They aspire to animate and redirect heartless totalitarian thought (exemplified by Heidegger's Nazi involvement) with the spirit of philosophical faith.

Ronnie's starting point is the premise of the *universal human potential to love.* Man is the potential to lead a realized life, by fulfilling the biblical commandment *to love thy neighbor as thyself.* Ontologically (potentially), we are this love. Failing to love is ontic (experiential); it is only contingent. This was Ronnie's recasting of Heidegger's famous ontological difference. Based on this principle Ronnie criticizes Spinoza when he excludes children, fools, and madmen from his ontological system. Spinoza here confuses psychology with ontology.

"No ontologist," Laing argues, "has the right to include out any human being whose action he finds unaccountable even though his behaviour may seem more strange than the birds in the garden" (R. Laing, 1954, p. 3).

This precept is the basis for Ronnie's critique of the psychiatric institution:

> To view others in terms of ourselves is a narcissistic fallacy.
> To the degree that the ontologist is psychologically narcissistic to that extent his ontology will fail in the task of awaking to relatedness and love.

Breaking down the commandment into six components we must

> 1st – love our neighbour unconditionally.
> 2nd – love is a verb, a way of relating not to an *it* but to a *thou.*
> 3rd – we must love each and every other neighbour – not a vague and indifferent universal humanity.
> 4th – we must recognize the otherness of the other person as different from myself. This is Levinas's ethical injunction not to reduce the otherness of the other to the same.
> 5th – love as myself means I have a reflexive relation to self that will influence other. If I am mistreating myself others also suffer.
> 6th – the *as* in "love as myself" expresses the correlation that exists between myself and the other. We exist in relation, never in isolation.

This sixth principle is the guiding theme for the development of Ronnie's social phenomenology. As a consequence of this principle, psychopathology can never be thought of in terms of a disease *in someone*; rather, it must always be seen as a *dysfunction in a relationship*. I turn now to Ronnie's (1960) justly famous work *The Divided Self* and the key concept of "ontological insecurity." This work is the fruition of his early phenomenological speculations and a manifestation of a lived phenomenology of love.

Ontological insecurity

To be sure, Ronnie had awakened to love. He was no doubt called to live as fully realized a life as possible, to live up to the truth of human potential. This meant overcoming the contingencies and the constraints in realizing loving relatedness. Ronnie was at this time completing his psychiatric training at Gartnavel Hospital in Glasgow. For him it was obvious that the treatment of long-term mental patients was anything but loving. Insulin injections, electric shocks, straitjackets, and locked wards were standard operating procedure. If a more loving environment was to be provided for his most chronic patients, to test the hypothesis that loving heals, then psychiatric institutional constraints, rules, roles, and conventions governing the relations between staff and patients would have to be transformed. What was obvious to Ronnie – the advantages of trying his "theory" out – was far from obvious to the hospital administrators. What won the day in the end was Ronnie's argument that the cost of replacing what the administrators thought would be the inevitably broken windows and furniture would be less than the drugs that would no longer have to be given. Opening up a space in which nurses allowed themselves to be with patients as other human beings was Ronnie's first attempt at a social phenomenological experiment. This became known as the "Rumpus Room" experiment, which Ronnie described in an article in the *Lancet* in 1955:

> In the last twelve months many changes occurred in these patients. They were no longer social isolates. Their conduct became more social, and they undertook tasks that were of more value in this small community. Their appearance and interest in themselves improved as they took a greater interest in those around them. . . . The patients lost many of the features of chronic psychoses; they were less violent to each other and to the staff, they were less dishevelled and their language ceased to be obscene. The nurses came to know the patients well, and spoke warmly of them.
>
> *(A. Laing, 1994, p. 58)*

However astonishing and gratifying this confirmation of the potency of a phenomenology of love to heal must have been, Ronnie was only just beginning to think about the question of why some more than others turn away from loving fellowship and become vulnerable to being labeled schizophrenic. This question led him to postulate the notion of "ontological insecurity" that he formulated in *The Divided Self*.

The project of *The Divided Self* (R. Laing, 1960) was to make madness intelligible. This would undermine conventional psychiatry, which defined insanity in terms of an abyss of unintelligibility that opens between the sane (psychiatrist) and the insane (patient). Initially Ronnie argues that it is not fear of death (Heidegger) but fear of the loss of primordial love that is the basis of anxiety. Anticipation of such loss is the pervasive experience of those insecure enough to become vulnerable to psychiatric diagnoses. Far from insane, their fear of the loss of love turns out to be a real and ever-present danger, especially insofar as the insecure often refuse to comply with family and social norms. What is the origin of this special vulnerability? Must it not stem from the earliest moments when consciousness could not lose itself in the enjoyment of ordinary life, or take for granted ownership of one's own existence? Instead, hyperreflexivity, a state of perpetual vigilance against the ever-present danger of loss of love dominated the consciousness of the insecure. The ontologically insecure experience others as threats to their existence, for example, through engulfment, petrification, or implosion. Ronnie was able to render intelligible the experience of ontological insecurity by transposing himself through an imaginative leap of substitution and putting himself in the other's shoes. The power of *The Divided Self* and its popularity was based on his brilliant and moving phenomenological vignettes of those suffering from ontological deprivation. As Ronnie states, "I have never known a schizophrenic who could say he was loved" (R. Laing, 1960, p. 38).

Without love, the life world and the relational world of meaningful involvement become stunted or collapse altogether. Rather than the healthy taking for granted of "givenness," the ontologically insecure withdraw from the given, refuse the given, and awaken to a nightmare. They awaken to an empty world without love. The meaning and music of their interpersonal relatedness has been muted, distorted, or lost. One turns away from one's fellow man in a desperate act of defense for survival. The profoundly unloved become locked in. They are out of this world – bereft, abandoned, exiled in a hell, hanging on to life by a thread. Their strategy is to benumb themselves, hide and camouflage themselves to escape from others and the anguish and pain of living without love, which means to feel somehow less than human. As Ronnie puts it, "a firm sense of one's own autonomous identity is required in order that one may be related as one human being to another otherwise any and every relationship threatens the individual with loss of identity" (Laing, 1960, p. 44).

Souls impoverished by the loss of love or the constant threat of loss cope using a variety of internal strategies that further their isolation and self-laceration. They create a false self system, pretending to lose themselves in a seriality of impersonations, and they dissociate from their embodiment, shutting themselves up in a subterranean atmosphere of despair and futility and affecting apparent indifference to the world and others, while in fact disguising their own fear of their potential for ultimate destructiveness.

If one assumes this strategy of anti-love, then "love" becomes more threatening and dangerous than hatred. The anti-existential being finds that he or she has descended into a vortex of nonbeing, into a "black hole." Ronnie's ability to render "schizophrenic" experience intelligible was never more poetically illustrated than in the case of Julie, his favorite Rumpus Room patient.

Julie, the ghost of the weed garden

How did it happen that Julie, "the ghost of the weed garden," came to refuse the given? How did love disappear from the garden? Her story is nothing less than a tragic fall. Julie was the proverbial good baby, but her mother's description of being a good baby – not demanding, no trouble weaning, clean from 15 months, did what she was told, never a trouble – sounded more like an existentially deadened baby. It seemed as though Julie never experienced or expressed her own desires, as if she did not know the difference between being good and being dead. The mother mediates the world to the infant; she establishes the earliest loving bonds. But what happens if the infant is allergic to and stifled by the atmosphere the mother and the family generate?

It appears that the child develops its own piercing vision, its own take on the truth but submerges this vision into the pretense of conformity. At a certain point, usually around puberty, the child attempts to establish and express its own identity, which produces a major crisis in a constricted family. As mother reports regarding Julie at this stage, "After all I've done for her how dare she accuse me of not having let her be." The child had overnight turned from good to bad. No sooner had this sea change occurred than Julie came to be regarded as crazy. Real conflict or dysjunction was intolerable and impossible for both daughter and mother.

Instead of continuing to confront her mother, saying that she was not letting her live, Julie started to say her mother murdered a child. The mother was relieved that Julie was not bad after all, that she was ill, mad. "She wasn't responsible for all the awful things she said" (Laing, 1960, p. 80). Hospitalization and a career as a chronic patient was Julie's destiny. Not until Ronnie's good ear deciphered her cryptic "schizophrenese" and established rapport was she released from her prison of isolation. She heard herself being heard for the first time in her life. Julie would call herself Mrs. Taylor.

> I'm tailor made
> I'm a tailoured maid
> I'm a tolled bell

That is, she was told, as if hypnotized, to pretend to be an individual. No one in her world could or would make sense of her viewpoint, whether he or she agreed or not. Everything she said and did confused her sense of self with not self. To love was dangerous: it was, to like, therefore to be like, to be alike, to be the same as, to be someone else, therefore to be dangerous to them and to herself as if she were someone else. Julie lived a death in life, an existential death. She called herself the ghost of the weed garden. There was no possibility of love anywhere but, as she told Ronnie, if you could go deep enough into the dark earth you would discover "bright gold" – or if you could go farther down you would find "the pearl at the bottom of the sea."

Phase II

Social phenomenology

Ronnie had arrived. He was "R. D. Laing." *The Divided Self* contextualized psychopathology within the perspective of a phenomenology of love and human relatedness. Ronnie was a Saint George. If he had not quite killed the dragon of psychiatry, he had mortally wounded it. Psychopathology could no longer be thought to be a disease in a person; rather, it must be understood in terms of an existential phenomenological disjunction between persons in family and social systems.

That families coerce their members to adhere to family norms, and that their violence masquerades as love, was for Ronnie evident. To document the phenomenological evidence, he interviewed in depth families of so-called schizophrenics. He described in *Sanity, Madness and the Family* (R. Laing & Esterson, 1964) the mystification and invalidation process within families and showed how family scapegoats come to be designated schizophrenics. He worked out some of the more overt interpersonal ploys for the stultification of love in families in *Self and Others* (1961), for example, the experiential techniques of collusion, disconformation, invalidation, pretense, and fantasy. He studied the deleterious effects of disjunctive perceptions and metaperceptions in a research on interpersonal perception in couples. He summarized Sartre's (1960) phenomenological reflections on group violence, and described how groups enforce by terror compliance to the group norms (R. Laing & Cooper, 1964).

However, by the 1960s Ronnie realized a barrier to the further development of his project, the awakening to love. He found that he was unable to awaken his profession or the public to the truth of his discovery. What must have been to this time his most disheartening moment was his research on normal families. In order to convince scientific workers in their own research terms of the validity of his "evidence" he had to demonstrate a difference between families of schizophrenics and normal families. The communication patterns and atmosphere in normal families unfortunately proved to be as or more stifling of love and truth in Ronnie's terms than the psychotogenic families he had studied. (He withheld publication of this study.) Not only did Ronnie meet with misunderstanding, indifference, and incredulity, he met with hostility from his psychiatric colleagues, his psychoanalytic associates, and families of schizophrenics, not to mention the pharmaceutical industry.

Ronnie by the mid-1960s became deeply disillusioned with his fellow professionals. Although no hippie, he in effect decided to "drop out." Yet, unexpectedly, at the same time Ronnie suddenly found himself catapulted to international prominence.

R. D. Laing was seen as a guru, illuminated. His message was supposed to be that the mad were sane and the sane were mad, and that what we needed was a social revolution. The founding of Kingsley Hall, the Dialectics of Liberation conference, and the creation of the Philadelphia Association were seen as seeds for this revolution. Ronnie became the center of "the scene," a heady mixture of poetry, philosophy, and freak-outs, Zen, yoga, acid, and all-the-way houses. Kingsley Hall was a radical experiment in a phenomenology of living that must have tested Ronnie's faith in love to the limit. It was at this point that his awakening to love did indeed force him to confront and challenge the political horizons, norms, constraints, and rules that governed conventional interpersonal relatedness, and thus subordinated love to power.

The politics of experience

In *The Politics of Experience* (Laing, 1967), Ronnie recognizes that ultimately it is the corruption of power, in families, institutions, or states that prevents the realization of love. A power struggle with an us-and-them scenario gets set up to justify social manipulation and control. The "them" can be schizophrenics, racial minorities, women, and the marginalized and disenfranchised as opposed to "us" normals.

From the margins of his own "scene," the Philadelphia Association, Ronnie embarked on the deconstruction of normality and its good conscience, anticipating Derrida. How society constructs its norms and values according to a polarized oppositional crediting and discrediting of good-and-bad, right-and-wrong polarities produces a grammar and politics of living. To stray from the socially designated "right" side puts us in the wrong and at risk. Laingian deconstruction begins with the reversal of conventional polarities in order to loosen polar oppositions. The us/them division is created through exclusion; thus, each opposite is defined by what it excludes.

By reversing the polarities of sanity and madness, Laing showed that there was more than a little madness in so-called sanity and more than a little sanity in so-called madness. Such a reversal of polarities is only an initial deconstructive gesture. In order to demystify power in the politics of experience we must learn to see through value polarities, which are always constructed on the basis of self-interest rather than love of the other. However, we are dangerously deluded if we believe our self-interest is to think in conformity with social norms. Quoting from the politics of experience, "What we call 'normal' [sane] is a product of repression, denial, splitting, projection, introjection and other forms of destructive action on our experience" (R. Laing, 1967, p. 27).

Our capacity to experience, hence to differentiate and judge fundamental polarities of experience in the field of reciprocal influence is so shrouded and veiled in mystification that anyone must undergo an intensive period of unlearning before they can begin to experience the world afresh, with innocence, truth, and love. It was this discipline of *unlearning* that provided the core of the PA's training or, rather, anti-training in phenomenological psychotherapy. It was only through a process of radical deconstruction of the "official version" of oneself and others that it was possible to meet another person in truth and love. As Ronnie put it, "Psychotherapy must remain an obstinate attempt of two people to recover the wholeness of being human through the relationship between them" (R. Laing, 1967, p. 50).

For Ronnie most of us are in shambles, head cut off from heart, heart from genitals. We are mostly victims of a conspiracy of mystification where violence masquerades as love, and love, which means letting the other be, nevertheless is used as a justification to manipulate and control the other's freedom. So-called schizophrenics at least have been successful at avoiding this sort of self-deceptive ego adaptation. Nevertheless, they run into disjunctive relationships with psychiatric authority (the social police force), and their liberty becomes endangered. So the question is left open-how do we deconstruct our self-deceptions, our lies that we take to be truths and our violence that we call love? Ronnie targets the family as the appropriate arena for more intensive deconstruction.

In *The Politics of the Family*, Laing returns to the theme of awakening to love. He writes, "Attempts to wake before our time are often punished especially by those who love us most. Because they, bless them, are asleep" (1969, p. 82). Anyone who wakes up and realizes that what is taken to be real is a "dream" is likely to be taken to be crazy. Ronnie reports a conversation with a celebrated philosopher who reckons he did not awaken from his postinfancy hypnotic state until over fifty. He had already written by then most of the works for which he is renowned.

In a nutshell, the phenomenology of the politics of the family is a deconstructive version of Sartrian group analysis (Sartre, 1960). Ronnie argues that members of families internalize reciprocally their family membership. The patterns and structure of these internalizations govern the interpersonal defense systems, self-narrations, and "knots," whereby members of the family try to maintain a constructed identity by means of regulating the perceptions of the other family members. We must study family dramas, scenarios, and the roles of the members, who often take up the scripts of their ancestors. For example, "little Jimmy is the spitting image of his grandfather." Social situations are a field of self-fulfilling prophesies. If someone is defined as the ill family member or as "schizophrenic" we can be sure this person is carrying the parcel for the whole family system. Families are rife with hypnotic instructions, such as rules for bringing up children. Parents are hypnotized by their parents and so on, along with the posthypnotic prohibition to prevent family members from remembering that they are carrying out hypnotic instructions. How much of who we think we are is what we have been hypnotized to think – for example, we are a good boy or girl?

Very early on we learn to make the following distinctions: inside/outside, pleasure/pain, real/not real, good/bad, me/not me, here/there, then/now. Rules for these differentiations are intergenerationally prescribed. Unless we "see through" the lens of these prescriptions we will see *through them* (that is, according to them), and there is a rule against knowing there is a rule. Psychotherapy is the process of awakening from the hypnotic induction and trance states of convention, the spell of the familiar, in order to reclaim responsibility for the way we see, and do not see, love and are unloving to our neighbors and ourselves.

Laing versus Freud

In contrast to Ronnie's social phenomenological approach, which is interpersonal, Freudian psychoanalysis is solipsistic and narcissistic.

Freud's metapsychological narrations are extensions of his narcissism, as he himself implies, although he only explicitly characterizes his opponents' theories as narcissistic. For Freud, the ego represses instincts and immediate gratification in order to defer and later achieve substitute gratification, egoic gratification, in reality. We overcome narcissistic wounds of separation and castration by telling ourselves stories that transform frustrated primary desire or libidinal energy into self-love and secondary socially acceptable enjoyment. This is the story of repression and the dynamics of the unconscious and its generation of conscious identity. Theorizing is seen in this light as amounting to no more than self-aggrandizing heroics. Freud criticized his critics and philosophers for being narcissistic but never reproached himself. To be sure, Freud's psychoanalytic practice of "just listening" provides an ethical or interpersonal dimension to his work. This is the practice that is in tune with social phenomenological therapy, which attempts to untie knots and dismantle "numbers" by letting the other be and be heard.

Moreover, Freud makes a sharp distinction between neurosis and psychosis, which Ronnie refutes. Psychosis is not in someone; it results from a disjunction between a so-called mental health professional and someone designated by family or friends as someone with a problem. Because what someone says may be disturbing to others, he or she may be classified as disturbed. Ronnie (Laing, 1970, p. 5) describes this in *Knots*:

> There must be something the matter with him
> because he would not be acting as he does
> unless there was
> therefore he is acting as he is
> because there is something the matter with him.

> He does not think there is anything the matter with him
> because
> one of the things that is
> the matter with him
> is that he does not think that there is anything
> the matter with him.

> Therefore
> we have to help him realize that,

the fact that he does not think there is anything
the matter with him
is one of the things that is
the matter with him.

Phase III

The final awakenings

In the final phase of his awakening to love Ronnie explored beginnings and end-
ings. He probed the unexplored region of intrauterine experience, on the one
hand, and the dark mysteries of how the lies of love may provoke transpersonal
catastrophe on the other.

In *The Facts of Life* (1976), Ronnie asks that we suspend belief or disbelief as he
tracks the traces of preoriginary life. Here is the place of the primordial differ-
entiation process where biomorphic distinctions first begin to happen, as we live
through the adventures of sailing down the fallopian tube, establishing a beach-
head at implantation, and pulsating to the rhythm of being nourished and sucked
dry by our placental surround. Must not these ordeals of primal survival during
gestation leave their imprint? Is it so far-fetched to suppose that these patterns of
prenatal experience are replayed in postnatal life?

Ronnie recounts story after story of his patients and others' lives that fit as just
such replays of one phase or another of fetal experience, if there is such a thing.
For example, it is commonplace to have patients who find it difficult to "get
into things." Could this be an implantation problem? Ronnie refers to these patterns of dynamic resonance as typologues, or the phenomenology of patterns of
experiential spaces. These typologues are actualized or instanced in life scenarios
or in the basic stories of world mythology. The fetal–umbilical–placental pattern
provides a metaphor for psychological and interpersonal interrelationships; in a
way, they figure this pattern. For example, when there is a fusion between mother
and daughter, this can be seen in terms of a refusal to give up a psychic umbilical
connection and a mothering placental surround. Life can be seen in terms of a rite
of passage. At each stage in life we confront and engage in ordeals that must be
negotiated and overcome in order for us to arrive and be fulfilled. Does not this
dynamic movement reflect its origin in the earliest and perhaps the most awesome
of life transformations, the movement from womb to world?

The lies of love

One of the last frontiers not taken up in systematic fashion by psychology, psychoanalysis, or phenomenology is the question of lies and deceit that come
between men and women or partners in love relationships. This question will
turn out to be the final ordeal from which Ronnie never completely awakened. He
shared vignettes of infidelity, jealousy, and deceit during his last workshops and

chronicled these in preliminary studies for a magnum opus on the phenomenology of the lies of love which he never lived to complete. I preview a few of these moments, as chronicled in his unpublished draft manuscript *The Challenges of Love* (Laing, 1989).

To open the question of the subliminal influence of lies, especially in relation to infidelity, even imagined infidelity, Ronnie loved to repeat a story told by a colleague. Ronnie speculates on the transpersonal effects of one person's thoughts on another's body, returning to his earliest project of a possible science of neuro-phenomenology. His colleague's patient asks about the wisdom of starting up an affair with a lady he recently met on a train. He is hesitant because of this rather strange "coincidence." His eyes met the eyes of the lady in question, a complete stranger, just before they came to their station. Without a word passing between them they exchange telephone numbers before getting off the train. A few days later he gets a call from the woman in question, who reports a rather bizarre event. Just as their eyes met before getting off the train, at exactly 3:32, her husband had a heart attack.

What happens when an affair is discovered and we find that we have been living in a false reality? Little has been said that addresses the explosive meaning pregnant in such situations. This is precisely what Ronnie proceeds to do. A major obstacle to developing a discourse on the question of male/female love, lies, and jealousy is language. Language is not used for the most part in gender-specific ways to discuss interpersonal relatedness. To say "I love you" is magic, but the power of the meaning of these words is always embedded in an interpersonal context. Ronnie gives an illustration of the almost magnetic power of these words themselves and their potential antithetical effects. He remembers a couple, who seemed perfectly happy, who came to see him. He at one point said to her, tell me you love me.

SHE: I love you.
HE: There's something lacking in your tone of voice.
SHE (after some temporizing): I love you but I'm not *in* love with you.
HE: Things could never be the same again.

He left her. They were both brokenhearted.

Ronnie proposes to map the grammatical interplay among *you*, *I*, and *me*, as well as *he* and *she*, as these players shift positions by their moves in the triangular games of love, lies, and jealousy. This ordinary grammar of human relatedness among the *I*, *me*, *you*, *we*, *us*, *she*, *her*, *he*, *him*, and *them* goes for the most part unnoticed, unconsidered, and undiscussed. Yet all the tangles, knots, and confusions of our life with one another center around our lack of clarity with regard to the use of these terms. For example, I may fail to realize that I am quite other than the you I am for you and you are other than the you I take you to be. Thus, we treat each other like components of ourselves rather than allowing each other otherness, rather than honoring our difference.

Jealousy arises when you become a you to him as you once were to me and I become a mere him to you both. I can't bear the thought that you could think of me as a mere him or her when you are with him or her. This is by far the worst betrayal – far worse than any sexual act. But who is the you that I love? The you for you, the you for me? Who is the me you love? The I that I am for me, the you that I am for you? Even though for all ordinary purposes we are able to cope with the unclarified and undifferentiated senses of what is going on between you and me, our love life drags us down into confusion. If a couple is an agglutinated mass of mistaken identities and a shift, a betrayal that is experienced as catastrophic, occurs one or both of them may become shattered, reduced to a heap of broken images. It has all come apart – "we" were a complete illusion. So does real love exist? Is mutual love and reciprocity possible, realizable? This vexed question about our own love life has hardly been explored. Awakening us to love is Ronnie's legacy and enduring relevance to phenomenology and psychotherapy.

Conclusion

In conclusion I return to the passage *love your neighbor as yourself*, and invite the spirit of Ronnie to an imagined conversation. The Hebrew reads *veaharta* (you shall love) *Lereakha* (your neighbor) *Kamokhah* (as yourself; Leviticus 19:18). In the first place, Levinas asks what does "yourself" signify? If we interpret the passage synchronically, there is a symmetry between oneself and our neighbor. My neighbor is another like me. This is the view of Buber, Rosenzweig, and Ronnie. Love your neighbor – he is like you – another, like you.

In Levinas's (1998, p. 91) reading we must pause before *Kamokhah*; the phrase then reads "Love your neighbor; this work is like yourself." Love your neighbor; he is yourself, it is this love of the neighbor, which is yourself. For the Bible, the other is always my priority. We can summarize the biblical teaching as putting the other, your neighbor, first. This Levinas claims is what it means to be "yourself." This is why Levinas insists on an asymmetry in interpersonal relationships, on a diachronic reading. The other is infinitely other and I am *obliged* by the face of the other to relate responsibly, to respond to his or her call nonviolently. The other must never become a theme for a discourse of knowledge, even Ronnie's proposed grammatology of gender difference. To be sure, he might well have replied, but does not a Levinasian require a better understanding of the grammar of sexual difference and the lies of love in order to operationalize ethics in practice? I leave this question open.

Note

This paper was presented at the symposium on "The Legacy and Future of R. D. Laing's Contribution to Contemporary Thought," sponsored by the Saybrook Graduate School in association with Free Association and the Existential-Humanistic Institute, in San Francisco, on March 13–14, 1999.

This paper first appeared in the United Kingdom in the *European Journal of Psychotherapy, Counselling and Health*, 2, no. 2 (1999), published by Routledge. Website: http://ivww.tandf. co.uk. Reprinted by permission.

References

Heidegger, M. (1927). *Being and time*, J. Stambaugh, trans. Albany: State University of New York Press, 1966.

Husserl, E. (1913). *Ideas pertaining to a pure phenomenology and phenomelological philosophy*, F. Kersten, trans. Dordrecht: Kluwer Academic, 1982.

Laing, A. (1994). *R. D. Laing: A Biography*. Peter Owen.

Laing, R. D. (1954). *Reflections on the ontology of human relations*. Unpublished manuscript, Glasgow.

Laing, R. D. (1960). *The divided self*. London: Penguin Books, U.K. 1965, first published Tavistock Publications.

Laing, R. D. (1961). *Self and others*. London: Tavistock.

Laing, R. D. (1967). *The politics of experience*. New York: Ballantine Books/Pantheon Books.

Laing, R. D. (1969). *The politics of the family*. New York: Pantheon Books.

Laing, R. D. (1970). *Knots*. New York: Pantheon Books.

Laing, R. D. (1976). *The facts of life*. New York: Pantheon Books.

Laing, R. D. (1989). *The challenge of love*. Unpublished manuscript, Going, Austria.

Laing, R. D. & Cooper, D. (1964). *Reason and violence: A decade of Sartre's philosophy*. New York: Pantheon Books.

Laing, R. D. & Esterson, A. (1964). *Sanity, madness and the family*. London: Tavistock.

Levinas, E. (1998). *The God who comes to mind*, B. Bergo, trans. Stanford, CA: Stanford University Press.

Mullan, B. (1995). *Mad to be normal*. London: Free Association Books.

Sartre, J. P. (1960). *Critique of dialectical reason*, A. Sheridan-Smith, trans. London: Verso.

9

R. D. LAING'S EXISTENTIAL-HUMANISTIC PRACTICE

What was he actually *doing*?

Kirk J. Schneider, PhD

Laing was one of the most celebrated clinicians of his day. At the 1985 Evolution of Psychotherapy conference (sponsored by the Erickson Institute), Laing spotted a disheveled bag lady (whom some would label psychotic) entering the lecture hall. Spontaneously, and in the middle of his talk, he walked over to the woman and began to converse with her. After some time had elapsed, and the woman's disposition improved, Salvador Minuchin, a celebrated clinician in his own right, stood and declared that Laing's contact with this woman was one of the finest examples of therapy that he had ever witnessed. Throughout Laing's formidable career, there has been a variety of such testaments to his work. Some of these testaments came from Laing himself and others came from those who witnessed his mastery.

In this essay I address two overarching questions: What was Laing actually doing in these sanctified encounters with clients – and how did he do it so quickly? I argue that part of what Laing was doing had already been eloquently outlined by existential-humanistic writers, as Laing himself conceded. But I also argue that Laing brought something unique to existential-humanistic practice, something that had not quite been characterized before and that has yet to be substantively articulated. Furthermore, I believe that this something is at the frontier, not just of existential-humanistic practice but of all practice that strives toward depth-psychological understanding as well. It is a seedbed for the future.

Before I begin, I want to enjoin all of you in the search for this "something" that made Laing's practice unique. As you listen to his commentaries and my own musings, I encourage you to investigate this enigmatic question with me – for it is by no means clear or readily articulated.

Some background about Laing's debt to existential-humanism is necessary first. Then, I elaborate on the "something" to which I earlier alluded, drawing on case illustrations from his practice.

Laing's debt to existential-humanism is clear, it seems to me, from the out-set. Beginning with *The Divided Self* (Laing, 1960) and extending throughout his entire intellectual corpus, Laing's focus has been on (1) the whole human being as opposed to part-processes, (2) the human being in his or her particular world or life context, and (3) the human being in relation to existence or creation. For me, one of the most stirring illustrations of Laing's existential-humanistic focus is his vase/face illusion at the beginning of *The Divided Self.* With this illusion, Laing brilliantly elucidates the angles, or stances, from which two or more people can be perceived. Depending on how one views the illusion, one may either per-ceive a vase or two opposing faces. Likewise, depending on how one views the gestalt of a human relationship, as Laing (1960) intimates, one may see a *Diagnostic and Statistical Manual of Mental Disorders* category, a neurochemistry system, an information-processing machine, a cauldron of instinctual drives, or a dynamic, evolving person. Put another way, one may experience another as an object ("vase") or a subject ("face"), with all attendant implications.

Let us consider these implications, for they are subtler than they at first appear. What does it really mean to take in another's face, for two people to really "face" one another? Have you genuinely opened to another's face of late? I have tried to do this more and more consciously since being inspired by Laing's analogy, and I have been daunted by what I have discovered. Like the eyes, the face is a win-dow on the world and perhaps on being itself. It is no accident that Emmanuel Levinas (Valevicius, 1988) chose the face as his touchstone for moral decision-making, for right action. If you can fully take in another's face, you are virtu-ally forced to be discerning in your response to him or her. The face not only encompasses one's personal experience but also opens out into the vast reaches of time, space, and creation; it is the mirror to all that we absorb. For Laing, to witness another's face and, indeed, being is a metaphysical exercise. (The smile, Laing [1960] remarked, is more than the "contraction of the circumoral muscles" [p. 31].) To face another is to radically open up to possibility, as well as to dread. Furthermore, Laing's metaphor deftly assists us to see the interconnec-tion between those who are called psychotic and those labeled normal, for if you genuinely open to the psychotic, you also open in some sense to the anxieties and possibilities in all of us, in the human condition. You open to the girl, for example, who feared that an A-bomb was ticking inside her, or to the patient who "feels crushed . . . even at the exchanges of ordinary conversation" (Laing, 1960, pp. 12, 163). The face opens to worlds beyond worlds, layers beyond layers of history, mystery, and even cosmology. In the face, Laing intimates, one can perceive the minutest impacts of family, culture, and biology; at the same time, one can detect the primordial forces of the universe at play – such as engulfment, impingement, chaos, and obliteration.

Laing's chief therapeutic concern, I believe, was honesty – in communicating, in understanding, and in healing. Laing's honesty was directly tied to his employ-ment of phenomenology – or fidelity to experience as lived. Laing was open to and highly encouraged maximal disclosure of experience. As he noted in one of his lectures, his aim was to help people *into* their existence, to help them be them-selves. At the same time, Laing was not casual in his promotion of this philosophy. He stretched the limits to be sure, but his approach was highly nuanced.

Integrative vision

Laing's therapeutic vision was integrative. Parallel to the Eastern notion of the Great Chain of Being, Laing conceived of human experience as a series of lev-els or domains, among them the biological, cognitive, sexual, interpersonal, and spiritual. How is the past connected with a person's current suffering, Laing (1985) inquired:

> Is it [related to] what was going on before [the person] came into the room . . . ? Is it [related to] events that have been going on for a number of years? Does it go back to childhood? Does it go back to birth? Does it go back to conception? Does it go back to before incarnation? Does it go back to before conception and one's last death? Does it go back to past lifetimes?

Laing's question was an ultra-radical one: Where in this wheel of existence, as he called it, is the person stuck, and how could one gain access to that "stuck place"? In order to stay maximally open to any experience that a person might relate to him, Laing cultivated that which he termed therapeutic suspension. By suspending both belief and disbelief, and by sustaining a disciplined naiveté, Laing was able to facilitate completely unanticipated discoveries, meanings, and resources within his clients.

Conditions for change

Presence was one of the chief means by which Laing fostered honesty (or authen-ticity). Ironically, however, one is hard-pressed to find the term *presence* in Laing's lexicon, perhaps because he felt it was overused. On the other hand, he used a variety of eloquent expressions to convey the essence of presence; one of these was attunement (or "at onement," as he put it). One of the first things Laing (1985) did when he sat before a client was to attune to (or "scan") their interrelationship. What are the feel, the tone, and the atmosphere of this interrelation, he would, in effect, ask, and how can one best address this feel, tone, and atmosphere? As suggested earlier, he would also inquire as to how can one find the "opening," the "chink in the armor" for accessing this person? Laing distinguished between intuition, which in his view sprang from the larger (transpersonal) self, and tech-nical judgment, which emanated from one's ego. Whereas intuition was relatively sweeping and direct, the ego, for Laing (1985), was a kind of "autohallucination," highly limited for his purposes.

One of the keys to Laing's cultivation of intuition was courage. In stark con-trast to this courage was that which Laing (1985) termed "psychophobia" – fear of the mind. He prided himself on lacking the former quality; however, there were humorous exceptions to this rule, particularly with the severely disturbed. For example, Laing (1985) tells the story of an Olympic weightlifter who came to see him for therapy following a fit of anger in which he had slammed his fist through a door. Laing took one look at the man and sheepishly referred him to "a good therapist down the street." On the whole, however, Laing viewed the medically distancing practices of conventional psychiatry as psychophobic in the extreme. One of the worst fears, Laing (1985) elaborated, was the fear of human beings, and in few places is this fear more evident than in mental hospitals. For me, this remark echoes Laing's commentary on the vase/face illusion. As suggested earlier, faces are terrifying reminders of our "Selves," in the larger sense, of our own awesomeness. To the extent we take our interconnectedness seriously, Laing continues, we cannot help but realize how vast it all is and how untenable our petty notions of normality, truth, or health. Even the Great Chain of Being must be questioned, intimates Laing, because it is hardly comforting – radically amazing perhaps – but not necessarily consoling.

Now I'd like to provide a few vignettes that eloquently capture Laing's approach. Following these descriptions, I will pose the question, "What the hell is Laing doing with these clients?" Laing (1985) states,

> I remember one occasion with a girl of seven years old. She was brought along by her father because she had stopped talking. He brought her into my room and he left. She sat on the floor, crossed her legs, and just sat there – not particularly withdrawn but certainly not looking as though she was interested to play or to have any conversation. She sat there like a sort of miniature Buddha, and I was sitting in my chair and I couldn't imagine how I might get to her. I asked if she'd like to talk and she had nothing to say. So I got off my chair and sat there on the floor in front of her. There was no plan that I worked out. She allowed me to touch the tip of her little finger with the tip of mine and gradually allowed me to touch the tips of [all] her fingers with the tips of mine. And I shut my eyes.
>
> I had a flash when I did that . . . a pang . . . of anxiety that she might do something to my face. Maybe I was picking up something from the tips of her fingers, but it went away. And I allowed myself to become completely absorbed in the kinesthetic sensations at the tips of her ten fingers. And for something like forty minutes or so, nothing [happened] except a gradually developing movement/dance with the tips of her fingers. . . . It became absolutely imperative that I not lose touch with the tips of any of her little fingers. And I imagine it began to feel as important to her as it did to me. After about forty minutes, I opened my eyes and as I opened my eyes I found her eyes opening just at the same moment, without a word having been spoken. So we withdrew our fingers from each other, and went back to my chair. I said to her, bring your dad along now if that's all right with you, and she nodded.

He told me later [that] as he was walking along the road with her towards his car he turned to her and said, "[W] hat went on between you and Dr. Laing?" She turned to him and said, "[I]t's none of your business!" And these are the first words she had spoken in about two months!

Laing (1985) goes on to describe a similar case of a 19-year-old woman in the grip of catatonia. She would drink her coffee in the morning, Laing reported, and come to a stop. She would freely walk about and freeze up. Eventually, she became so panic-stricken that she lapsed into hours of paralysis. Laing had one session with her that he described as an "interpersonal meditation." He further described the sensation of being suspended in time and space with her. Soon after that session, Laing reported, the woman did something very smart: She took a job as an artist's model and in effect "marketed her catatonia." But beyond this cleverness, he elaborated, she was gradually able to move normally again.

Laing's "stances": a preliminary sketch

What then, are we to make of these vignettes? First of all, they are at the very least remarkable, if true. Second of all, they are rife with potential interpretations. Before I offer some, however, I wish to be clear about one point: In no way do I intend to formalize that which is unique, spontaneous, and ineffable in Laing's style – these are sacrosanct. That which I do seek, on the other hand, is to derive some general principles from Laing's approach that may assist others, in their own unique contexts, to become commensurately inspired.

My reading of Laing's healing, then, rests on the provision of three basic conditions or stances: presence, invoking the actual, and vivifying resistance (Schneider, 1998; Schneider & May, 1995). Presence refers to Laing's capacity to hold and illuminate that which is palpably (immediately, affectively, kinesthetically, and profoundly) relevant within his clients and between himself and his clients. Invoking the actual refers to Laing's capacity to assist his clients into that which is palpably relevant (or charged) as a conduit to their liberation. Finally, vivifying resistance pertains to Laing's capacity to assist his clients to overcome the blocks to that which is palpably relevant.

Let me elaborate this perspective in the context of Laing's work with the seven-year-old mute girl. This girl, it seems to me, was both terrified and eager at some level to break out of her shell. Probably owing to past trauma, her entire world was designed to constrict, to petrify, to deaden, and, conversely, to keep her from venturing out, taking a risk, and declaring herself. Both literally and figuratively, her world had silenced her. Laing, on the other hand, was able to provide conditions or stances through which she could come *into* herself, *into* her voice. Through presence (holding and illuminating that which was charged), Laing was able to connect with her and contain her struggle, and she, in turn, felt safer to explore herself; by invoking the actual (reaching out with his hands), he was able to invite her to embody that which was emerging (e.g., risk, courage, connection), and by vivifying or silently bringing her attention to that which blocked her emergence (e.g., fear), Laing was able to catalyze her will to overcome that blockage. Another way to frame this formulation is that Laing held up a series of mirrors to his client. The mirrors of presence and invoking the actual helped the girl to perceive that which was emerging in her (e.g., the yearning to expand, assert, and declare herself), whereas the mirror of resistance helped her to perceive (reassess, overcome) that which hindered her from emerging. Taken together, these mirrors enabled the girl to survey her "battle" (that which was emerging vs. that which was blocked), sort out the stakes in that battle, and risk the decision to overcome that battle. Her rebuke of her father in the aftermath of therapy was a natural consequence of her self-realization.

I think it is no accident that Laing (1985) looked to ancient methods of healing to describe his work; very little that is modern seems parallel. Laing, for example, equates his approach with that of ancient Greek physicians who utilized an "incubatorium" to minister to the sick. The incubatorium, according to Laing, was literally a snake pit in which the ailing were immersed. The ailing person would receive a message from the gods, so the story goes, and convey that message to an overseeing priest who would administer the treatment. Laing also equates his work with an ancient Egyptian sect called the Therapeutae (from which the term *therapy* is derived). This sect, according to Laing, cultivated the high art of attention or presence as a healing practice.

What then are we to make of Laing's analogies to incubatoria and Therapeutae, to meditations, and suspensions of space-time? I think what we are witnessing here is a prophetic call to a future therapeutic age. In this future age, the therapy of the day will be hardly recognizable by today's standards, yet may be a lot closer to the esoteric healing standards of ages past. I would go so far as to say that the therapy of tomorrow will be an "energetic" therapy. Instead of relying on the overt or the categorical, such a therapy will emphasize the preverbal/kinesthetic field within which the participants interact. That the "New Physics" (e.g., Rupert Sheldrake's "morphogenetic fields" and David Bohm's "implicate order") echoes this visionary direction is no accident. For each of these perspectives – including Laing's – converges on mutually influencing energies, nonlocal resonances, and "field" harmonics (Feinstein, 1998).

One last note, for those who are skeptical of Laing's claims – and there is reason for such skepticism – Loren Mosher, a former Laing associate, has conducted a series of investigations of Laing-style sanctuaries. In his investigation of Soteria House, for example, he found that at two years, the outcomes were "in no way worse . . . and on many measures better than" those for a conventional psychiatric hospital (Mosher, 1997, p. 5; see also Carlton, Ferriter, Huband, & Spandler, 2008; Mosher & Menn, 1978). Specifically, the Soteria data revealed that patients had "fewer readmissions, less outpatient care, better jobs, left home more often, and had far less medication" than their conventional patient counterparts (Mosher, personal communication, March 7, 1999). These data provide much to ponder, it seems to me, in this "decade of the brain" and much to consider about the politics that are driving the science.

So where does this leave us, twenty five years after Laing's death? With a psychonaut, a pioneer, a startling new horizon.

Note

This paper was presented at the symposium on "The Legacy and Future of R. D. Laing's Contribution to Contemporary Thought," sponsored by the Saybrook Graduate School in association with Free Association and the Existential-Humanistic Institute, in San Francisco, on March 13–14, 1999.

Psychoanalytic Review, 87(4), August 2000 © 2000 N.P.A.P.

References

Carlton, T., Ferriter, M., Huband, N., & Spandler, H. (2008). A systematic review of the Soteria paradigm for the treatment of people diagnosed with schizophrenia. *Schizophrenia Bulletin, 34,* 181–192.

Feinstein, D. (1998). At play in the fields of the mind: Personal myths as fields of information. *Journal of Humanistic Psychology, 38*(3), 71–109.

Laing, R. D. (1960). *The divided self: An existential study in sanity and madness.* Middlesex, England: Penguin, 1969.

Laing, R. D. (1985). *Theoretical and practical aspects of psychotherapy* [Cassette recording no. L330–WIA]. Seminar at the conference on "The Evolution of Psychotherapy," Phoenix, AZ, and available from the Milton H. Erickson Foundation, Inc., 3606 N. 24th St., Phoenix, AZ 85016–6500.

Mosher, L. R. (1997, May). *R. D. Laing and alternatives to mental hospitals.* Paper delivered at the conference "In the Wake of R. D. Laing," London, England.

Mosher, L. R. & Menn, A. Z. (1978). Community residential treatment for schizophrenia: Two year follow-up data. *Hospital and Community Psychiatry, 29,* 715–723.

Schneider, K. J. (1998). Existential processes. In L. S. Greenberg, J. C. Watson, & G. Lietaer, eds., *Handbook of experiential psychotherapy* (pp. 103–120). New York: Guilford Press.

Schneider, K. J. & May, R. (1995). *The psychology of existence: An integrative, clinical perspective.* New York: McGraw-Hill.

Valevicius, A. (1988). *From the other to the totally other. The religious philosophy of Emmanuel Levinas.* New York: Peter Lang.

10

PSYCHOTHERAPEUTIC COMPASSION IN THE TRADITION OF R. D. LAING

Theodor Itten

> Try your best to treat others as you would wish to be treated yourself, and you will find that this is the shortest way to benevolence.
>
> – *Confucianism: Mencius VII.A.4*

Compassion is an emotional understanding with empathy for others.

The etymology of *compassion* is Latin, meaning "suffering with." More involved than simple empathy, compassion commonly gives rise to an active desire to alleviate another's suffering. Yet, not doing for, but doing with the other. It is a sharing. We all know, all over this planet Earth, compassion is at the root (radical) of all religious faiths. The so-called Jewish Christian, Zoroastrian, Hinduism and others . . . *Golden Rule of treating others* is "Do to others what you would have them do to you; Do not do unto others whatever is injurious to yourself; Do not do to others what would cause pain if done to you." In Hindu spirituality compassion is *ahimsa*, a Sanskrit word that stands for "refraining from harmfulness." Buddha is credited with saying, "Compassion is that which makes the heart of the good move at the pain of others. It crushes and destroys the pain of others; it shelters and embraces the distressed." The Arabic word for compassion is *rahmah*; foremost among God's attributes for Muslims are mercy and compassion. For Ronald David Laing this is camaraderie among equals by the grace of the Almighty.

In our training group (which ran from 1976–1981) Laing would often ask, "What do you do when you don't know what to do? Do you just do something or other as an intervention, or leave it to chance?" Maybe one could speak to the unconscious, if that is you know how to do this, or, one could listen to Francis Huxley, longtime friend of Laing and a seasoned social anthropologist who suggested the alchemical task to "make of our self a vessel." We psychotherapists are skilled in empathy and have learned to be fully attentive to another human being when he or she is in our presence. She or he might suffer from various psychological aliments, which present themselves as patterns of behavior and experience, regarded by folks with a diagnostic view as "pathological." Another position to start from could be, "wait and see," to look for what will come out of a sign, and to see it as showing us the path of healing we need to embark on together.

The household communities, operating since 1964 under the auspices of the Philadelphia Association (PA), are founded on the principle of offering asylum, where one can have, if one desires and wants, a pleasant room of one's own, while other people see to it that the basic human needs are cared for: food, warmth and shelter. In the PA we try to hold a balance between care, concern, attention, mindfulness and letting be. Laing, speaking in 1989 on Kingsley Hall, to Bob Mullan, said,

> Things are so complex, so let's take the simplest instance you can and concentrate on it. I thought, well, maybe if there were a few people who were imbued with this sort of thing – Buddhist mediation – and were living together with people who were in disturbed states of mind, they all might get themselves tuned. They might settle down, and maybe the most important therapeutic factor was the presence of other people in a balanced, wholesome, healthy, sane state of mind.
>
> *(Mullan, 1995: 173)*

One of the main reasons for my invitation to speak to you here – and I am ever so pleased to be a stand in for Andrew Feldmar – must lie in the fact that I have lived, besides having been one of Laing's apprentice, in a therapeutic household, the Archway Community, of the Philadelphia Association London, from the autumn of 1976 to the summer of 1977. The houses I lived in were 27 Shaftsbury Road and 132 Tollington Park Road, North London. I speak to you not only as someone who trained in Community Therapy within the PA but also as someone who has had to pause, be patient, wait and trust through what disturbed me, and made me disturbing. In February 1981, four years after leaving the households, I graduated, and I was elected an associate member of the PA in spring 1981. Ronnie Laing and I remained friends until his early death, at the age of 61. Presently I am 61 years old and still an ordinary member of the PA.

Some of the rules that were helpful for me, and others, in the PA, were the following:

1 All the rules are open to be questioned, including this one.
2 If you need support in whatever way, existential, psychological, social, economic, physical, ask for it.
3 Self-regulation, auto-rhythmia is fine, up to the point where it trespasses onto others.

Cure or heal? The miserable situation might anyway change, from the outside in. Yet we also live our lives from inside out. As social anthropologists and psychotherapists we tread the paths of the unknown when we accompany those who have searched out our company for a while. Usually they want to change something about how they go about their lives. In front of us lies an unmapped landscape, with scarcely a familiar landmark in sight. A few, however, are known to us – bequeathed to us as myths, as a pantheon of legends large and small. They serve as a handy cosmology, a vast invisible umbrella over our individual existence, conferring an illusionary sense of protection by making some sense of what is happening. By such visions and imaginings we alleviate the fears of the soul. Some seek a rapport with this unknown realm, calling it the collective unconscious; they project a grand vision of the dark and unwelcome side of our personality that lies in the shadows.

By practicing the healing art of psychotherapy I am opening up a place (space) and time for another human being, coming into a meeting with me. She or he can then begin to talk freely and securely in confidence. First of all, there is trust, that as patient I will not be harmed by those I am consulting. In a therapeutic conversation there is always already compassion from the side of the therapist, holding the floor, maintaining the ebb and flow of "rhythm, tempo – the timbre and pitch of the words that are in the paralinguistic's. There is . . . music of words. There are, as well, kinesics – concerted movements involving arm, hand, finger, leg, the positions of our bodies in the chairs, set at 90 degrees to each other" (Laing, cited in Amantea, 1989[1]: 141). Laing's words here come from his videoed presentation at the first Evolution of Psychotherapy Conference, held in Phoenix, Arizona, in December 1985, where he conducted an in vivo therapeutic intervention, with a so-called card-carrying schizophrenic woman, called Christy. Laing continues:

> The paralinguistic and kinesics – the music and the dance were much emphasized . . . but most "professionals" are amazingly impervious to all that. It is a question of the complete opera, with singers, costumes, sets, backdrops and orchestra, versus the mere libretto. You are publishing the libretto (the verbal content) without the music (the pitch, timbre, rhythm, tempo, the paralinguistics) and without the choreography (two symmetrical chairs placed precisely as intended) and the balled (kinesics). . . . There is a lot of technique there. Many people like Christy do not connect with 'content' alone, if the sound and movements of the therapist are, in effect, autistic. That is, if the therapist in his/her presence manifested through sight and sound is effectively selectively inattentive to 99 percent of the sight and sound of the patient/client.
>
> *(Laing, in Amantea, 1989: 142)*

Laing in effect demystified a transpersonal reality, by communicating with Christy in an interpersonal way – projecting into awareness a transpersonal field, so to speak, that envelops our encounter, that is, *the* encounter and which in the normal course of things we seldom dare to know. There are more things in heaven and earth than are dreamt of in *our* philosophy.

In the ensuing question time, Christy mentions the reason why she is doing better than before the interview with Laing. "I think that's because you know how to share minds, it's because he knows how to tap into other people's minds. (Looks at Laing) You know on a subtle level – not by asking questions" (Amantea: 160). Laing found, she said, the place where her mind had wandered. He affirmed her perception of reality, before giving her a chance to consider changing it. Thus, she quit putting mental energy, as she remarked, into a conspiracy model. Psychotherapeutic passion is, when good enough, an experience of communion.

In psychotherapeutic time and space we entertain deep subjectivity, both in service of and in trepidation of "objectivity." Embarking on this journey into the underworld we discover, with the help of trust and therapeutic commitment, how subjective reflections on our experience are not to be violated by reasoning objectivity. A daring familiarity with such deep subjectivity characterizes all of Laing's travels through this terrain, utilizing the tools which the late Roger Poole (1939–2003) catalogued as "description, comparison, deployment, perspectives, sympathy and re-organisation of sheaves and profiles" have enriched us with a measure of "truth about the totality of the psychic background" (Poole, 1972: 128) of the families Laing and Esterson (1964) studied.

We all know by now that Laing was strongly influenced by Kierkegaard, especially the *Concluding Unscientific Postscript*, which assisted him in his desire to establish a rapport with the subjective reality of the person before him, someone who was, in the language of his chosen profession, first and foremost a patient. Being informed by existence philosophy, means to ponder continuously on concrete lived and experienced subjective reality. This became a necessity when faced with someone who was living in a state of "ontological insecurity," swimming in dire straits, closed down, despairing and desperate for respect. With Kierkegaard to hand, Poole (2005: 105) writes, "Laing has now what he needs for the analysis of despair, the battle between 'the self' and 'the false self.'"

Trusting his fellow witness in despair, sickness unto death, confusion and existential dread, Laing practiced variants of what Poole termed both direct and indirect communication in order to comprehend even the most seemingly odd behavior and see in it the person's unique answer to the problem of insufferable situations. Laing perennially reached for authenticity, the gold standard in psychotherapy. In *The Divided Self*, he wrote,

> This provides striking confirmation of Jung's statement that the schizophrenic ceases to be schizophrenic when he meets someone by whom he feels understood. When this happens most of the bizarrerie of which is taken as "signs" of the "disease" simply evaporates . . . The main agent in uniting the patient, in allowing the pieces to come together, to cohere, is the physician's love, a love that recognises the patient's total being, and accepts it, with no strings attached.
>
> *(Laing, 1960: 180)*

Laing ventured into this territory, but unlike Freud, with no defensive sword and shield in hand, a leap into a boundless empty space between, where the healing relationship of patient and therapist could come to be, a place where love is indispensable, to making sense of the world.

Therapeutic passion

> For Socrates, the unexamined life was not worth living, the examined life can be pretty rotten too. It all depends who is doing the examining. The unfortunate individuals whose minds attract the scrutiny of the modern state usually find the experience profoundly traumatic, and sometimes disturbing to the point of permanent psychological debilitation.
>
> *Hawkes (2013: 7)*

To attend a joint examination of life with passion is to be patient in endurance of ill or illness, suffering. Hence compassion, as I explained in the beginning of my talk, is to suffer with another, to feel pity. More often than not experiencing an imbroglio in living can be harrowingly painful. Since a lot of people have complained to me that after they have been to mental hospitals/psychiatric clinics of how, in the grip of their hopelessness, they were treated in a condescending manner, we want to make you the reader aware of how madness can hinder and stifle *all* action and engender profound upheaval. How then to hear authentic communication, when it is most needed? The late James Hillman[2] (1926–2011) was a daring expert in present-age journeys to the underworld of the soul. Madness, if not shunned away by anxiety, is a profoundly ancient experience of a gargantuan emotion. Let's hear what he has to say,

> From its point of view, it's walking in the door with a message, but you sit in the room and it knocks the door down and you think, "Shit, this is only bringing me disruption," but what does it carry in its hand? I think what it's walking in the door with are the Gods. I think the madness is the messenger of the Gods. And that's Plato, not Freud. Different forms of what Plato called mania, each of them associated with a different God. So the madness is calling us to the Gods, in one way or another either as frenzy or as a love or as a ritual initiation into a new kind of life. Something more important than usual life is going on. It is drawing us out of one thing and toward something else.
>
> *(Hillman & Ventura, 1993: 169)*

The holy madness of Eros has to be served, otherwise, the profane silliness of everydayness catches up with confusion. Holl's prose brings in the four players of the Gods of madness: Apollo, Dionysus, Aphrodite and the poet's muse, the so-called White Goddess. Socrates mentions to Phaedrus, that in days of old, madness was held to be a valuable gift. True, some saw it as an evil,

> but in reality, the greatest blessings come by way of madness, indeed of madness that is heaven-sent. It was when they were mad that the prophetess

at Delphi and the priestesses at Dodona achieved so much for which both
states and individuals in Greece were thankful; when sane they did little or
nothing.

(Plato, 1978: Phaedrus, No. 244b: 491)

With Jung we have learned again, against the protest of modern psychiatrists
that the Gods are in the disease. Called or not called, they are always there whether
you believe it or bit. For Hillman (1993: 169–170) insanity is the description of
"what the human being does in relation to that mania. That is, it follows the
wrong God, or it serves its God in the wrong way. It doesn't understand the ritual,
or it literalizes the ritual. It gets inflated it takes the mania to itself, takes credit for
it, "the thoughts that come through me are mine, not the Gods,'" or it says, "I am
an instrument of the Gods, I'm their favorite son or chosen person." Of all the definitions of madness, Theodore Roethke's is a firm favorite: "What's madness but
the nobility of soul at odds with circumstance?" Roethke's example was found in
a poem, but there are other perhaps less charming ways of thinking about insanity
and madness which use various language games to prop them up. We know them
as the biochemical, neurological, genetic, sociological, psychoanalytical, childhood dysfunction and abuse models. From description to reality – one suffused
with contradiction, where people snap at the point of no return. I turn now to the
story of Angel, one of immediacy in the search for the hidden dimension to life.

Experience with Angel

Jeff called. It was a lush evening in the summer of 1979. He described his problem
with Angel, his former lover, who visited him over Christmas. Now she keeps
throwing tantrums, shouting in the house, being a burden on his housemates. She
can't stay any longer. He would like, together with Angel, to drop in on us in the
Villa Therapeutica, a place in Islington, North London. He asks me to put some
time aside for both of them. Maybe Angel can even stay at the Villa Therapeutica,
temporarily, of course. They arrive in the late evening. They tell their stories.
After two hours it's time for them to depart. Then Angel stands, shouts louder and
louder, throws her hands in front of her flickering eyes. "Where am I? What am
I doing here?" she asks. "What answer does she hear within herself?" I ask her in
return. "I need a room, a quiet place to think. I don't want to carry on playing
other people's games. I want to be protected. To stretch out my hand, and touch
another hand." While she is answering, Angel plays with her hands in front of her
eyes. The silence that follows takes hold of our hearts. This is enough for a first
time.

A few days later Angel comes to visit again, eyes filled with fear. "I don't have
anything left," she says. "I just see a hole." While she tells stories about her life,
she weeps and gesticulates as if conducting her mental melody. After an hour and
a half I have to leave her. She sinks to the floor, says, "Now you have just killed
me," Silence! I kneel down next to her and massage her back, gently and slowly.

Angel calms down. After a while she gets up and leaves. I see the many dimensions of her story of suffering vanish into one another like breaking waves. The symbolic roads! I am Angel's audience and listeners. In this way I become part of her story, and her secret stories, told here for the second time, a part of me. Which great story plays host to our own individual ones? Angel wants to empty herself, talk herself free, and talk right to the end, in the here and now. She is afraid of this.

I wake up. It is half past three in the morning, and Angel is standing in my restroom in the villa. "What's wrong?" I ask her from the in-between world of dreams. "I'm frightened," she says, "of the voices downstairs in my room and of my thoughts as well. I can't sleep. I'm exhausted." "Angel," I reply, "light a candle." She does so. I go back to sleep. After several hours, she wakes me. "I'm going," she says. "The dawn (Eos) is coming. I'm not frightened in your room, so now I can sleep downstairs in my room too. Can I take a candle with me?" "Of course." Angel and I found ourselves in a therapeutic situation that allowed her experiences, and the stories which until that point she had repressed, to flame freely. There are no more self-defense games. She is exhausted. Where love is, there is also pain and care, shame and death. We are loving creatures who can also wound unintentionally. There are places we linger as we wander through the country of the mind. It's Angel's last day. She wanders about the villa, alert and bold. She calls me from the airport. "I need another few Marks to get me home. Can you help me out?" This takes the biscuit. "Sure," I say, "I'm on my way." I go there on the Honda 340 and hand over the money. "Have a good journey." Back to the cover of *Time Out* magazine, this week's title: "Blind Faith." Is there any other sort of faith? Over the course of this single week, Angel moved along the path of experience in a healing ritual, from going crazy over newfound emptiness and quiet, to a new departure on the road homeward to herself.

> On closer understanding, however, the ritual may be found not only to be self-directed but also to have a socially directed message, conveyed in a privately elaborate code. It becomes the psychotherapist's task to decode it. Sometimes, if the patients trust one enough, he will decode his signals himself, or explain them retrospectively after he has given up the ritual.
>
> *(Laing, 1966: 332–333)*

Style

You are how you are at the present moment. I live my style as psychotherapist and psychologist. Character style is fated, is set as a habit, is continuously reinforced with sentences of faith, wherever they initially came from. What is then open to change? How I live the person I have become and will be, embedded in the self, rooted within a given family clan finding itself in a society, culture and religious pantheon. Soul determines all and in silence is the basis of our music or song of life. "Silence is not only present before the beginning and after the end, but during the piece" (Brendel, 2002: 173). As a psychotherapist I practice being in company with undivided attention, clarification, reframing, co-presence, cultivated intuition, spontaneity and sensibility. Humanitarianism and psychotherapy both aim to alleviate suffering by harmless means. "It is in everyone's interest – patients, families, taxpayers," stated Laing in 1984, on the occasion of the Silver Jubilee of the Richmond Fellowship, "that the response of society to this situation be as efficacious at all levels as it can possibly be. . . . Therefore, whatever else our society feels called upon to provide for people in this form of distress, by way of regimes and therapies of whatever varieties, we should not forget, as the Italians seem to have done, that it is both necessary and feasible to set up small-scale genuine asylums or sanctuaries for those of us who would be lost, literally, without them." Epidaurus in Greece, the healing center of the Asclepian healing arts, was in operation from round 600 bc until about ad 200. Asclepius, son of Apollo, disciple of Cherion and friend of dogs and snakes, having underworld connections with Hades and Dionysus, is still the healing God of therapeutic communities, such as the Philadelphia Association or Soteria houses. This tradition held that there is a power or energeia, which attracts an illness, brings it into the open and can heal it. Therefore, in order to heal, that energeia had to be actualized or cultivated. This was done by a process of incubation. This took place underground, in snake holes, where the patients, after cleansing and singing rituals, spent a day and a night in healing sleep. Some say it was for three days and, according to other writers, involved the use of psychedelic substances, as well as the company of snakes. On reemerging the patient would tell his or her healing dreams and visions to the therapist, who often did nothing but listen attentively with unconditional love. The content of the healing dreams would direct and form the basis of the treatment. Imagine someone allowed to go through a psychosis as a natural cycle, as a breakthrough to the true self, as the beginning of a healing journey. And you as an aide or professional helper can partake in this adventure of natural healing, without the interference of chemical straitjackets, to experience a reality based on the authority of one's own psyche, rather than power- and theory-based authority. This is compassionate psychotherapy in rapport with another person. People are invited to drop their past suffering, change their habits in a self-determined and free fashion, knowing that due to living and being lived, by the unconscious, we have new moments to get stuck. The art of living is to get out of the place we are caught in first.

In an interview with the Greek journal *CHIOS*, Laing (1984) had this to say:

> I call my type of therapy Integral Therapy, because integral means the whole and that means that I don't confine myself say to practising so called psychotherapy or psychoanalysis or any particular method . . . I regard myself as a priest of Asclepius . . . a method of healing which is incubation . . . the skilful method of helping people out of catastrophic states of mind that they want to be helped out of themselves. That is therapy. And the main factor in this skilful means, in this method of therapy, is one's own presence, one's own relationship to the universe.

Our world, our experience of the world and our selves are one. Silence can be such a delight, when we can listen to the inner voice, who tells each one of us – like the unconscious we are – a set of truthful instructions of what is to be said and done. When I follow this inner voice or calling, this talent will set me free in my individuation. In case I ignore and go against this truth voiced from the soul, this not hearing will turn against me and make me ill or harm me otherwise, with panic, put down, low self-esteem and, obviously, low self-confidence. Here is the weed in the imagined garden of health and healing. In musing on the hatred of health, Laing goes on:

> We could not fear and hate health until there was a will to the health we fear and hate. Until or unless we have a clear vision of the answers to these six questions, embedded in the sentence: "Who, or what, needs to be healed, of what, by whom, how?, we won't get far along the Way. We shall just be taking a stroll down another garden path which ends in another cul de sac".
>
> *(Laing, 1987b: 84)*

Laing, like Rycroft his training psychoanalyst, had a gifted intuitive sense of the healing grace with their patients. Both could also be mischievous, rebellious, deeply serious and generally aware of their blind spots, which often lead to sabotage one's own creative self. The politics of truth in psychotherapy is to de-doctrinize and de-dogmatize technic and methods of modalities of psychotherapy, in order to cure it of its ideology. In summarizing his work for the *Oxford Companion to the Mind*, Laing wrote,

> There is so much that goes on between us which we can never know. The necessity of this ignorance, and the impossibility of any satisfactory criteria of decidability when it comes to the validation of particular attributions of a personal and interpersonal order, have led those who wish to cultivate the art of the soluble to abandon this area of uncertainty and enigmas. However, this domain does not evaporate because the objective look does not see it. The great divide between fact and feelings is a product of our own schizoid construction. In reality, the reason of the heart and the physiology of the brain coexist and must be interdependent. We cannot construe this reality, however. We cannot explain it; much less can we understand it.
>
> *(Laing, 1987a: 418)*

Ultimately, what Laing was referring to can only be lived through. Often we know the hard way, to become more and more tolerant that we cannot modify our behavior patterns despite all the insight gained by having undergone psychotherapy. What we can do is how we live these and to disidentify ourselves from those familiar habitats (mostly family) which set them going in the first place. Yes, we in the PA, past and present, cultivate and nourish a sense of wholeness, some like to call it a gestalt, to understand how we live our life, and how we are lived, by the unconscious, what the trouble is that disturbs our calm smooth sailing. Laing concluded his interview with Anthony Clare for the BBC's Radio 4 broadcast on July 14, 1985, with an honest lament that he had neither theological answers nor explanations for life and death. Laing:

> What do I think of people who have? Well at the very least good luck to them, and at the very most, if they have found a reconciliation for suffering, life, death and spiritual terms which is consistent and coherent and true, then I very much regret that such a vision hasn't come my way. I'm not unaware of the words that could be used to formulate such a view of things, but it hasn't come my way that I've been able to have that type of joyous clear shining eyes that some people who devote themselves to suffering have. If it's true I hope that I can see it's true, and if it's not true than I would rather be in a state of confusion than believe something that is consoling which isn't true. I don't want to trade in the truth for illusions.
>
> *(Clare, 1993: 216)*

As psychotherapists we can reach a mode of living with a truth, which leaves no final consolatory words. Remember John Yossarian in Joseph Heller's (1961) *Catch-22*: "If he flies, he is crazy and doesn't have to fly as a bomber pilot; but if he doesn't want to fly bombers, he must be sane, and thus has to take off. That's some crazy catch, don't you think?"

No longer ashamed of whom I am, this is the beginning, middle and end of the process and experience of metanoia.[3]

Notes

1 Amantea (1989: 143–153) presents the encounter between Christy and Laing in its entirety.
2 See Russell (2013) for an extensive discussion of Hillman's work.
3 See Laing (1972).

References

Amantea, C. (1989) *The Lourdes of Arizona*. San Diego, CA: Mho & Mho Works.
Brendel, A. (2002) *Me of all people: Alfred Brendel in conversation*. Ithaca, NY: Cornell University Press.
Clare, A. (1993) *In The Psychiatrists Chair*. London. Mandarin.
Hawkes, D. (2013) Renounce! *Times Literary Supplement* (TLS) 12, July 2013, 2754, London, p. 7.
Heller, J. (1961) *Catch 22*. New York. Simon & Schuster.
Hillman, J. & Ventura, M. (1993) *We've Had a Hundred Years of Psychotherapy and the World's Getting Worse*. San Francisco: Harper Collins.
Laing, R. D. (1960) *The Divided Self*. London: Tavistock.
Laing, R. D. (1966) Ritualization and Abnormal Behaviour. *Philosophical Transactions of the Royal Society of London. Series B, Biological Sciences*, 251, no. 772, 331–335.

Laing, R.D. (1972) Metanoia: Some Experiences at Kingsley Hall, London 1968. In H.M. Ruitenbeek (Ed.) *Going Crazy – R. D. Laing and Beyond*. New York: Bantam Books.

Laing, R.D. (1984) CHIOS Interview, R. D. Laing Collection, Special Collections Dept. University of Glasgow Library, MS Laing L 157.

Laing, R.D. (1987a) Laing's Understanding of Interpersonal Experience. In R. L. Gregory (Ed.) *The Oxford Companion to the Mind*. Oxford. Oxford University Press.

Laing, R.D. (1987b) Hatred of health. *Journal of Contemplative Psychotherapy*, IV, pp. 77–86.

Laing, R.D. & Esterson, A. (1964) *Sanity, Madness & the Family. Vol. 1 Families of Schizophrenics*. London: Tavistock Publications.

Mullan, B. (1995) *Mad to Be Normal – Conversations with R. D. Laing*. London: Free Association Books.

Plato (1978) *The Collected Dialogues, Including the Letters*. Edited by E. Hamilton and H. Cairns. Princeton, NJ: Bollingen Series, Princeton University Press.

Poole, R. (1972) *Towards Deep Subjectivity*. London: Allan Lane.

Poole, R. (2005) R. D. Laing's Reading of Kierkegaard. In S. Raschid (Ed.) *R. D. Laing – Contemporary Perspectives*. London: FAB. pp. 100–111.

Russell, D. (2013) *James Hillman – The Life and Ideas*. New York: Helios Press.

11

A NOTE ON LIVING IN ONE OF R. D. LAING'S POST-KINGSLEY HALL HOUSEHOLDS: PORTLAND ROAD

M. Guy Thompson, PhD

Kingsley Hall was the first of Laing's household communities that served as a place where you could live through your madness until you could get it together and live independently. It was conceived as an "asylum" from forms of treatment – psychiatric or otherwise – that many were convinced were not helpful and even contributed to their difficulties. Laing and his colleagues, including David Cooper and Aaron Esterson, leased the building from a London charity and occupied it from 1965 to 1970. The house was of historic significance, having been the residence of Mahatma Gandhi when he was negotiating India's independence from British rule. Muriel Lester, the principal trustee of Kingsley Hall, agreed that Laing's vision for its use was faithful to its long-established humanitarian purpose. Kingsley Hall was leased to his organization – the Philadelphia Association – for the sum of one British pound per annum.

In 1970 the lease expired and Laing moved his, by now famous, operations to a group of buildings that were acquired by various means. Esterson and Cooper departed, and a new cadre of colleagues and students who shared Laing's unorthodox views about the "nontreatment" of schizophrenia joined him. They included Leon Redler, an American; Hugh Crawford, a fellow Scotsman and psychoanalyst; John Heaton, a physician and phenomenologist; and Francis Huxley, the nephew of Aldous Huxley and an anthropologist. Numerous post-Kingsley Hall houses gradually emerged, each adhering to the basic "hands-off" philosophy that had been initiated at Kingsley Hall. Each place, however, was different, reflecting the personalities of the people who lived there as well as the therapist or therapists who were responsible for each house.

By the time I arrived in London in 1973 to study with Laing there were four or five such places, primarily under the stewardship of Leon Redler and Hugh Crawford. I opted to join Crawford's house at Portland Road. Though it was essentially like the others, I was drawn to Crawford's personality and the unusual degree of involvement he effected with the people living there. While some of the houses went to extraordinary lengths to adopt a hands-off approach to the members of their household, Crawford employed a more engaged, in-your-face intimacy that I found challenging yet inviting. Most of the people living there were also in therapy with him, an arrangement that was unorthodox, though had its advantages. Getting in wasn't easy. Since there was no one officially "in charge," not even the therapist who visited regularly, there was no one from whom to seek admittance. No one was paid to work there, not even the therapist who was responsible (but not in charge). And because I didn't happen to be psychotic, I lacked the most compelling rationale for wanting to join. Some of the students I had met told me how they had visited Portland Road and, while sipping tea, offered to "help out." "What's in it for you?" they were asked. When they replied that, being students, they wanted to learn more about psychosis and what it meant to be mad, they were summarily rejected. Having failed the test, they were never invited to return.

It occurred to me it would take some time, as with any relationship, to gain sufficient trust to be welcome. I attended Crawford's seminars on Heidegger and Merleau-Ponty, went to the occasional open house that welcomed strangers, and slowly made my presence felt. Eventually I was invited to participate in a "vigil," a group of around-the-clock, relay of two-person teams commissioned to accompany a person who had succumbed to a psychotic episode. These affairs usually lasted a couple of weeks, sometimes longer, before they abated.

In my first such experience, a man in his twenties was in the throes of a manic episode, in Laingian terms, a psychotic "voyage" of self-discovery. Having managed to stay cool and not panic in such situations, I suppose I proved I could be counted on and sensitive to the extreme vulnerability of the people living there. After six months or so, I was finally invited to live at Portland Road. Crazier people fared better. Like Laing, I had struggled with depression since childhood. My mother committed suicide when I was fourteen, and I was still struggling with the guilt I felt at not being able to prevent that. But depression was not usually a rationale for living at Portland Road. In Britain, just about everyone was depressed because of the weather, so that was hardly out of the ordinary. Typically, a person who was interested would call, say he or she was going through a crisis or had simply reached the end of his or her tether, and he would be invited to come around to visit. On arrival, everyone who lived there, a dozen people or so, would meet with the visitor. The person, in turn, would have the evening to him- or herself in order to make his case heard. What were people at Portland Road looking for? By the same token, what criteria do psychotherapists use in evaluating a prospective patient's suitability for undergoing therapy? At Portland Road this was especially problematical because many of the applicants were not interested in therapy and, if they were, had a hard time finding a therapist who was willing to work with them off medication. Still, there were similarities between the two frames of reference.

Freud, for example, had looked for patients who, irrespective of how neurotic they happened to be, were nevertheless prepared to be honest with him. The fundamental rule of analysis assumes a capacity for candor. Similarly, at Portland Road people were expected to be candid with the people to whom they offered their case, no matter how crazy they might be. The residents who conducted the interview were looking for a sincerity of purpose and a hint of good will beneath all the symptoms the interviewee was saddled with, seeking, no matter how crazed or crazy, to contact that part of his personality that was still sane.

To complicate matters further, every applicant had to be admitted unanimously. One negative vote and you were rejected. Yet, once in, the new member could count on the unadulterated support of everyone living there, because of the fact that everyone supported his moving in. The sense of community and fellow-feeling was extraordinary. So was the frankness with which everyone exercised his or her "candid" opinions about everyone else. The effect could be startling, as one was slowly stripped of the ego that was so carefully created for society's approval. I soon realized why candor is something most of us prefer to avoid, however much we complain about its absence. Again, the similarity to the psychotherapy experience was unmistakable. But now, instead of having to contend with merely one therapist for one hour a day, at Portland Road you were confronted with an entire cadre of relationships, all of whom engendered transference reactions, all of which you had to manage and work through.

I would now like to introduce Jerome, a twenty-year-old man who had been referred to Laing by a psychiatrist at a local mental hospital. Jerome was a rather slight, dark-haired and extremely shy person who, in a quiet and tentative manner, told us the following. Over the past two or three years Jerome had developed a history of withdrawing from his family – mother, father, and a younger sister – by retiring to his bedroom and locking himself in. His parents would try to cajole him to come out of his room, and when that didn't work they became angry and threatened to punish him if he did not open his door. Jerome refused to budge. Eventually, his parents contacted the local mental hospital for help. Jerome was then forcibly taken from his room and removed to a hospital via ambulance and restraints. Once there, he persisted in his behavior and refused to speak to anyone. All the while, he couldn't say why he was behaving this way or what he hoped to gain by it. He simply believed that he must.

He was soon diagnosed as suffering from catatonic schizophrenia with depressive features. A series of electroconvulsive therapy (ECT) sessions was administered, and before long Jerome was returned to his ordinary, cooperative self. Six months or so later he repeated the same scenario: withdrawal, removal to hospital, ECT, recovery. Never any idea as to why Jerome persisted in this behavior was ever determined. But each time he repeated it, a lengthier course of treatment was required to bring him back "to his senses." He and his family endured this routine on three occasions over a period of two years.

The psychiatrist who contacted Laing confessed that his colleagues at the hospital had thrown in the towel with Jerome and vowed that if he were admitted to the hospital again he wouldn't leave. This, now, was the fourth such episode. On this occasion, when his parents implored Jerome to come out of his room he replied that he would on one condition: that Laing would see him. Jerome had read *The Divided Self* and concluded that Laing was the only psychiatrist he could trust not to "treat" him for a mental illness.

When Jerome visited Portland Road, he recounted what he wanted. He wanted a room of his own, to stay until he was ready to come out. We were asked to honor his request, and with some trepidation, we agreed to his terms. I single Jerome out, of all the other people I came to know at Portland Road, because he presented us with the most serious challenge we had ever had to face. Due to the nature of his terms, Jerome effectively deprived Portland Road of its most effective source of healing: the communion shared by the people living there. Jerome's plan undermined the philosophy that Laing and Hugh Crawford had formulated, a sense of fellow-feeling that honored a fidelity to interpersonal experience, no matter how crazy or alarming a person's participation in that process was. We felt that Jerome was entitled to pursue the experience he felt called on to give way to, even if the outward behavior his experience effected was problematic. Although a person's experience is a private affair, the behavior with which one engages others is not. Because the two are invariably related, the philosophy at Portland Road was to tolerate unconventional behavior to an amazing degree in order to facilitate the underlying struggle that person was engaged in.

The conventional psychoanalytic setting, for example, places enormous constraints on a person's behavior, including the use of a couch to facilitate candor. At Portland Road, you were obliged to *live* with the behavior that everyone else exhibited, so the course of a given person's behavior was unpredictable, and sometimes violent. In other words, there was an element of risk in living in such conditions because no one knew what anyone else was capable of and what lengths some might go to in order to be "true" to what he or she was experiencing, authentically.

True to his word, Jerome took to his room and stayed there. He had his own room, which no one saw him come in or out of. Although it wasn't uncommon to forgo the occasional meal, the way Jerome removed himself from the household was extreme. No one even saw him sneak downstairs for food in the middle of the night, or to use the bathroom. Our sense of worry soon turned into alarm. Jerome apparently wasn't eating anything, and it became increasingly clear that he was also incontinent. We tried talking to him. Out of frustration we said, "This wasn't part of our agreement," to turn us into a hospital where we would have to take care of him. "Oh yes it is!" Jerome insisted. Still, Jerome wasn't in any ostensible pain. He didn't seem especially depressed, or anxious, or catatonic. He was just being stubborn! He insisted on doing this his way, even if he could not or would not explain why.

We reminded Jerome that we had put ourselves out on a limb for him, keeping his parents in the dark while he was jeopardizing his health. Where was the gratitude, a gesture of good will, in return? Jerome refused to discuss his behavior or to explore his underlying motives. Nor would he acknowledge his withdrawal as a symptom that was generating a crisis. He simply submitted to, and was inordinately protective of, his private experience, the details of which he refused to share. Jerome eventually agreed to eat some food in order to ward off starvation, as long as we brought it to him. The stench of his incontinence became onerous, though Jerome was apparently oblivious to it. Not surprisingly, he soon became the topic of conversation each evening around the dinner table.

"What are we going to do about him," we wondered. Ironically, he had transformed Portland Road into a mental hospital. We were constantly concerned about his physical health, his diet, and the increasing potential for bedsores, which he eventually developed. He continued to lose weight due to the meager amount of food he was eating. Either we could tell him he had to leave or we had to capitulate to the extraordinary conditions he presented us with. As news of our dilemma leaked out, Laing became increasingly nervous. Once Jerome developed bedsores he was in danger of being taken to a hospital for medical treatment. Compounding everything else, Jerome couldn't keep down the meager amounts of food he was eating and vomited it up frequently. Whether this was self-generated or involuntary, we didn't know.

None of us possessed the expertise or inclination to serve as a hospital staff. Who was going to clean him, bathe him, and all the other things that were essential to his survival? Some of us eventually consented to be his nursemaid in order to keep his condition stable. At least he was alive and more or less coping. But how much longer would we have to wait before Jerome finally came out of it and abandon his isolation?

Four more months went by. By now Jerome's family insisted they visit and threatened legal action if we wouldn't permit them to. We weren't, however, about to let that happen. Crawford implored us to remain patient and let things take their course. Laing, however, was especially worried, but given our determination to see this through, he agreed to support us and keep Jerome's family, who had by now complained to him, at bay. Meanwhile, Jerome continued to lose weight and was becoming ill. Now, six months into this, we faced a real crisis. Jerome developed bedsores, but he continued to resist talking to us or to relent in his behavior. On the contrary, he bitterly protested our efforts to bathe him and even to prevent his starvation.

We finally decided that a change of some kind was essential if we hoped to see this through to a satisfactory conclusion. We decided that Jerome needed to be in closer proximity to the people he lived with, whether or not he wanted to. The threat to his physical health and the lack of contact, in the most basic human terms, was alarming. If he could not, or would not, join us, perhaps we could join him. So we decided to move him into my bedroom to share. In deference to the sacrifice of my previously private room, others agreed to bathe Jerome and feed him on a regular schedule, change his bed sheets, spend time with him, and endeavor to talk to him, even if he refused to reciprocate. We gave him therapeutic massages to relieve the loss of muscle tone and for some physical contact. We resigned ourselves to the fact that we had, whether we liked it or not, become a "hospital," however reluctant we were to. We felt confident, however, that his condition was bound to improve.

In fact, his condition stabilized, but that was about all. I got used to the stench, the silence, the close quarters. But it didn't help my depression, sharing a room with a ghost who haunted the space but couldn't occupy it. I needed something to relieve the deadness that now permeated our shared space, so I invited the most floridly "schizophrenic" person in Portland Road, another young man who believed he was Mick Jagger, to move into our room with us, making it three who were sharing the room. This new person, who I will call Mick, serenaded Jerome morning and night with his guitar – which he had no idea how to play! – and probably made Jerome feel even crazier than before. But hey, at least it was a livelier, if more insane, arrangement, and with all the commotion and Jerome's complaining I soon recovered from my depression. Whether Jerome liked it or not, our "rock star" guest was here to stay, and I admit to the guilty pleasure I felt in the comfort that Jerome was not in complete control of our lives.

Before long a whole year had transpired, but there was still no discernible change in Jerome. In the meantime, a number of crises had occurred between Jerome's family and Laing, Laing's growing impatience with us, our impatience with Jerome, and, finally, between ourselves and Hugh Crawford for not supporting our numerous efforts to have Jerome removed from the house. We were ready – eager! – to admit defeat and resign ourselves to an unmitigated failure. Jerome's condition was apparently interminable. His "asylum" with us had become for him simply a way of life. It seemed obvious to us now that this was all he had really wanted from us, to live in the squalor he had generated around himself.

The time, in the immortal words of Raymond Chandler, staggered by, and the urgency of Jerome's situation gradually became a commonplace, and somehow less urgent to resolve. Life continued at Portland Road independent of Jerome's situation. Others had their problems too, which were addressed in the communal way that was our custom. Another month slipped by, and then another, until I finally lost track of the time and stopped counting. Jerome had long ceased to be the nightly topic of conversation, and his presence had become a fixture, like the furniture in the house. Nobody even noticed when the year-and-a-half anniversary arrived since Jerome had arrived at Portland Road. We had become so accustomed to his odd definition of cohabitation – the baths, the linen changes, the serenades – that we hardly noticed that evening by the fire when Jerome nonchalantly sauntered downstairs to use the bathroom. When he was finished he flushed the toilet, peeked his head into the den to say hello, and quietly returned upstairs. To put it mildly, we were in a state of shock and pinching ourselves to make sure we weren't dreaming.

An hour later, Jerome came back, summarily announced that he was famished and effectively terminated the fast that had reduced him to 90 pounds of weight. This was a Jerome we had never even met: talkative, though shy, but suddenly social nonetheless. We couldn't believe our eyes and ears. How long, we immediately worried, would this last before he returned to our room and his isolation?

By the next day, Jerome had obviously taken a new turn. He was finally, if inexplicably, finished with whatever he had been doing, engaged in God knows what manner of bizarre silent meditation. Naturally, we wanted to *know*. "What on earth were you up to, Jerome, all that time by yourself?" I asked him. "What was it you were getting out of your system?"

I don't think any of us expected an answer. We didn't think that Jerome had one, but it turned out that he did. He told us that the reason he had isolated himself all that time, for a year and a half, was because he had had to count to a million and then back to zero, uninterrupted, in order to finally achieve his freedom. That was all he had ever wanted to do, over the past four years, since his first compulsion to withdraw into his bedroom at home. No one had ever let him do it.

But why, we asked, did it have to take so long? A year and a half! Did it have to take that much time? We had given him his way, hadn't we? According to Jerome, yes and no. After all, we didn't just let him be. We intruded and interfered, talked to him, played music, gave him massages and generally distracted him from the task at hand, his counting. He said that every time he got to a few thousand, even a few hundred thousand, someone broke his concentration with a song, a massage, or whatever, and he was obliged to start counting all over again, from the beginning. The worst, he said, was when we added the guitar player! "But why didn't you just *tell* us," we asked, "what you were doing? We would have eagerly obliged, if only we knew what the deal was." "That wouldn't have counted," Jerome shot back. "It was essential that you let me have my way, but *without having to explain why.*"

Apparently, it was only when our collective anxiety over Jerome's behavior subsided, after the anniversary when we finally gave up and backed off, that he was able to complete the task that he had set himself to accomplish. We had eventually, without entirely appreciating its significance, submitted to his conditions, permitting him to get on with, and submit to, his own self-imposed mission of whatever mad inspiration had compelled him to count to a million and back again, uninterrupted, without excuse or explanation.

The unorthodox nature of the "treatment" that Jerome received at Portland Road is impossible to compare with conventional treatment modalities. Nevertheless, the question is invariably asked: Did it really "work"? And if so, how? Nearly forty years later, Jerome has never experienced another psychotic episode again. He soon left Portland Road, resumed his life, and proved to be an unremarkable person, really, ordinary in the extreme. Naturally, we wondered why Jerome had felt the need to withdraw in the first place. What were the dynamics, the unconscious motivation that prompted such a radical solution to his problems? These were questions Jerome couldn't answer. It is telling, and doubly ironic, that Jerome didn't need those questions to be answered *in order* to repair what he, in his shattered condition, couldn't himself comprehend.

This story won't make much sense to anybody who attempts to glean from it an identifiable treatment philosophy, unless they take into account the central importance that Laing gave to the inherent problem of freedom in every therapy experience. This was a concern that had also preoccupied Freud in the development of his clinical technique, just as it did the existentialist philosophers, such as Kierkegaard, Nietzsche, Heidegger, Sartre, with whom Laing was principally identified. How does one "help" those who are in some measure of personal jeopardy without impinging on that person's inherently private, though socially intelligible, right of freedom?

Freud's solution to this problem was analytic neutrality, the cornerstone of his clinical technique. It followed the ancient dictum "Do no harm," what Laing recognized was a form of benign neglect. In many ways, Jerome's experience at Portland Road was a perfect example of benign neglect put into practice. The respect we tried to pay this young man was all that any of us felt qualified to offer. We didn't understand what was the matter with him, nor did we pretend to. We weren't sure what would help or what might make matters worse, so we did as little as possible. Following the principle of neutrality, we employed benign neglect as unobtrusively as we could. Neither Laing nor Crawford directed the treatment, because there was no "treatment" to direct.

The way that we struggled with and responded to Jerome's impasse as it unfolded will no doubt be regarded as reckless, indulgent, dangerous, even bizarre by the psychiatric staff of virtually every mental hospital in the world. His behavior – intransigent, stubborn, resistant – would no doubt be met with an even greater force of will, determination, and power than his own. Who do you suppose, given the forces at play, would ultimately "win" such a contest? Naturally, the use of medicating drugs would be brought to bear, and electric shock, as well as whatever form of incarceration is deemed necessary.

Few, if any, psychoanalysts believe it is possible to treat such an impasse with analysis. Yet, our treatment of Jerome was arguably a form of analysis, stretched perhaps beyond its limit. Because Jerome refused to talk, we were obliged to let his behavior do the "talking." D. W. Winnicott, Harry Stack Sullivan, Frieda Fromm-Reichmann, Clara Thompson, and Otto Allen Will, Jr., are only some of the prominent psychoanalysts who helped people in this kind of crisis. Some have recounted the many hours they spent with patients who were silent, letting time run its course until something broke through the impasse their patients were struggling with. Who would deny that Jerome resisted treatment? But what manner of treatment can a person wholeheartedly submit to when it coerces it's way in, without invitation or compassion? And let's be frank about this, without love. It seems to me, on reflection, that it was our love for Jerome that finally had its way when we backed off from all of our efforts to "help" him, when we were able to just let him be, as he had asked us to, and allow him to join our community, but on his terms, not ours.

Love is a hard thing to pin down, because there are many types of it, and not all of them are applicable to the therapeutic process. Jerome was searching for the truth, his truth, and was determined to find it, whatever the cost. In a manner of speaking, his journey was a search for *authenticity*, to be capable of being the person he was, however unpleasant or demanding that might appear to others. He had spent his life cowing to others, and the time came when he had had enough. What he wanted from his family, and the psychiatrists who treated him, was the freedom to be real, or genuine, without airs or pretense. Jerome couldn't spell this out; few of our are able to. But he knew, somewhere in his soul, what he had to do, and what the freedom to be himself would feel like. When you think about that, his journey was not just an act of desperation, it was an act of courage, where everything was on the line, come what may.

Laing saw his role as one of helping the people who came to see him "untie" the knots they had inadvertently tied themselves in. He believed this entailed extraordinary care to not repeat the same types of subterfuge and coercion that had gotten them into those knots in the first place. Jerome had tied himself in a knot, and had come up with his own solution as to what he needed to do in order to untie it, including his insistence on doing this silently. That we were able to get out of his way and facilitate his task was nothing short of a miracle.

This degree of non-intrusion in the context of psychotherapy is a rarity. Those therapists who believe it is incumbent on them to run a "tight ship," who maintain their authority over their patients at all costs, and who reduce the therapy experience to a set of techniques that can be learned aren't likely to embrace a method of "treatment" that is as modest in its claims as it is cautious with its interventions. Jerome taught me that techniques are of no use when all a person is asking is to be accepted for who he is, unconditionally.

12

"HUMAN, ALL TOO HUMAN"

The life and work of R. D. Laing interview

Douglas Kirsner, PhD

Introduction

During 1975 and 1976 I had the good fortune of spending some months living in 74 Portland Road in London, the Philadelphia Association (PA) household
that Hugh Crawford ran (to the extent that anyone could run it.[1] I vividly recall
visiting the Cassell Hospital in Australia – famous for psychotherapy with very
disturbed patients – and telling the staff what daily life in that house was like.
Even they were shocked!) In the basement of that house was the headquarters of
the PA that R. D. Laing still actively chaired. (Only "chaired" since it was next to
impossible to lead such an eccentric bunch of individualistic skeptics; in any case
Laing seemed constitutionally unable to keep many followers for long). Down
there it was like the Freudian unconscious – anarchic, timeless, creative, unconventional and unpredictable though to some extent interpretable. It was really an
antiorganization where rules were left at the top of the stairs. As home to the PA's
many seminars and workshops there was always some activity, at least from late
afternoon on. When there weren't animated seminars (dwelling, existentialism,
psychoanalysis, phenomenology, Buddhism, asylums, Lewis Carroll, etc.), yoga
and meditation workshops were taking place.

I was beguiled. I had been interested in Laing for years and even written a
book, *The Schizoid World of Jean-Paul Sartre and R. D. Laing* (Kirsner, 1976/2003).
I argued there that both Sartre and his disciple Laing started out from a schizoid
problematic, one that nonetheless addressed very real and significant psychosocial
problems in the modern world. So in the Portland Road basement by day I found
myself rummaging through some of the old PA archives, reading Laing's careful notes of Sartre's works. At night I attended lectures and seminars, including
Laing's ruminative lectures which were at that time certainly quite wonderfully
absorbing and creative.

Of course, I spent time with Laing and other members of the PA. I once asked Laing why his general influence was not that great. He replied that there was no Laingian technique, that there was no Laingian School. I am sure he was right, but there was more. Although he was charismatic, Laing's personality was such that he could not really sustain a movement with disciples. He was often narcissistic and could appear as a trickster, somebody indefinable and unpredictable. A skeptic at heart, he was no dogmatist. He was a chameleon who was not really graspable in his essence. People had very different takes on who their "Ronnie" was and what he believed in. Nobody owned him, not the left, the anti-psychiatrists, the Buddhists, not even the PA that he had founded. Although he obviously loved being famous, Laing could not relish it properly since he was always frightened of losing his identity by being categorized. Laing was too starstruck by his own image, overawed by his own reputation and role. This was strange for such a serious student of Sartre on self-deception – he seemed to have the delusion that he was "R. D. Laing".

But fortunately Laing was never reducible to his reputation. When Sartre was asked why he was studying Paul Valery who his critics dismissed as merely a "bourgeois intellectual", Sartre responded that while it was certainly true that Valery was a bourgeois intellectual, not every bourgeois intellectual was Paul Valery. I felt the same about Laing. While Laing no doubt had major problems (alcohol, drugs, narcissism, etc.), there can be no doubt that, despite these problems, he made exceptional contributions.

What were these exceptional contributions? Throughout his varied career Laing focused on many things: schizophrenia, birth and prebirth experience, the family, the impact of the modern world of science and technology, yoga, politics, the impact of psychiatry, patients' rights, the vagaries of love, and many more. But there was a vital link permeating all of them, which originated with what is central to Sartre – the distinction between two realms, the human and the nonhuman, and the consequences of treating human beings as though they were objects or things. Like Sartre, who began with the radical ontological division of the world into human and nonhuman, "being-for-itself" and "being-in-itself", existence and essence, free and unfree, Laing took as his starting point that no matter how alienated they were, every human being was free and needed to be treated as a free agent. On this premise, it is inappropriate to talk about human beings in "thing" language; language about things or processes is never appropriate for ultimately understanding human beings.

While Laing was influenced by many philosophers and psychoanalysts, the extent to which Laing was a thoroughgoing follower of Sartre's philosophy has been greatly underrated. In fact, I do not believe that Laing can be fully appreciated without recognizing the central role of Sartre's philosophy in it, for their starting points that divided being into free and determined beings were identical. Without recognizing Laing's allegiance to Sartre's stand point many of Laing's interests and perspectives appear unconnected and arbitrary. Laing's fascination with Sartre went back to his youth. David Cooper told me how Laing pored over

Sartre's *Being and Nothingness* through many nights, black coffee at his side. Laing and Cooper published their summaries of some of Sartre's later work including his *Critique of Dialectical Reason* to which Sartre wrote an appreciative foreword in 1963. It is worth quoting from it:

> Like you I think that we cannot understand psychic troubles *from outside* . . . I believe also that one cannot study nor cure a neurosis without an original respect for the person of the patient . . . I maintain like you I believe, mental illness to be the issue that the free organism, in its total unity, invents to live in an unlivable situation. For that reason, I attach the greatest value to your research, in particular to the study that you have made of the family milieu taken as group and as series and I am convinced that your efforts contribute to our approaching the time when psychiatry will be, finally, *human*.
>
> (Laing and Cooper, 1964, p. 7, my translation,
> emphasis in the original)

Clearly, Sartre assumed that mainstream psychiatry treated people as things.

Sartre took it as axiomatic that the human world was based on our praxis, agency and freedom and was irreducible to definitions of essences. Our being was always in question. Laing's landscape was essentially Sartre's – our essential freedom, self-deception, experience and its violation, the terror of the group, fear and intrusion of others, mystification, being for others as hostility and objectification. First and foremost, we must understand human beings as agents, as producers, as praxis. For Sartre our behavior was always intelligible and it was self-deception to ignore that. Since we started as agents who were condemned to be free, we could not escape our freedom. On the other hand, the nonhuman world was that of things, of identities, of essences and processes.

Laing took the implications of Sartre's schema very seriously. A "science of persons" and not of things was central to *The Divided Self* (Laing, 1965). Laing's abiding concern was with the implications of the intrusion of natural science into the human arena such as the scientific look or birth as an exclusively medical rather than a human event. For the schizophrenics of *The Divided Self* the fact that they were persons meant that they were free and (if they wanted) could produce potentially intelligible communications through their actions. Word salads were red herrings produced to mystify others (they may also have helped to mystify their selves). Laing claimed that the schizophrenics deemed by conventional psychiatry to be beyond all reason as victims of illness processes could be regarded instead as agents whose experience was potentially understandable and rational when seen as intentional acts within a context. They were using Sartrean self-deception as a way of trying to live in what they saw to be an unlivable situation. But why would one not want to be free? For Sartre the answer was clear: with freedom comes responsibility that cannot be avoided. Laing almost certainly overrated the magnitude of the patient's choices in schizophrenia – by challenging the role of unconscious factors as well as organic ones, he was left with little alternative. But he had tried to redress the balance a little in favor of the schizophrenic as human and acting meaningfully rather than as merely the victim of an organic process.

For Sartre, whose collected essays appeared as a series titled *Situations*, all free human actions took place within a setting, within certain parameters, as though they were on a stage where, although the scene was set, the actors could script the actions. For Sartre all actions occurred within a structured context that had an impact in a specific way with a particular person. Like Sartre, Laing always focused on context as a way of understanding those social events that seemed irrational. If we situate the context, we may better empathize with the specific intentions of the free subject. Laing utilized a systems theory approach with the concept of meta-context – the context of a context – to understand the hidden rationality in a situation, especially because meta-contexts by definition were not observable.

Laing completed *The Divided Self* in 1956 before Sartre published *Search for a Methods* and *Critique of Dialectical Reason* in France in 1960. After *The Divided Self* Laing moved from an interest in the meaning in the intrapsychic life of the individual through the context of interpersonal space of two persons (self and others) which following the later Sartre is locatable within the group or family context. In *Sanity, Madness and the Family* (with Esterson) and *The Politics of the Family* (1971) Laing was interested in how the family constellation provided the context in which individual schizophrenic experience could be understood as a rational strategy. For Sartre and Laing this group context existed within a society which was part of the context of the Total Social World System, which is, in turn, part of the cosmos. In *The Politics of Experience* (1967) Laing understood the Total Social World System as providing the social context in which schizophrenia was an understandable reaction. In *Knots* (1970) and in parts of *The Politics of Experience* (1967) Laing even allowed for the possibility of mystical experience to explain seemingly irrational experience and behavior in terms of the biggest meta-context of all. Mysticism was about as far as contextualizing could go, and Laing went to Ceylon to meditate in 1971. Of course, Sartre was too much a rationalist to make Laing's further move of situating the social world within the mystical. But the methodology of investigating particular "situations" illuminates Laing's basic approach and abiding project because like Sartre, Laing appreciated individuals in their singularity at the same time as they represented something more general. Context for Sartre and Laing was the human equivalent to cause in the nonhuman world. To the extent that context provided the parameters of choice we are all in Sartre's term, "universal singulars", where we can cross-reference an individual with his or her time. Laing was sensitive to and respected the unique experience of individuals whom he did not suppose that he understood because he was an "expert" in mental illness. When he wanted, Laing had an uncanny ability to hear and empathize.

Laing was to psychotics what Freud was to neurotics – he listened to their stories to help to understand their meaning in terms of wishes and intentions, not of organic processes. Challenging conventional mores and approaches, Laing was, as M. Guy Thompson (1998) has pointed out, in the Greek tradition of skepticism where little or nothing was taken for granted. Dichotomies, such as "inside–outside", "mind–body", "self–other", "society–individual", "mad–normal", were, as he would have put it, "up for grabs". Philosophy, especially existential philosophy and phenomenology, suffused his work with the clinical data gleaned from his work as a psychiatrist and a psychoanalyst as live material to further explore the humanity or lack of it in the human world. Laing was particularly offended by the stand of Karl Jaspers and modern psychiatry that there was a category of human beings – psychotics – who were "un-understandable". There was, according to Jaspers, an unbridgeable "abyss of difference" between psychotics and the rest of us (Kirsner, 1990). Not that there weren't some obvious differences, but they were, for Laing, a challenge rather than a bridge that could never be crossed. For Laing, whatever else it was schizophrenia was always a social event taking place within a social context needing to be understood in order to situate the experience and behavior of the psychotic. Whatever might be happening inside the person, clearly there were dramatic and significant events occurring outside, in interpersonal space and outside that in the broader social contexts. Laing was the major figure who helped loosen up the mind-set of "us" the normal diagnosers about "them", the mad. He was bent on searching for the interpersonal and social context of the diagnosis of psychosis and its impact (see Kirsner, 1990).

Moreover, there was the issue of perspective – radically different consequences accrue from the initial stance of seeing someone as a person or as an object. Since the observer was always part of the observational field, how one treated someone impacted how they reacted and how they were seen. Along with phenomenological thinkers in general, for Sartre consciousness was never independent but always consciousness of something – one's stance determined what one saw. This phenomenology of ways of seeing is clear in Laing from the beginning. In *The Divided Self* Laing wrote,

> Man's being . . . can be seen from different points of view and one or other aspect can be made the focus of study. In particular, man can be seen as a person or thing. Now, even the same thing, seen from different points of view, gives rise to two entirely different descriptions, and the descriptions give rise to two entirely different theories, and the theories result in two entirely different sets of action. The initial way we see a thing gives rise to all our subsequent dealings with it.
>
> ·   *(1965, p. 20)*

Laing took the implications of one's point of view much further in his later work – he made the concept of "the normal" itself a focus of investigation and critique. This is epitomized in one of Laing's very best pieces, "The Obvious", Laing's contribution to the Dialectics of Liberation conference in 1967 (Laing, 1968). (David Cooper, who edited that collection of lectures into a book, told me that he considered them as encapsulating the one or two essential things that each contributor had to say in his or her life.) Etymologically, the "obvious" is that which stands in front of us. The story Laing told about the woman holding her three-year-old out of a sixth-story window to show how much she loved him by not dropping him was, for Laing, an example of the crazed terrorism of hyper-normality. The normal stance for Laing was so warped as to be anti-human, as not treating people with the respect and dignity appropriate to human beings. Our reflex to obey, encapsulated in the Milgram (1974) experiments, was the result of treating people as though they were behaviorist machines. The double meaning of *dia-gnosis* as "seeing through" or seeing through social reality demonstrated the central issue that the perspective one adopted determined what one saw. Treating humans as persons had vastly different consequences from treating them as machines or things.

In Laing's later work the basically subjective and human was made to stand in stark contrast to a technocratic and objective scientific approach. Thus, his interest in the birth process, prebirth experience, the way the mind has been seen in mech-anistic terms, and the technological worldview of knowledge without love can be seen in the context of Laing's interest in human agency as a primary explana-tory factor in the human world. After *Knots* (1970), he wrote a play, *Do You Love Me?* (1972), a self-indulgent book of Laing's conversations with his children, and another self-indulgent book, this time of sonnets. But there was also *The Facts of Life* (1976), where he investigated the possibility of prebirth experience as pro-viding a template for later seemingly unintelligible behavior and experience. He raised the question as to what would happen to our worldview if we allowed our-selves to think whether there was some degree of intentionality in life before birth. It also focused on prebirth experience and the technological fix of psychiatry. *The Voice of Experience* (1982) discussed experience, technology, psychiatry and once again the possibility of prebirth experience and *Wisdom, Madness and Folly* (1985) was an autobiography of his early years and his years of becoming a psychiatrist.

Freud thought that slips of the tongue and other marginalia of the psychopa-thology of everyday life could provide us with important discoveries about the nature of the human mind. I think that, for Laing, schizophrenia played a similar role in providing a way into understanding the lost world of human experienc-ing. I think one of the reasons that Laing so often felt he had been misunder-stood is that his project was far larger than understanding schizophrenia. It is as though Freud were saddled with the discovery of Freudian slips as his major achievement – Freudian slips were a waystation and not any kind of end point. I think Laing's end point is the role of the loss of the world of valid experience as the problem of our age. This has consequences for our view of the world beyond "normality", such as the place of science and how alienated medicine becomes when we think that it is an achievement for a woman to be able to read a news-paper while she is having a baby. Issues about the central denial and violation of the realm of experience in the modern world persisted for Laing until the end of his life. His interest in Francis Mott's strange ideas about prebirth experience, the importance of the voice of experience and its relation to the scientific "look", the asylum post-Kingsley Hall communities in London, which were all aspects of a living phenomenology, what we did to ourselves and others in order to not see what we experience. Scientific objective rationality systematically contributed to the destruction and invalidation of the primacy of experience as providing specifically human data. In his social phenomenology Laing illuminated a specific type of sensibility to experience, a natural way of being alive to oneself and others which he felt had been lost.

Of course, there was his last yet unpublished book about love, an issue that pervades his work. How is love between two human beings possible? If we love somebody, we love them as they are in their own being or "is-ness". To love somebody for Laing is to leave them alone as they are in their unique difference from us. For Laing the modern world seemed beholden to a soulless scientific "knowledge without love" as the astronomer C. F. von Weizsacker put it (see Laing, 1976, pp. 151–152). How could knowledge without love yield knowledge of love? From Laing's perspective, the only way to humanize science was for it to assume human premises (Laing, 1976, p. 142).

How was love possible in the modern world in which people seemed increasingly to be treated as objects? The name of the organization he founded with others in 1964 to deal with human distress, the Philadelphia Association, was derived from the idea of "brotherly love". The PA's main concern was with people "whose relations with themselves and others have become an occasion of wretchedness" and to "come to a better understanding of how we occasion our suffering and joy, of the ways we may lose ourselves and each other, and find ourselves and each other again" (Philadelphia Association, 2015). Laing was always concerned with the disjunctions between people that prevented simple, natural love from occurring. For Sartre and Laing, no matter how alienated we humans are from ourselves or others, we are always free agents to some extent. The assumptions of science when it involved humans demanded fundamental questioning for Laing since the starting points of the human and nonhuman approaches were radically different and thus led to different conclusions. Treating persons as things implied that one inevitably reached conclusions about things and not people. That was Laing's basic existential critique of psychiatry, which was a paradigmatic instance of a "heartless" approach that no matter how "humane" was fundamentally flawed by confusing people with things, talking about humans in nonhuman terms. That is why "experience" is such a basic datum for Laing, why the violation and mystification of experience was always so important and why "sensibility" to the nuances of others' experience was so essential for Laing. Therefore, the underlying reason that Laing focused so much on "the scientific look", on the heartlessness of psychiatry, on invalidation and the circles of deceit that lead to mystification, on the difficulties of love (of oneself and others) was the degree to which (even inadvertently) we treat others or ourselves as things instead of as free agents. Laing argued from *The Divided Self* onward that there was the world of difference between treating somebody as a victim of processes or as a being whose actions were the result of intentions.

Laing's approach was existential, phenomenological and experiential – concepts such as "ontological insecurity", the violation, invalidation and mystification of experience, alienation from who we and others are, the impact of deception were definitively human terms for understanding the human situation. In one lecture I recall Laing telling of the impact on an elderly woman when she found out that her husband had been having an affair for twenty years. Her whole sense of reality was destroyed. The problem was not so much the affair as the effect on her sense of who she was having lived with such a fundamental deception for so long. What perception or what person could now be worthy of trust?

In his 1964 preface to the Pelican Edition of *The Divided Self*, Laing wrote,

> Freud insisted that our civilization is a repressive one. There is a conflict between the demands of conformity and the demands of our instinctive energies, explicitly sexual. Freud could see no easy resolution of this antagonism, and he came to believe that in our time the possibility of simple natural love between human beings had already been abolished.
>
> *(1965, p. 11)*

During the 1980 interview about the human condition that follows, Laing reminded me again of Freud's comment. This is the passage from *Civilization and Its Discontents*:

> Among the works of the sensitive English writer, John Galsworthy . . . there is a short story of which I early formed a high opinion. It is called "The Apple-Tree", and it brings home to us how the life of present-day civilized people leaves no room for the simple natural love of two human beings.
>
> *(Freud, 1930, p. 105n)*

I think that this passage indicates something central to Laing's own abiding view of the world so vividly expressed in *The Politics of Experience*, Laing's version of *Civilization and Its Discontents*. It is scarcely accidental that Laing's last and unfinished work was devoted to the history of love. But while the regrets for what has been lost may be similar for Freud and Laing, Laing's view strongly contrasts Freud's. Laing was an irremediable romantic, reminiscent of Jean-Jacques Rousseau, who argued for the natural goodness of men and women before their corruption by civilization: "Man is born free but everywhere he is in chains" (1968, p. 14). We cannot predict, Laing once said, the behavior of animals in their natural state from the behavior of animals in captivity. Freud adopted a tragic view of human existence that assumed malaise to be inherent in culture – Freud had an antiromantic Hobbesian view of the human condition. And this is Sartre's view as well. While, as I have been arguing, Laing followed Sartre in so much, he diverged greatly on this issue. For Sartre the problems of human relationships were not attributable to human history but were inscribed in the nature of being-for-others itself. But for Laing, our problems lay ultimately in treating people as objects and not as human. I think Laing's view of human nature, certainly as expressed in *The Politics of Experience*, was a romantic one: we are inherently and naturally good if only the world would leave us alone. Love was possible if not for the inroads of civilization. Schizophrenics might be in a better state if only psychiatrists would not interfere with them. And people would be more human if technocrats did not treat them as things. We get the sense of a simple, natural human state of affairs from which we have become estranged. On this view, we are, as the Scottish Christians of his youth would have put it, "corrupted".

Laing romanticized what it is to be human partly in reaction to the prevalent ways of looking at humans in nonhuman terms. But his strength lay in his stance as a skeptic who challenged the presumption of knowledge by those who looked at humans from a standpoint appropriate for looking at things. Some of his popularity was in his questioning of established claims to knowledge, especially about mental illness issues. His strength lay in his questioning of the impact of looking at the human world in nonhuman terms and in providing glimpses of the possibilities of a more human world where relationships were a good deal more humane.

Laing made such significant contributions to our approach to mental illness and psychiatry that many of his ideas have come to be widely accepted. Nowadays, for example, psychotics are accorded far more respect than before; the way that interpersonal relations can be subject to mystification and invalidation is assumed; the role and function of the family in relation to mental illness is taken seriously; the potentially intrusive role of psychiatry is taken for granted. We are fortunate that there is a good deal more material in addition to his published books and articles in the form of lectures, notes and other documents. The lectures were especially valuable because Laing was often at his best in more informal situations when he could ruminate well beyond his writings. The number of books about Laing is testament to the interest, value and esteem in which he is held. I can only hope that Laing's executor will be able to see his way clear to releasing the material for the scholarly, and ultimately public, consumption that it deserves.

Laing was no ideologue and never gave easy answers to difficult questions. This is reflected in the following interview I conducted with him in his London office on February 22, 1980, which is among his most far-reaching and interesting. The interview about his views on the human condition provides insights into the way Laing saw important issues such as the ones that I have been highlighting as central to his stance. They remain very relevant today. This interview was originally broadcast on Melbourne radio station, 3RRR, as part of a series I codirected in 1980, *The Psychoanalytic Revolution*.

In 1985 Laing told me of David Cooper's death at fifty-eight from a heart attack. Since from firsthand experience I knew Cooper to be a chronic alcoholic, I asked Laing if this could be related to Cooper's drinking. Laing totally dismissed this possibility, saying that alcohol had no role in heart attacks. From Laing's denial of what is the well-established relation of alcohol to heart disease I should have known better than to express surprise when Laing then lit up a cigarette. He told me that those experts on breathing and meditation, Buddhist gurus such as Chogyam Trungpa all smoked. Obviously, Laing also denied the established relation between smoking and heart disease. Sadly, we all know what happened: Laing, who smoked and, like David Cooper, regularly drank to excess, died early from a heart attack. Nobody could deny that Laing, in the words of one of his favorite philosophers, Friedrich Nietszche, would always "live dangerously".

For me the vagaries, complexities, strengths and weaknesses of Laing's life and work can be summed up in another of Nietzsche's memorable phrases – Ronnie Laing was "human, all too human".

Interview

Do you see yourself as a cultural pessimist or a cultural optimist? Or aren't these categories very useful in relation to the human condition?

I suppose I'm an optimist on Mondays, Thursdays and Saturdays and a pessimist on Wednesdays and Sundays. I haven't got a philosophical position that justifies either optimism or pessimism. As I live them, anyway, these terms are more moods. They are of interest phenomenologically, but I don't think the mood proves anything, and I don't think anything proves the mood. We can feed a pessimistic mood with any amount of social observation, fact and pseudo-fact. And an optimistic mood can be fed also. I don't actually think in those terms, and I can't construct a stable linear view of history. History is so vast that my mind is completely boggled by the thought of all the different aspects of living that have gone into the human story so far. In what sense this is better than that, and how you can assess these against innumerable and continually changing factors, is beyond my mind to compute.

A writer like Kafka seems to see the world as a prison without bars, as in many ways you saw the world of the schizophrenic in The Divided Self, *or Beckett, who doesn't seem to see any way out, or the early Sartre – we're condemned to be free at the same time as being abandoned. We have all these parameters in our existence, within which we can act. I wonder whether you feel that there are various parameters of our existence which could be described as the human situation?*

Whether our souls or minds have any sort of autonomy apart from our physical existence, we live our life in a physically mortal frame. One thing that is certain is death. What death is, however, seems to me an essential, baffling mystery. Apart from observing it (which only tells you what you see – it doesn't tell you what it is that one is looking at), the only way we could possibly know about it is to remember having died. And some people say they do. But what people say is always open to a scale of plausibility and implausibility, possibility and impossibility, probability and improbability. And so, what one makes of what anyone says will fit into a scale of credibility.

My mind works the same way as in the existential frame that it is apparently in the nature of man to question his being. Man is the being whose being is in question to himself. It doesn't look as though there are any other creatures that we've come across, except the human race so far, that have this peculiarity.

What is your stance on the world — your take on it — what is it like today for you?

My perspective is of the kind that I don't have a model to which I can refer it. I can't say it is like a prison, a womb, a tomb. I think it was Max Beerbohm from whom I first heard, "Life is a prison without bars". If a metaphor did fit, then I wish it would come to mind! I would even justify my inability to say what the world looks like by arguing that it is in the nature of the world not to be "putable" into an objector an image that one can stand out of. There is no image that one can make, which is the totality of all images in the ground of the possibility of everything. You can't put the infinite set of all into a model or an image that has a boundary on which one is on the outside looking. I don't share the internal world, or the world that used to be for Giordano Bruno, and up to maybe the time of Galileo, of the world as a vast animal, all alive. I don't feel it in terms of a schema of any particular spatial centeredness in the world that is related to any particular theological or existential significance.

I grew up with the idea of these vast infinite spaces of Pascal. I don't feel alienated. I don't feel I strayed into this universe by some mistake or absentmindedly or for some reason I've forgotten. I feel quite at home, basically in harmony. But I've got a real sense of shuddering and terror at the way human life can turn on anyone. Things that can happen to people don't look at all pleasant, and I'm very thankful that in my life so far I've been spared a lot of terrible things that one actually encounters. As Sophocles said, "Terrible is life" . . . It's not unmitigated. I don't have a sense of a continued abyss of utter end or nihilistic dissolution of all significance and meaning of things that I value and cherish. I don't know how to account for any of this universe. In reflecting upon what my position seems to be, I don't see why we would expect to be able to account for any of it.

In Freud's theory of civilization he claims that basically we are pretty narcissistic and what we want is satisfaction of the pleasure principle. But then, à la Hobbes, we unite for a better long-term goal. Civilization is just a compromise. Freud does see human beings as not particularly lovely individuals. In many ways we are basically pretty destructive, as well as, of course, being creative.

Oh yes. I don't recognize in the way I look at my fellow creatures and myself that I've hardened into a misanthropic stance. I've never gone through a period of catastrophic disillusionment, a soured or a jaundiced view of people. Freud claimed for himself that he had a "friendly attitude" to human beings. At the same time, he didn't see why in any sense of the term that he could make any sense of, that you should be expected to love people at large, as he found many people quite unlovable. He disagreed with that injunction or command.

Also, in *Civilization and Its Discontents*, he brings up the short story by John Galsworthy, "The Apple Tree". A student on holiday in Wales has a brief romance with a farmer's daughter, just before World War I. He is upper class; she a peasant. He goes back to finish his holidays in Brighton. Soon the girls with their tennis racquets and the rest of it capture his attention. He forgets about her completely.

Many years later he happens to be on holiday in Wales. He remembers he had this affair there as a student and discovers that the girl committed suicide when he didn't come back for her, as he had vowed he would. Freud said this story showed how simple, natural human love is no longer possible in our civilization.

I don't agree that you can culture out love. There is a lot to he said for one of the pleasant developments of our civilization. I am basing myself here, for instance on other people, social historians, like Louis Stone (in *Sex, Marriage and Family History from 1500–1800* with apercus about the nineteenth century). He makes a very strong case that the development of our industrial civilization, money circulation and the dissolution of the romantically cherished structures that went 200 to 300 years ago opened out space for women and men to develop something like a friendly relationship to each other, to be able to look at each other, to choose each other out of personal taste to a considerable extent, to develop on their own avowal and take their destiny in their hands between themselves, to take the decision to live together if they wanted, to part if they wanted, to have children if they wanted. I like all that sort of thing. I am a sufficiently "corrupt" (I say that ironically) product of my times that I actually prefer the thought of living now than any other time I can think of. Just for the little time since the end of World War II in Europe, however long that is going to last, has been a remarkable period of comparative peace. Comparative, I mean, just in this particular location on the planet or anywhere where people haven't got the knives out, or the helicopters, or the machine guns – where people have a chance to sit down and get on with living a peaceful life and making something of it, I mean, that's the sort of place I would like to be.

But a lot of people would see you as a herald of a sort of nonalienated life to come in a totally different society. They've read The Politics of Experience *and taken it that we are all half-crazed, half people in a really crazy world. Is there a question of being misunderstood?*

I suppose it depends on the tone of voice in which one says that, and the look in the eyes – whether it is said in a frenetic, frantic way or whether it is said in some other tone of voice. If we take the world's well-known spiritual teachers from the Buddha to the Judeo-Christian tradition, to the Greek tradition and the Islamic tradition, it's said all over the place that most people by any rigorous standards are pretty daft. We don't give any credit to even the state of mind of people – our own great-great-great-grandparents – we think we have to make allowances for it, they didn't know any better. Have a look at how many women were burned a year in Europe for years – only about twenty generations back – apparently about 100,000 a year is a low conservative estimate out of a population of about 6,000,000. An incredibly large number of women were picked up in the middle of the night from their beds, trundled along in carts at 3 a.m. – it could happen here or anywhere – these guys were going around picking up women and putting them into dungeons and torturing them and burning them. Any student in the first year of a philosophical course is expected to begin to realize that the unreflective ordinary state of mind, as soon as one looks upon it, is practically bound to discover innumerable, epistemological errors – deep programmed epistemological errors – so I don't think I'm saying anything unusual there.

You have been taken as that, though, haven't you?

I was taken by quite a lot of people who raved. The education people divided into two camps over *The Politics of Experience*. Some of them who were on the inner side of education knew the echoes, resonances and reverberations of what I was saying. But they deeply resented that thousands of people read that in that form for the first time – that was their introduction to all that. They read me before they had read Sartre or Hegel or before they had even heard of Kierkegaard, or before they had ever thought of reading Plato or Aristotle. Psychoanalysts did not like the idea that thousands of intelligent students were reading for the first time (at fourteen or earlier) these thoughts about Freud or psychiatry before they had read anything else, getting misled and misinformed and led astray. And the other side of those people who were positioned to make that critical judgment loved it, of course. They liked that because they felt my point of view was sympathetic with theirs.

You actually did chime in with the mood of the 1960s, characterized by the Dialectics of Liberation Conference.

Yes. Most of *The Politics of Experience* was written in the late fifties and early sixties, and given in lectures, in professional and academic circles. Then, without me knowing that it was happening, a whole year of American college students picked it up and it became a campus best seller. Well, it never had that fate anywhere else. And of course since the Americans with their *Tibetan Book of the Dead*, Tim Leary and then *The Politics of Experience* – it was all over the world. The American students, what could they have read like that? Herbert Marcuse is not the same as that. He's not an existentialist; he is a Marxist-Freudian.

Sartre had never got to that generation in America, and Camus was now too old for them. So here was quite a young guy in his thirties just writing. But all this passed me by. I didn't realize it had been happening until I came back from India. I realized that for three to four years there must have been a lot of stirring up of all sorts of issues that people were debating and that my contribution had become part of that conversation and that debate. But I found it extremely disheartening that any bit of meaning in what I'd intended to say had got overgrown with so many weeds of misunderstanding, deliberate distortion. Or if not misunderstanding, in some cases then construing the words of what I said in quite a legitimate way, but not in the way I intended.

Many people would regard you as a radical. For example, in writing The Politics of Experience *you were one of the first people who took experience seriously as a central motif. Yet you don't cut it off from our interactions with our fellow human beings. Related to that of course is your work in psychiatry and anti-psychiatry. I know that's not something you particularly want to be associated with.*

I don't see how anyone could see me as a radical in a political activist sense. And I certainly would not say that I don't like to be thought of as radical. It's a nice word to bask under the warmth of, like *profound* and so forth.

In talking about the place that one gives experience to, it is really a matter of taking our human life cycle from conception to death. There are certain critical moments in that life cycle physiologically and as adults we experience . . . It is very difficult to say what one means by "experience"! There is an attitude of mind that simply seems to say that what we as human beings experience doesn't matter at all. It's got no metaphysical significance to speak of. It's mainly a nuisance as far as scientific truth is concerned. Practically no experience can be believed naively.

When it is believed it's almost as though what one said is that experience is a psychosis of matter – that experience is itself another countable aberration in the universe that knows nothing of it, and gets on its own way apparently without it. And yet it is only through it that we know anything at all. So there's a complex problem of different orders of this scientific methodology. The way one looks and what one sees and what comes into view. And what is revealed or concealed according to how one looks at anything at all.

I don't know the base word for a "looking at" that has been described by Foucault as this look of observation, inspection, monitoring and surveillance – we "look at". This is the look with which we look at people under certain circumstances. My dentist gives me nitrous oxide and a local anesthetic and as far as he is concerned he is not out of touch with me as a human being, but he is giving all his attention to an objective problem which I am paying him to, I hope, ablate, subtract, eliminate, strip of his look any subjectivity that he has that is not going to contribute to his skill at drilling into my root. I am not asking for personal feelings or for him to be aware of the phenomenology of dentistry. I am not asking for that at all. And that's fine.

But then it applies to the way I die, it's applied to the way my children are taught to speak and move. It's applied all over the place. And I dislike that impinging, transgressive spread and that encroachment on the on-goings that are being looked at and examined and dissected and controlled and started and stopped in that way. There's no way you can look at anyone that way, it's an instrumental look, and I don't want be at the receiving end of that unless I am able to keep that look as a slave that doesn't become my master, that I'm in control of that look. I can use that look, I can pay someone to look at me in that way and stop looking at me in that way when I want them to stop. He can't take over my whole life with that look. He can't take over something as profoundly important in every sort of way symbolically, socially and physically and the way I want to live my body or the way a woman wants to have a baby; I find that that's an insufferable transgression. So that's one side of things that unites in my mind as a common factor in the domain of psychiatry, the domain of medicine in general in the domain of midwifery and obstetrics and all this field of thanatology, I suppose thanatology is here to stay now – no wonder.

But that sensibility has been with you since the beginning – that the critique of standard institutional psychiatry has been exactly of that nature. It's been an attack on a knowledge which is not guided by love, which is really interested only in control and manipulation.

I do not in the slightest claim to be a rare human being, insofar as I'm capable of feeling. I'm not saying that scientists and psychiatrists who exclude this mode of being with and feeling with from their scientific work are incapable of it in their personal lives. But this sort of psychiatrist has developed a stance to his professional work whereby he feels that he's almost professionally culpable if he doesn't look at people that way. The way doctors learn how to do that is to start off with a dead dogfish and move on to a dead human being, a corpse. Then we kill a frog and put it through all sorts of numbers from smashing its head to cutting its head off and pithing its spine and seeing all the different parts twitch. Then you eventually cut it all up, into bits that are still twitching. And then you have a bit of muscle or a bit of nerve from this frog. And then you learn how nerves and muscles work and then you move to patients in hospital and you start studying diseases and you can get a ten-pound frog muscle that twitches, you start testing reflexes in neurological conditions. And in the movement from muscle nerve twitch to the tendon reflex no person has entered the horizon – there's no human being. There's a neurological condition, you're simply looking at this bit of something with a tendon doing things to a piece of stuff. In some mysterious way there is a person attached, in some way connected, if only legally.

But at any rate there's a patient there. It's neurology; you're studying the nervous system and you're not really concerned with the personality of someone who's got pneumonia, except to give them a tranquillizer if they won't lie quiet. There's all sorts of objectives, studies that you can do. You can classify behavior even as an objective thing that people now suffer from Type A or Type B behavior, people with different sorts of heart conditions. You now suffer from your own conduct; your conduct has become reified, objectified. The agent has been abolished, and by reversal has become pacified, and people now suffer from pathological syndromes of behavior. So, instead of Manfred Bleuler or Ted Lidz in their descriptions of having a girl in their clinic or office who's scared stiff of them, they are doing an interview with acute excitement and a mute catatonic schizophrenic whose nervous system needs to be toned down because there is too much sensual arousal.

From the moment of entering into the whole system they've never even seen a person there. When I started psychiatry, I thought it was a branch of neurology! I was interested in the brain; my first job was in a neurosurgical unit. I was into this: how do these disorders of the body affect the mind? I wanted to know how the brain affected the mind. So I looked at people in this way. I never thought there was any other way to do it though I hadn't lost my fellow feeling like the rest of my fellow students. But when I came to a patient I de-listed the complaint. I did an examination trying to find out what was the matter. And what was the matter was some sort of delineable if possible, pathological condition or syndrome, or set of conditions. So I went through all this stuff with people in psychiatry and as you quickly discover, you've got to discover it yourself. You examine them all over backside forward, upside down and so forth, and there is nothing the matter with them physically and no pathological stuff.

When it came to people who are schizophrenic, I looked at people like that, and there was nothing the matter with them. I couldn't make this out. Apart from what the textbooks say — textbooks go into primary, secondary or first-rank symptoms of schizophrenia — what psychiatrists in actual clinical practice go through in diagnosing someone who is schizophrenic is that it is someone who is different. They never diagnose anyone who they felt was essentially the same as them as schizophrenic. It is a way of expressing, as I said, in *The Divided Self*, that disjunction. I think that for every sociologist, as well as psychiatrists, and anthropologists, that's abundantly clear that it is a disjunction that generates the diagnosis. But the disjunction is of a peculiar order. I can't understand this person who is inaccessible to me. As Jaspers says, it is on the other side of an abyss — his psychic life is different from mine. I repeatedly found that I felt I could understand this person perfectly well with no particular difficulty. I didn't see how or why other people would draw that line where they did. I still don't know why, actually.

It doesn't mean to say there isn't an abyss. If someone is on the other side of an abyss he doesn't cease to be a human being because I can only wave at him across a vast abyss, because he speaks another language, has made up a language of his own, is in a different inner space, is on a trip, or freaked out, or lost or confused. Now, the psychiatrists say the reason why that communication has broken down to me and you is that there is something the matter with you which makes you unable to communicate with me, or with anyone for that matter. Or yourself properly. And so that is why I can't understand you. It's because you're not capable of making yourself understood and you're not understandable. *Verstehen* therefore is out of the question. It's a complete error of reading of the situation to apply *Verstehen* modalities to a situation that is only explainable, it is not understandable.

Again, I am amazed that nonpsychiatrists still have to be intimidated by psychiatry. All the hermeneutics of this problematic, how psychiatrists are allowed to get away with being vested with such power over such a crude issue! I mean, that would be all right if it was said in conversation as an insult to someone. "You are just making no real sense at all, and it's not even good for you to be allowed to speak. Your mind is so confused. And the reason why it is so confused is that I can't understand a word of what you're saying and that's that". In decent human dialogue if I feel that about someone, I don't feel impelled then to work them over with therapeutic vigor, rigor and zeal. Well, that's all right with me, I don't expect to understand everyone. Possibly there are quite understandable reasons (if I knew what they were) why he doesn't want to be understood. I don't have to stretch my imagination too far to imagine someone in that position. What I cannot however, do is move into a sympathetic or empathetic mode while remaining in a "looking at" mode, it is a contradiction of terms. The interesting thing is, that lack of understanding, applied with that look, in fact, extends essentially to everyone, not really just schizophrenics. If you think that schizophrenia is a name that a psychiatrist gives to someone who can't understand, then Bleuler was quite prepared to say that he couldn't understand 90 percent of people who are tinged with schizoid or schizophrenic symptoms. It is quite often said that if psychiatrists could diagnose people at will, one in ten of any group of people would be definitely down the hatch. I mean how can this be taken seriously?

Szasz says that you really champion the schizophrenic, that you think that it's wonderful to go through voyages of discovery, of inner space, and they are really better people in a sense than the usual.

Since *The Politics of Experience* I haven't given a long exposition in a book of my own position, but I have done many interviews in which I have said again, I think that some people, who for a variety of reasons get in dislocated and social space, getting out of position, being insufferable, not breaking the law in any gross way but act in such a way that no one can stand them any longer. This is a point that Hugh Crawford has particularly made, and he is absolutely right. No one was ever sent away to hospital for schizophrenia if the company that they were keeping wanted them just in any ordinary way to be around. Either frightening, or worrying or alarming or putting people off . . . So there is no question that there are people who get into positions of being diagnosed as schizophrenic or go into unusual states of mind or so forth. People get diagnosed as schizophrenic or whatever state of mind, in terms of their likeability in general, or in terms of the vices and virtues, in terms of the Robert Burns sort of thing – "A man's a man for all that", whether you're daft of not, I don't think they're any better or worse than you or me. I said this is degrading, as it is. Sociologically, it stigmatizes, it places someone down and it strips a person of their total legal rights to their own body, to their own time, to their own money, to their own words, to their own utterances, to their own thoughts, etc., etc. So I agreed with Goffman and other people, yes this is a degradation, this is degrading. It invalidates the person quite explicitly and turns them into (in an obvious, justifiable pun), at the same time an invalid and an invalidated person.

So I said I'm doing that. So the screams went up from some quarters that I was idealizing schizophrenics, as Nathan Ackerman, the American family therapist, said, "You're a schizophrenia lover, Ronnie, That's why they can't stand you!" So I'm just going to say that I'm going to treat this person on equal terms with me. If he behaves in a way that is insufferable to me, I'll deal with that accordingly. I might even deal with it by the use, or the power to use the diagnosis of schizophrenia. Though I've never had occasion to move in that type of setting, I am glad to say, for years now.

Note

1 The Philadelphia Association was a charitable institution in London established by R. D. Laing and others in 1964. It challenged conventional ways of dealing with mental and emotional distress. Beginning with Kingsley Hall, a number of communal therapeutic households were set up under its auspices. In addition to maintaining therapeutic households, the Philadelphia Association continues to conduct psychotherapy, psychotherapy training and courses.

References

Freud, S. (1930). *Civilization and its Discontents*. In *The Standard Edition of the Complete Psychological Works of Sigmund Freud, Volume XXI (1927–1931): The Future of an Illusion, Civilization and its Discontents, and Other Works*, 57–146. London: Hogarth Press.

Kirsner, D. (1976). *The Schizoid World of Jean-Paul Sartre and R. D. Laing*. Hillsdale, NJ: Humanities Press/Brisbane: University of Queensland Press. Reprinted by Other Press, New York, 2003.

Kirsner, D. (1990). Across an Abyss: Laing, Jaspers and Sartre. *Journal of the British Society for Phenomenology* 21(3), October, pp. 209–216.

Laing, R. D. (1965). *The Divided Self*. New York: Pelican.

Laing, R. D. (1967). *The Politics of Experience and the Bird of Paradise*. Harmondsworth, UK: Penguin Books.

Laing, R. D. (1968). The Obvious. In D. Cooper (ed.), *The Dialectics of Liberation*, 13–33. Harmondsworth, UK: Penguin.

Laing, R. D. (1970). *Knots*. London: Tavistock.

Laing, R. D. (1971). *The Politics of the Family and Other Essays*. London: Tavistock.

Laing, R. D. (1972). *Do You Love Me? An Entertainment in Conversation and Verse*. New York: Pantheon.

Laing, R. D. (1976). *The Facts of Life*. London: Allen Lane.

Laing, R. D. (1982). *The Voice of Experience*. New York: Pantheon.

Laing, R. D. (1985). *Wisdom, Madness and Folly: The Making of a Psychiatrist*. London: Macmillan.

Laing, R. D. and Cooper, D. (1964). *Reason and Violence: A Decade of Sartre's Philosophy (1950–1960)*. London: Tavistock.

Laing, R. D. and Esterson, A. (1964). *Sanity, Madness and the Family*. Harmondsworth, UK: Penguin Books.

Milgram, S. (1974). *Obedience to Authority*. New York: Harper and Row.

Philadelphia Association (2015). What is the Philadelphia Association? http://www.evo lutionaere-zellen.org/html/finger/finger8_12/finger10/phili.html Retrieved from the World Wide Web, March 8, 2015.

Rousseau, J.-J. (1968). *The Social Contract*. New York: Cosmo Books.

Thompson, M. G. (1998). Skepticism and Psychoanalysis: Toward an Ethic of Experience. *fort da: The Journal of the Northern California Society for Psychoanalytic Psychology* 4(1), Spring, pp. 44–53.

INDEX